P9-DGV-361

THE Human
Equation

Jeffrey Pfeffer

The Human Equation

BUILDING PROFITS BY PUTTING PEOPLE FIRST

Harvard Business School Press
Boston, Massachusetts

Copyright © 1998 by the President and Fellows of Harvard College

All rights reserved

Printed in the United States of America

02 01 00 99 98   5 4 3 2 1

Table 1-1 on page 8 and Table 7-1 on page 200: Reprinted by permission of the *Wall Street Journal*, © 1996 Dow Jones & Company, Inc. All Rights Reserved Worldwide.

Library of Congress Cataloging-in-Publication Data

Pfeffer, Jeffrey.
    The human equation : building profits by putting people first /
Jeffrey Pfeffer.
        p.   cm.
    Includes bibliographical references and index.
    ISBN 0-87584-841-9 (alk. paper)
    1. Success in business.   2. Corporate profits.   3. Personnel
management.   I. Title.
    HF5386.P576   1998
    658.3'14—dc21   97-27510
                                                                 CIP

The paper used in this publication meets the requirements of the American National
Standard for Permanence of Paper for Printed Library Materials Z39.49-1984

Contents

Preface

THIS BOOK IS a sequel to an earlier work that both explored the effects of high commitment work practices on organizational performance and sought to understand the reasons why these manifestly effective ways of managing the employment relation weren't more commonly or readily adopted. After publishing *Competitive Advantage Through People* in 1994, I taught the material in both a required MBA course on human resources at Stanford and in executive seminars all over the world, and this experience, along with a number of outside developments, convinced me of the need for this book. First, additional data became available that make a powerful business case for managing people effectively as a source of outstanding organizational performance. Second, I developed even more of my own experience with organizations that were managing people effectively, and I also enjoyed contact with and learned from organizations that were trying to change but having difficulties doing so. From all of this field experience I acquired a better understanding of the factors and issues associated with implementation and learned more effective ways of assisting organizations in thinking about human resource issues.

But perhaps my biggest reason for writing this book was that I was particularly intrigued and troubled by the trends I observed in management practices as well as by some reactions to the ideas in the earlier book. I was told, both by practicing managers and by people such as John Paul MacDuffie, who reviewed *Competitive Advantage Through People* for the journal *Administrative Science Quarterly,* that at least some of the dimensions of high performance work systems that I had highlighted as being important, such as employment security, might be of value but were nonetheless decreasing in frequency. In fact, the ability and willingness of U.S. firms to downsize and restructure was argued by some observers to be a source of the resurgence in the competitiveness of many American companies. Nor was this the only example of a discrepancy between what theory and research prescribed and what firms were doing. Contingent work was on the rise, diminishing the connection between people and their organizations even as businesses claimed to be seeking a committed and motivated work force. Individual piecework and a return to the control-oriented ideas of Frederick Taylor seemed to be enjoying a resurgence even as "empowerment" became an increasingly overused word. Even as evidence accumulated about the slow diffusion of more effective work practices, sympathy for any role for public policy or collective action, paradoxically, decreased. And so it went.

It was as if the trends in actual management practices were moving in one direction while the evidence grew supporting practices based on an opposing approach. Consequently, I wanted to explore the two possible explanations for this dichotomy. One is that I and many others were simply wrong in our ideas about these issues. The second was the possibility that much of the conventional wisdom, at least as represented in the U.S. business press, and a great deal of current management practice was inconsistent with both logic and data. Organizations might be incurring long-term organizational problems for short-term palliatives.

In doing the research and writing for this book, I have come to understand that ideas with both empirical and logical support that seem on the surface to be common sense often aren't implemented and sometimes aren't even recognized. Simply put, common sense is not all that common. The incorrect implication frequently drawn is that if something isn't being done, it must not be as useful or worthwhile as is thought. This idea of adaptive, rational behavior is deeply ingrained, but it is not invariably correct. I have had conversations with Louis Uchitelle, who writes about work-place issues for the *New York Times,* during which we have shared the observation that sometimes people in organizations simply don't practice basic common sense, don't behave strategically, and aren't always thoughtful or logical about the policies they implement. As I learned that my observations about the role of labor unions, new employment arrangements, compensation practices, and, for that matter, government action defied both conventional wisdom and dominant ideology, I frequently heard comments to the effect that "everyone is doing (or thinking) something else, so what can we do?"—even as the speaker recognized the folly of current organizational arrangements.

From considering these challenges and ideas, I developed two insights that I believe to be common sense but which are nevertheless not widely held or implemented: First, it is almost impossible to earn above normal, exceptional economic returns by doing what "everyone else" is doing—prosaically put, you can't be "normal" and expect "abnormal" returns; and second, it is also impossible to achieve some lasting competitive advantage simply by making purchases in the open market—something that anyone can do. It became clear to me that I needed to write another book in which I more directly confronted the most unhelpful and incorrect variants of "conventional wisdom." So, here it is.

Acknowledgments

MUCH OF WHAT I have learned has been from others, and I have been truly fortunate to have had the help of many colleagues and access to numerous organizations in considering how to build high performance organizations. I highlight here only the most important recent contributors to my education. I am enduringly grateful for what they have provided me. Needless to say, the conclusions and what I have done with the information and insight they have so generously furnished are my responsibility.

I have been lucky to have had the opportunity to meet and interact with a number of business people and organizations from whom I have learned a great deal. Peter Hartz of Volkswagen, whom I met at a World Economic Forum meeting, was kind enough to share with me his thoughts about the Volkswagen cultural change and a book, *The Company that Breathes,* that documents how Volkswagen has handled having too many workers and the resulting very difficult labor negotiations. Elmar Toime of the New Zealand Post made a number of his senior managers available for interviews, provided background information, and shared his own philosophy developed in the course of helping to lead a truly remarkable transformation of a state-owned enterprise. Dennis Bakke and his colleagues at AES were exceedingly generous with their time and information as I wrote a case on this unusual organization; they helped me to understand the trade-offs between specialization on the one hand and learning and innovation on the other. AES people, and the people at Southwest Airlines who permitted Charles O'Reilly, Peter Webb, and me to visit and write a case, take having fun at work seriously, but they also share, in common with many of the other managers in high commitment work systems I have met, a fundamental belief in the value of all employees, not just those that have advanced degrees or other credentials. Hal Bennett, an entrepreneur in the Bay Area, has frequently reminded me of the importance of "fun" as an organizing principle as well as of the importance of effective management of people. He has been a source of energy, wisdom, and support.

Dave Spence of Boise Cascade has served both as a model of what might be done in managing people and as a sounding board for ideas. Marsh Campbell of Magma Copper (now a subsidiary of BHP) provided me with information on Magma's transformation of their labor relations and the results they achieved as a consequence. Lynn Williams, formerly head of the United Steelworkers of America, explained the changes in bargaining in the steel industry and the subsequent results. Bob Beck, formerly head of human resources at the Bank of America and now at Gateway 2000, has over the years been an important source of ideas and insights. Charlie Bressler at the Men's Wearhouse, Ron Eastman and Ruth Grouell at Geron, and many, many other people and organizations have provided information, inspiration, and insight.

After I had written a draft of the manuscript, a number of people were exceptionally generous with their time and their knowledge, helping to improve succeeding drafts. Beth Benjamin, a former doctoral student of mine now working at RAND, furnished not only helpful comments on the writing, numerous examples of the points, and insightful discussion of the issues, but also provided me with a number of extremely useful documents on the state of labor law and labor relations in the United States. Brent Keltner was kind enough to share with me his dissertation research on banks in the United States and Germany—data that dramatically illustrate two different ways of thinking about the work force and achieving economic success. Mark van Beusekom and Harrie Regtering of the Netherlands Participation Institute sponsored a conference and visit to Europe and provided numerous materials illustrating the applicability of these ideas in the Netherlands as well as information on employment relation practices and the institutional and legal environment in Western Europe. Morten Hansen, another former doctoral student of mine, was, as usual, candid, thoughtful, and helpful in providing comments on the manuscript.

I have benefited from the insights and comments of the MBA students who have taken both the elective and required versions of my course in human resources. Furthermore, my thinking has been enriched by the various executives whom I have encountered in programs both at Stanford and at specific organizations where I have taught. They have invariably provided questions, examples, and wisdom that helped me to develop my ideas.

Other readers of various versions and parts of this manuscript have also made extremely helpful comments. Charles O'Reilly did his customary, brilliant job of reading and commenting on an early draft of the manuscript, asking difficult questions about audience and focus and challenging me on a number of substantive issues. Francine Gordon of the Boston Consulting Group was kind enough to provide both detailed and general feedback as well as words of encouragement on the project. Tanya Menon furnished comments and a perspective that were both useful and distinct from what others had provided, and I appreciate her time and thought.

I am very grateful to the Human Resource Initiative at Stanford Business School for their support, in research time, travel expenses, and research assistance. Katrina Jaggears, my assistant, provided her usual exceptionally high level of support—something I never take for granted. I am here in 1997 to write this book because of the care and skill of Drs. James Avery and Joel Klompus in 1993, and I will always appreciate who they are and what they did.

It has been more than twelve years since I met the Amazing Kathleen. During that time, she has encouraged me to write for a wider audience and has taught me more than I have learned about many things. Not much would be possible without her love and support. To know her is to experience life in a different way.

Introduction

SOMETHING VERY STRANGE is occurring in organizational management. Over the past decade or so, numerous rigorous studies conducted both within specific industries and in samples of organizations that cross industries have demonstrated the enormous economic returns obtained through the implementation of what are variously called high involvement, high performance, or high commitment management practices. Furthermore, much of this research serves to validate earlier writing on participative management and employee involvement. But even as these research results pile up, trends in actual management practice are, in many instances, moving in a direction exactly *opposite* to what this growing body of evidence prescribes. Moreover, this disjuncture between knowledge and management practice is occurring at the same time as organizations, confronted with a very competitive environment, are frantically looking for some magic elixir that will provide sustained success, at least over some reasonable period of time.

So, even as firms desperately seek success and the evidence for at least one important source of economic success—how firms treat their people—accumulates, many if not most organizations are doing precisely the opposite of what they should. Rather than putting their people first, numerous firms have sought solutions to competitive challenges in places and means that have not been very productive—treating their businesses as portfolios of assets to be bought and sold in an effort to find the right competitive niche, downsizing and outsourcing in a futile attempt to shrink or transact their way to profit, and doing myriad other things that weaken or destroy their organizational culture in efforts to minimize labor costs—even as they repeatedly proclaim, "people are our most important asset."

Our first task in this book is to consider what are the real sources of organizational success and, indeed, if it is actually still possible to build firms capable of achieving sustained levels of outstanding performance. So, the first two chapters explore the relationship between how firms manage people and the profits and performance they earn. The returns from managing people in ways that build high commitment, involvement, and learning and organizational competence are typically on the order of 30 to 50 percent, substantial by any measure. We will see, from both quantitative evidence and qualitative case examples, that it is more important to manage your business right than to be in the "right" business. Success comes from being able to effectively implement a competitive strategy, not merely from having one.

When we next consider the basic elements of high performance organizations, in chapter 3, and a framework for implementing and aligning these practices, in chapter 4, we will begin to understand why, in spite of the extensive literature documenting the extraordinary economic returns that can be achieved, so many managers don't implement these ideas. Many of these management principles seem to fly in the face of both conventional wisdom and common, increasingly dominant, practice. There is a dramatic increase in contingent work arrangements, for example—use of part-time, temporary, or contract employees—as well as a growing reliance on corporate downsizing, both of which diminish the connections between people and their organizations even as the organizations using these strategies claim to be seeking a committed and motivated work force. Individual piecework and a return to the control-oriented ideas of Frederick Taylor and the scientific management school are enjoying a resurgence even as the word "empowerment" becomes so overused as to be trite. Organizations are obsessed with reducing their pay rates even as the evidence grows that (1) labor rates are not the same thing as labor costs, (2) in many industries, labor costs are not the most important or even a significant component of total costs, and (3) many alternative and frequently more effective competitive strategies are available. While the evidence accumulates demonstrating the slow diffusion of more effective work arrangements, sympathy for any role for public policy or collective action to assist the implementation process, paradoxically, steadily decreases. Because of this disjuncture between evidence and practice, the second part of this book explores some of the ideas that most diverge from current practice and examines both the logic and the evidence suggesting that what currently passes for conventional wisdom and sound thinking is, for the most part, neither wise nor logical.

But, you may be thinking, aren't these trends in employment practices—contingent work; downsizing; substitution of employment security with "employability"; individual, performance-based pay; and eschewal of government or institutional involvement in the labor market—most pronounced in the United States? And aren't business organizations in the United States among the most competitive and innovative in the world? Aren't organizations around the world seeking to emulate these "new" employment practices? (I put "new" in quotes because, as we will see later, the current trends simply promise a return to the way employment was organized more than one hundred years ago.) The answer to these questions is generally yes, but don't make the mistake of confusing success that occurs "in spite of" some set of behaviors with success that results "because of" a set of practices. I first heard Marshall Goldsmith, a noted consultant on leadership, use this distinction in a seminar. He noted that when people reached high leadership positions, attainments that attested to their success, they tended to see *everything* they did as contributing to that success. Marshall pointed out that some of their success was "because of" particular behaviors, but some of their success occurred "in spite of" other behaviors that were actually counterproductive. A similar analogy holds for organizations. It is important to understand which practices actually contribute to success and innovation and which ones get in the way. It is imperative not to be seduced by glib generalizations based on either a too-aggregated or a misleading interpretation of the evidence.

Our understanding of the real effects of various management practices is also hampered by a tendency to see behavior as invariably adaptive or rational. This perspective leads to the assumption that if something is not being done, it must not be very useful, and, conversely, that if some management trend is accelerating, it must be because of its ultimate wisdom and effectiveness. But these assumptions are not always correct. Practices supported by evidence and logic, even some that appear in many instances to be common sense, may fail to be recognized and implemented. Simply put, in the world of organizational management, common sense is not always all that common.

For those of you who are tempted to say as you read this book, "but what you are proposing isn't what everyone else is doing," I will remind you that it is not likely that you are going to be able to achieve outstanding economic success simply by doing what everyone else does. Prosaically put, you can't be "normal" and expect to achieve "abnormal" returns. This suggests that success comes to those organizations that have the wisdom and courage to find their own path. In hindsight, it is easy to see how the decision at Wal-Mart not to outsource its transportation but to keep its trucking fleet in-house helped it to achieve competitive advantage through its distribution system. In hindsight, it is easy to see how Southwest Airlines's strategy of ignoring the hub-and-spoke system typical of other airlines—a system once described as optimally designed to bring the maximum number of unhappy people together at the same place at the same time—helped the airline to succeed. In hindsight, it is clear how Motorola's commitment to training as part of its quality process helped it to achieve substantial economic success. But at the time those organizations did what they did, many observers thought them foolish or foolhardy. Of course, being different may mean that an organization will do worse rather than better than most of its competitors. But, firms should not pay high executive salaries merely to find leaders who can copy what others are doing—imitation simply should not be that expensive to obtain. What organizational leaders should do is to cultivate the wisdom, knowledge, and courage to figure out the basis of competitive success and to implement that knowledge, regardless of what others are doing or saying.

A second fundamental idea relevant to adding value and profits to organizations is that just as a firm cannot achieve outstanding economic success by doing what everyone else is doing, it cannot achieve sustainable competitive advantage and exceptional results merely by making purchases on the market. What one organization can buy, others can, too. Any firm can call Manpower or Kelly Services for temporary help. Any firm can contract out. What provides long-term advantage are those things that are core to the firm and not readily duplicated by competitors—and purchases on the open market cannot be sources of unique or distinct capabilities.

The foregoing implies that to make the connection between people and profits, organizations are going to have to think a little differently and manage a lot differently than many of their competitors, at least in the United States. And that is exactly right. In the end, making the connection between people and profits entails confronting how we think about work, organizations, and the people in them. What matters is managers' point of view. When you look at your work force, do you see the source of your organization's sustained success and your people as the only thing that differentiates you from your competition? Or do you, like so many, see people as labor costs to be reduced or eliminated; implicit contracts for careers and job security as constraints to be negated; and mutual trust and respect as luxuries not affordable under current competitive conditions, to be replaced by some optimal compensation and incentive arrangements that attempt to make trust unnecessary? How we look at things affects how they look and what we do. A case can be made that with the right point of view and perspective, implementation of the practices that can help achieve enduring profits through a people-centered strategy is actually not that difficult. With the wrong perspective and point of view, implementation of these ideas may be almost impossible, regardless of how many programs are implemented or how many consultants are hired. So, it all comes down to how you and your colleagues view your organization and the sources of its success and whether you have the wisdom and courage to act on those insights.

I. PEOPLE-CENTERED MANAGEMENT AND ORGANIZATIONAL SUCCESS

1 ◆ *Looking for Success in All the Wrong Places*

*T*RY THE FOLLOWING EXERCISE in your organization. Ask your colleagues to name the firms that have enjoyed the largest stock market returns over the past twenty to twenty-five years and to state why. This question effectively uncovers individuals' views about what makes organizations successful over long periods of time and reveals how people think about the sources of sustained competitive success.

I have done this exercise many times, and the results have been amazingly consistent—respondents' conclusions about the source of long-term success often are not very accurate. The firms named in response to this question almost invariably have a number of elements in common. First, many are large, consistent with an implicit belief that success comes from having access to economies of scale and the associated cost efficiencies. This quest for size drives the incessant wave of mergers and consolidations, even though the available evidence indicates that most mergers not only do not generate the anticipated economic benefits, they also frequently fail to produce even positive economic returns.

Many of the companies named are global, consistent with the realization that we move in a global business world and that success comes from having a global presence. Many of the companies listed lead their markets. This follows the conventional view that a dominant market share is the key to success.[1] Many of the firms mentioned are in high-technology industries, because of the general belief that the road to riches is paved with technology and that the key to success lies in having some technological edge. Most of the firms have some distinct brand or product technology that precludes ready imitation. Belief in the importance of a brand or technology for outstanding and sustained performance is premised on the idea that to enjoy economic success over a protracted period, firms need some barriers to imitation so that economic returns cannot be eroded by new competition. Most people see such barriers to competitive imitation as residing in trademarks, patents, technology, or brand image. In addition, many of the companies mentioned in this exercise have sought success in part by becoming lean and mean, by cutting people and other costs as a way of enhancing profit margins.

When people do this exercise, many begin by thinking first about what industries have prospered. They assume that being in the "right" industry—an industry that has barriers to entry, limited rivalry, and market power with respect to its customers and suppliers—is important for success. Conventional wisdom maintains that industry matters a great deal and that choosing the right competitive niche, therefore, is one of top management's most critical tasks. Finally, many people think of firms known for their brilliant strategy. Again, conventional wisdom emphasizes the importance of strategy as a source of success.

Emphasis on strategy and market position as the basis of success has brought rapid growth to the strategy consulting industry. It has also fostered a frequently-espoused view that the chief executive's task is primarily concerned with formulating the right strategy for the firm. This process, presumably, depends on data and analysis, following a strategic direction established at the most senior levels in a firm or division. "Our mental image of the strategic process . . . is of decision makers sifting information received from lieutenants and gleaned from written reports."[2] Unfortunately, as we will soon see in this chapter, little evidence exists to show that being in the "right" industry matters much for firm growth or economic success. Further, we will find that the emphasis on strategy as the most critical activity is also somewhat misplaced. A study of Japanese manufacturing companies reveals that "executives in superior Japanese companies seem to do comparatively little of what is usually thought of as strategic planning. Instead . . . they spend more time overseeing organizational dedication to the 'basics' of competitive advantage."[3] Those basics are things such as product and service quality, customer satisfaction, and operational excellence—

the not-so-glamorous but essential elements of business process implementation. It is my observation that in many instances, senior managers of the most successful firms worry more about their people and about building learning, skill, and competence in their organizations than they do about having the right strategy.

The first task of this chapter will be to show that much of the conventional wisdom about the sources of sustained success is wrong—inconsistent with the available evidence. Companies do not have to be large, do not have to go through waves of downsizings, and do not have to be technologically sophisticated, the market share leader, or even global to enjoy substantial economic returns. More important than having a strategy is the ability to implement it.

The management issue is simple and compelling: If you seek success in the wrong places, you are likely to waste a lot of effort, focus on the wrong things, and, in the end, overlook some of the real sources of competitive leverage—the culture and capabilities of your organization that derive from how you manage your people. This is a more important source of sustained success than many of those so commonly mentioned, because it is much more difficult to imitate or understand capability and systems of management practice than it is to copy strategy, technology, or even global presence. This source of economic success is largely based on a perspective that sees the development of people-based strategies as crucial for long-term economic performance. The second important task of this chapter is, then, to illustrate how a firm's perspective on managing people affects both its approach to its business and, as a consequence, its economic performance.

HOW CONVENTIONAL WISDOM IS WRONG

A number of studies provide evidence that the conventional wisdom of business strategy—that industry matters a great deal in affecting economic success—is simply wrong.[4] One study related the creation of shareholder value, defined as the increase in stock price plus dividends, to both the firm's revenue growth and to industry growth rates. The research, covering more than 1,800 companies traded on U.S. stock exchanges with a market capitalization of more than $500 million in 1994 dollars, found that "industry growth rates are almost completely unrelated to the likelihood that a company will be able to create superior value for shareholders over a 10-year period. . . . [A]n analysis of the data shows that companies in slow-growing, more mature industries are somewhat more likely to create superior returns for shareholders than companies in fast-growing industries."[5] In fact, industry growth rate explained precisely *0* percent of the variation in the fraction of companies in an industry that were top performers in terms of creating shareholder value.[6] Even company revenue growth, although much more important than industry growth rate, had only a moderate effect on shareholder returns. Revenue growth, over a decade, accounted for about one-third of the variation in the firms' returns to shareholders.[7]

So much for the importance of being in the right industry. What about size as a source of competitive success? To examine this, I went to the *Value Line Investment Survey* and gathered, for the most recent year available, either 1995 or 1996, the following three pieces of information for each firm within a given industry (industry categories are defined by Value Line): size, as measured by total revenues; profits as a percent of the total capital employed; and profits as a percent of net worth or shareholder's equity. These latter two measures provide an indication of how effectively the firm employed its capital and what it earned on its equity. The investment survey covers eighty-three nonbank industries, with eighty industries of five or more firms included, enough firms to make the analysis meaningful. For each of these eighty industries, I computed the correlations between revenues and the two measures of profitability: percent earned on total capital and percent earned on net worth. Since industries differ greatly in many characteristics, analysis within industries offers a useful control for common industry factors such as overall industry conditions. The analysis permits one to answer the following question: Within each industry, what is the relationship between size and profitability?

What did this analysis reveal? In thirty-five of the eighty industries considered, that is, in about 44 percent of the total, a *negative* relationship existed between sales and the percent earned on total capital. The average correlation between revenues and the percent earned on total capital across the eighty industries was just .09, which means that, on average, less than one percent of the variation in returns on total capital can be accounted for by sales revenues. If we consider returns to shareholder equity, the results are only slightly more favorable for those who believe size matters. In this instance, only thirty-one out of the eighty industries exhibited a negative relationship between sales and the percent earned on net worth. The average correlation between revenues and the returns earned on net worth across the eighty industries was just .11, again indicating that a very small portion of the variation in returns, about one percent, can, on average, be explained by size.

One cannot conclude from this, of course, that size is never important. Some industries show relatively strong relationships between sales and returns to total capital and net worth, industries such as grocery stores, drug stores, and stores selling household products. But in many industries, the relationship between size and profitability is either negative (as in railroads, home appliances manufacturing, and homebuilding, for instance) or essentially zero (for instance, in the auto and truck industry, air transportation, and medical services). Other things being equal, big is probably nice. But as a source of success and profitability, size, in many instances, is simply not very important.

What do the data indicate about the importance to earning outstanding returns of being in a high technology industry? In 1996, *Inc.* magazine's list of America's 500 fastest-growing companies was headed by a consumer-products distributor, a toothbrush maker, and a human resources service company[8]—none of them high technology industries. From 1987 through 1995, ServiceMaster, a company in the low-technology business of providing cleaning and other services, such as facilities management, to hospitals, educational organizations, and companies as well as various home-care services to consumers, earned an average return on shareholders' equity of almost 82 percent, a much higher return than was earned by either Intel or Microsoft, or, in fact, by the two combined.

In spring 1996, two sources provided lists dramatically illustrating that high technology was not necessarily the route to success, although it could be, and that high returns could be made in industries that enjoyed little market power and were, in fact, quite competitive. First, the *Wall Street Journal* published a list showing how one thousand major corporations treated their shareholders, in terms of one-, three-, and five-year returns, and other lists showing the best and worst firms in terms of one-, three-, five-, and ten-year returns. The *Journal* article also included a ranking of eighty-eight industries based on five-year shareholder returns. Second, also in 1996, *World Link,* a magazine published by the World Economic Forum, listed the two hundred fastest growing companies (measuring growth in terms of earnings per share) from around the world. At the outset, let me note that even a five-year period is a fairly short span for assessing performance. In a five-year period, specific industry conditions or stock market fads can loom large, and one can profit simply by being in the right place at the right time. Returns over ten- or even twenty-year periods are probably more useful for examining sources of sustained economic success. Nonetheless, the results are still instructive.

Table 1-1 reproduces the list of the top fifteen industries in terms of shareholder return as reported in 1996. Although the top two in 1996, semiconductors and software, are, obviously, both high technology industries, most of the rest, except for biotechnology, office equipment, and communications, are in highly competitive industries in which technological advantage plays only a small role in ensuring success.

Table 1-1   THE FIFTEEN BEST-PERFORMING INDUSTRIES, BASED ON FIVE-YEAR AVERAGE SHAREHOLDER RETURN

Industry	Five-Year Average Return
Semiconductor	45.0%
Software and processing	39.8
Eastern banks	36.3
Recreation-toys	35.8
Western banks	33.9
Medical/Biotechnology	30.7
Securities brokers	30.4
Southern banks	30.0
Office equipment	30.0
Communications	29.4
Lodging	27.9
Diversified financial services	27.7
Money-center banks	27.5
Casinos	27.3
Industrial technology	27.1

Source: John R. Dorfman, "Surprise: The Entire Tech Sector Fails to Win Hands Down," *Wall Street Journal,* 29 February 1996, R4. Reprinted by permission of the *Wall Street Journal,* © 1996 Dow Jones & Company, Inc. All Rights Reserved Worldwide.

Many of the high performance industries were in finance and banking, in which, during the 1980s and early 1990s, rivalry was intense, product innovation and new entry was spirited, and firms had little market power with respect to customers or suppliers. Considering the entire list (not reproduced here), reveals other surprises. Restaurants (ranked twenty-sixth) provided a higher return to shareholders than did medical device manufacturers (ranked twenty-eighth). Footwear firms (ranked thirtieth) finished ahead of pharmaceuticals companies (ranked forty-seventh). The computer industry ranked seventy-eighth, behind industries such as automobile parts (thirty-fourth), heavy machinery (twenty-ninth), and even railroads (ranked thirty-third).

The *Journal* published the same lists in 1997, showing similar results. Once again the top performing industry was semiconductors, with communications technology ranked second. But the third best performing industry was lodging, with an average five-year return of 31.1 percent, followed by heavy machinery, Western banks, and oil drilling. The software industry ranked seventh, followed by money-center banks, Eastern banks, aerospace and defense, conglomerates, pipelines, and Southern banks. The fourteenth-best return was earned by diversified financial services, and auto manufacturers ranked fifteenth, with an average five-year return of 22.7 percent.[9]

The *Journal*'s listing in 1996 of the twenty-five companies with the highest ten-year returns included a number of high-technology companies such as Amgen (biotechnology, ranked second), Micron (semiconductors, ranked eleventh), and 3Com (computer networking equipment, ranked twenty-third). But it also included retailers such as Home Depot (ranked fourth), a shoe company (Nike, ranked thirteenth), and a number of medical service providers such as St. Jude Medical (ninth), Pacificare Health Systems (eighteenth), and United Healthcare (seventh).

Table 1-2 presents *World Link*'s list of the twenty-five international firms ranked in terms of five-year growth in earnings per share, compiled from a set of more than 11,000 publicly traded companies. The compilers noted that the list was constructed on the basis of five-year earnings per share growth because "revenue and profit figures are distorted by acquisitions or disposals, while market value is highly dependent on the fortunes of each individual market."[10] This list shows even less of a high technology dominance than does the *Journal*'s. Many of

Table 1-2 TWENTY-FIVE WORLDWIDE COMPANIES WITH HIGHEST
FIVE-YEAR EARNINGS-PER-SHARE GROWTH RATES

Company	Country	Industry	Five-Year EPS Growth
Rogers Corporation	U.S.A.	Electronic parts	169.44%
Amgen	U.S.A.	Biotechnology	144.68%
Swiss Life Insurance	Switzerland	Insurance	130.84%
The Allen Group	U.S.A.	Electronics	127.62%
Chase Manhattan	U.S.A.	Banking	125.80%
Hudson's Bay Co.	Canada	Retailing	125.48%
Newbridge Networks	U.S.A.	Electronic equipment	119.83%
Clear Channel Com.	U.S.A.	Telecommunications	108.99%
Public Service of N.M.	U.S.A.	Electric utility	106.92%
Amagerbanken	Denmark	Banking	104.31%
CJ Vogel Draht	Germany	Financial services	100.94%
San Miguel Brewery	Hong Kong	Brewers	96.81%
Trak Auto Corp.	U.S.A.	Retailing	92.41%
Kolb & Schule	Germany	Apparel and textiles	91.09%
Lam Research Corp.	U.S.A.	Semiconductors	88.35%
Morgan Keegan	U.S.A.	Securities brokerage	85.27%
Natl. Western Life Ins.	U.S.A.	Insurance	81.64%
Designs Inc.	U.S.A.	Apparel retailing	80.83%
Volt Information Sci.	U.S.A.	Information services	78.12%
Sedlbauer	Germany	Electronic parts	75.53%
Astra Compania	Argentina	Exploration and drilling	74.94%
Metro-Richelieu	Canada	Grocery retailing	74.73%
Mines de la Lucette	France	Metal production	71.42%
United Dominion	Canada	Mining and manufacturing	71.29%
IHC Caland	Netherlands	Shipbuilding	70.40%

Source: "Profit Growth: The World's Top 200," *World Link* (March/April 1996): 46.
Reproduced from *World Link,* the magazine of the World Economic Forum.

the firms operate in very competitive industries, providing services such as securities brokerage, insurance, banking, and retailing. Interestingly, a number of the firms are based in comparatively high-wage, Western European countries, such as Germany, the Netherlands, Switzerland, and Denmark. These companies' success, despite operating in highly unionized, high-wage countries, belies another element of conventional wisdom: that the only way to succeed in an era of global competition is to enjoy the benefits of a largely unregulated, non-unionized, and low-wage environment.

Another piece of today's conventional wisdom holds that the way to economic success is to cut costs, thereby improving profit margins and stock price and leading to other good outcomes. One of the quickest ways to cut costs is to cut people, so downsizing has become quite fashionable. Analysts Gertz and Baptista note that "Whether they call it cost cutting or downsizing or restructuring or reengineering, a great many U.S. firms have been actively pursuing strategies to make themselves smaller: fewer employees, fewer operating units, and fewer subsidiaries."[11] Again, a moment's reflection will suggest that this strategy is unlikely to provide sustainable advantage over any significant period of time. Laying off employees can be done by any organization with sufficient stomach for the task. Anyone can hire an investment banker to dispose of assets such as divisions or facilities. Downsizing does ensure that the resulting organization winds up smaller. But downsizing, by itself, cannot fix problems with products or services, with time lags in launching new products or services, with quality, or with any of the other myriad factors that help to determine success in the marketplace. In fact, as we will see in chapter 6, evidence exists that downsizing, with its significant costs in employee morale and motivation; potential quality problems; and diversion of attention to costs, job loss, and fear—and away from customer service, revenue growth, and innovation—does not even effectively reduce costs.

Does downsizing, in fact, provide great returns to the firms that do it? A study of one thousand large U.S. companies found that "investors place a much higher value on companies that improved their bottom lines through revenue growth than through cost cutting. . . . The reason for this clear preference . . . may be a recognition on the part of investors that gains made through cost cutting represent either a single event or one that can only be repeated a limited number of times."[12] The highest growth in absolute stock market value was achieved by companies that were able to increase both revenues and profits faster than average for their industry over the five-year period between 1988 and 1993. This study also found virtually no correlation between company size and revenue growth rate. It is not the case that companies must be small to grow, as the experience of Wal-Mart, Hewlett-Packard, and Motorola, among many others, attests. What about the importance of being in the right industry? This research also found *no* correlation between industry growth rate and the growth rates of companies within each industry. Rather, "the greater variation is between companies *within* industries, rather than among industries themselves. Within a given industry, the range of performance between the fastest-growing and the slowest-growing companies is greater than the range of performance between the fastest- and slowest-growing industries."[13]

Do you need to be global to be successful? It doesn't hurt, but it isn't necessary. Southwest Airlines is by far the best performing airline, but it operates only in the United States. Wal-Mart, the discount retailer, has provided exceptional economic returns, as have firms such as Home Depot (building supplies) and Staples (office equipment and supplies), even though these companies have only recently begun to locate any facilities outside of the United States. The number one ranked firm in the *Wall Street Journal*'s 1997 list of top performing companies over a ten-year period, with a total return to investors of an astounding 60.6 percent per year for ten years, was Concord EFS, a company in the business of providing payment-processing services, "which means handling credit- and debit-card transactions. . . . The company long has catered to small merchants and has carved out lucrative niches among trucking companies and grocery stores."[14] All of its business is in the United States.

These facts and analyses reveal the problems with our intuitions about the sources of success. Virtually no connection exists between organizational success and industry characteristics. Some very successful organizations operate in terrible industries. Wal-Mart has done quite well in an industry one-third of which was in bankruptcy in the early 1990s. Southwest Airlines produced a stock market return of over 21,000 percent between 1972 and 1992 and has been profitable in each of the past twenty-four years, a record unmatched by any other airline in the world except Singapore Airlines. After 1978, entry into the industry has been virtually unrestricted and there have been numerous new companies and intense competition. Meanwhile, between 1991 and 1992, some 40 percent of the U.S. airline industry either filed for bankruptcy (for example, Continental Airlines, America West, Trans World Airlines, and others) or ceased operations completely (as did Eastern Airlines). Furthermore, the evidence shows little or no connection between success over time and being a particular size or having a dominant market share. Southwest Airlines has enjoyed growth in revenue and profits that place it among the leaders in the airline industry. But it is far smaller than United, American, or Delta and holds a relatively small share of the national air traffic market. MBNA is smaller than Citicorp in its share of the credit card market, although it has enjoyed faster growth and better profitability. In the recent past, Chrysler has been more profitable than General Motors, in terms of return on sales, shareholders' equity, or total assets, even though it holds a smaller share of the automobile and truck market.

These facts about the sources of success are of more than just academic interest. The problem with looking for success in the wrong places is that organizational leaders take actions based on these faulty beliefs and, in the process, often cause irreparable harm to their organizations. They downsize—and do so in a mean-spirited fashion—thereby creating a death spiral for their organizations. They emphasize finding a magic strategic silver bullet to solve operational problems that come from how they treat their employees and the resulting level of innovation and performance. They seek economies of scale instead of economies of scope. In all of this, senior managers create economic damage that they, with their golden parachutes and generous severance arrangements, seldom pay for. By focusing on the wrong things, they pay too little attention to different, sustainable bases of competitive success, and thus are prone to managing their firms into economic decline.

STRATEGY OR IMPLEMENTATION?

Success comes from delivering value to your customers, and the ability to deliver value comes from having sound conceptions of what customers want and value and of how to organize and manage people to produce that value. Success frequently entails implementation rather than coming up with great ideas, simply because in the current world, implementation is much more difficult. As a senior officer at a major strategy consulting firm said to me, "*Finding* the answer is relatively easy; *doing* the answer is frequently impossible." Nonetheless, firms often pursue a strategic fix to what are fundamentally operational problems.

Consider, for instance, United Airlines. In the early 1990s, it faced a problem. Southwest Airlines had entered the intra-California marketplace and by 1994 had more than 50 percent of that market. United's concern was that much of its total profits came from its Asia Pacific routes. In 1996, for instance, United's revenue from that region constituted one-third of the firm's total revenues, and this market was experiencing substantial growth. Many of United's flights to the region departed from the gateway cities of Los Angeles and San Francisco. A strategic analysis led to the conclusion that the company needed control over its feeder traffic and could not simply cede the California market to Southwest. United came up with a "strategy"—imitate Southwest in its low fares, high levels of customer service, and even its look. Ground agents were put in shorts, athletic shoes, and golf shirts. Fares were slashed. The company used only Boeing 737s, the same plane that Southwest used. Finally, to be profitable and cut costs, United set itself the goal of turning its planes around in twenty minutes.

Unfortunately, executing that strategy proved to be a lot more difficult than coming up with it in the first place. My colleagues and I observed that United took more than thirty-five minutes to turn its planes around, meaning that initially it was always late and subsequently had to adjust its schedules. Service, delivered by flight attendants who were not part of the organization's employee ownership, was not always friendly or courteous. Indeed, in a move that some describe as bold, United recently embarked on an advertising campaign acknowledging the hassles of flying. I agree that the new advertising campaign is bold, but it also seems quite nervy—instead of trying to fix its service problems in what is, after all, a service industry, United is simply admitting its poor performance and making a joke out of it. As a consequence of its inability to match Southwest's costs (because of differences in asset utilization), on-time performance, or service, United has begun to pull out of many of the routes in which it directly competed with Southwest.

After 16 months, Shuttle by United has retreated from many Southwest routes and admits it hasn't gotten as close as it had hoped to Southwest's low costs. And Southwest has not only regained traffic lost initially to the Shuttle but also *increased* its California business. . . . One year ago, the two competed directly on 13% of Southwest's routes. Now United overlaps on only 7% of Southwest's routes. Southwest says California . . . now has fuller planes, better revenue and stronger profit than the rest of its system.[15]

Or, consider the case of Kaiser Permanente, a very large, old, health maintenance organization with a large base in California and a national presence. Competition in the provision of medical services has intensified substantially over the past several years. Kaiser was traditionally much less expensive than its fee-for-service competition and even than other HMOs. Kaiser, however, owns its own hospitals and buildings and, as a consequence, could not always offer lower prices than contracting networks that basically purchased excess capacity in the medical system at above marginal cost but well below the average cost of building and providing those services. Kaiser, however, did have one potential advantage: Most of its doctors were also partners, and because the system was completely integrated, no bureaucracy blocked access to care. Getting a referral to see a specialist or being admitted to the hospital did not require pre-authorization. Presumably, this permitted the organization to save money by not having the myriad clerks who now virtually run U.S. medical care, and it should also have permitted Kaiser to offer a more patient-friendly service. Finally, the system had a quality emphasis and a database that made measuring and managing quality feasible, as well as a strong social mission and a committed, long-term work force. These human assets and cultural values should be important strengths in the fierce competition for patients.

When Kaiser began to confront competitive stress—it was no longer the least expensive provider of medical services, in part because some of its competitors were trying to buy market share by aggressive pricing—the organization's response was unfortunate. Instead of focusing on implementing systems and practices that would permit it to generate the skills and behaviors required for competitive success, it responded by laying people off in an effort to cut costs and by reorganizing. Layoffs simply demotivated people and produced turnover—easily accomplished in a health-care environment in which strong administrative talent is in short supply. Reorganization made work for the consulting firm that recommended it, but it did not solve the basic issues of service implementation that would actually address issues of costs and quality.

Kaiser and United both sought solutions to operational issues in strategic "fixes," neither of which were completely successful. But it is easy to see why they did so. Many firms sell strategy analysis and consulting, and it is obviously tempting for an organization facing competitive challenge to seek help outside itself. Moreover, the strategic solutions always look so good. They have a precision and logic that is often compelling. Seldom asked is whether or not the strategy has much chance of being successfully implemented or whether the strategic solution solves basic operational problems or merely diverts attention and effort into new markets and new structures. It is often easier and substantially more seductive to manage something—a strategy—that is analyzable and can be reasonably readily changed, as contrasted with dealing with the day-to-day details of operations and implementation. Those problems are less glamorous, less interesting, but most importantly, much harder to solve.

Successful organizations understand the importance of implementation, not just strategy, and, moreover, recognize the crucial role of their people in this process. Consider, for instance, Norwest, a diversified financial services organization. In 1997, the company ranked twenty-second on the *Business Week 50,* a ranking of all Standard and Poor's 500 companies based on eight financial criteria: revenue growth, earnings growth, and total shareholder returns measured over both one- and three-year periods; net margin; and return on equity. Also in 1997, Norwest was named in the annual *Fortune* magazine survey of customer satisfaction as the best bank, tying Keycorp for the top spot. Between 1988 and 1996, the company achieved a 21 percent compounded annual growth in revenues and 24 percent compounded annual growth in net income. Richard Kovacevich, the CEO, had this to say about the relative importance of strategy and execution: "I could leave our strategic plan on a plane, and it wouldn't make any difference. No one could execute it. Our success has nothing to do with planning. It has to do with execution."[16] And what is the basis of Norwest's effective execution? Knowing the business, having good shared values, implementing advanced technology? "They're all important. But none are as important as talented, professional, motivated people who care. That's our real competitive advantage."[17]

A similar point of view is held by Tom Farmer, the founder and CEO of Kwik-Fit, the market-leading supplier of automobile repair services in the United Kingdom and the Netherlands, with a total of 726 stores and sales of $461 million at the end of the 1995 fiscal year. Between 1991 and 1995, earnings per share increased 55 percent in the difficult and competitive business of supplying tires, batteries, mufflers, brakes, and similar services. I had the opportunity to meet Tom Farmer when we were both on a program in London. Waiting to give our talks, I chatted with him about his philosophy and perspective on strategy. Tom disdained the common obsession with finding some magic strategic "fix." He said, "In a service business, there is only *one* successful strategy—to provide your customers outstanding value and service—customer delight." And, he recognized that customer service depended on having people who felt good about the organization and would, therefore, care about the customers. He has built the business on his recognition that people are the company's most valuable asset—the all-important contact with the customers—and the key to success.

Robert Waterman has provided an important insight on the connection between strategy and effectively managing people. He recognized that organization—people, culture, capability—are important sources of competitive advantage. People *are* the strategy.

> Organizing to anticipate and respond to customer needs . . . seems like a simple idea . . . it's at the heart of what we ought to mean by *strategy*. . . . For many managers, strategy . . . has meant either coming up with a brilliant idea or slamming the competition. . . . The companies I researched *do* look for sustainable competitive advantage. . . . They get a sustained advantage from the way they organize, not from the brilliant idea. Because they persist where others give up, they accomplish the most difficult part of strategy . . . implementation, that is, getting what is often a simple idea done and getting it done right.[18]

Success comes from successfully implementing strategy, not just from having one. This implementation capability derives, in large measure, from the organization's people, how they are treated, their skills and competencies, and their efforts on behalf of the organization. Fixing an organization's management practices may be more difficult than readjusting the strategy, but the payoff is often much greater. Managers are always well-advised to solve the real problem—not the one they would prefer to solve or are able to solve. This obvious recommendation is, unfortunately, all too often violated in practice.

MANAGEMENT PERSPECTIVE AND IMPLEMENTING PEOPLE-CENTERED STRATEGIES

How leaders diagnose and think about competitive conditions and business opportunities affects how their organizations manage people and, as a consequence, economic performance. An example drawn from banking in the United States and in Germany dramatically illustrates how different ways of responding to increased competition—in one instance centering the response on maintaining people and developing their skills and competencies and in another instance seeking to eliminate people and thereby reduce labor costs—produced very different results.

German and U.S. Banks' Response to Increased Competition

Suppose you were the chief executive of a bank at the beginning of the 1980s and could readily foresee the increased competition that was coming because of the deregulation of financial markets and the entry of new competitors. How would you respond? If you were like many bank executives in the United States, what you saw when you looked at your organization were costs—branches and people—fixed assets that would burden the organization in the coming competitive environment. You probably thought the best way to succeed was to become the lowest cost provider of financial services and, therefore, became cost driven. Since many of your costs were people costs, it seemed reasonable to attempt to reduce those costs as much as possible. Moreover, because some fraction of your costs were incurred in providing customer service, you might try to figure out how to deliver these services less expensively through automation, reduce or eliminate services, or charge for each service provided. On the other hand, if you were a senior bank executive in Germany, unionization, codetermination laws, and various labor regulations—as well as social custom—made the wholesale elimination of people virtually impossible. "Stuck" with your people, what you needed to do was to turn what to many may have looked like a cost or a liability—your people—into an important competitive asset. This could be accomplished by pursuing a high service, relationship-based strategy that involved cross-selling more financial services to your existing customer base—competing on the basis of service and economies of scope rather than on the basis of price and economies of scale.

The story of the two different paths pursued by German and U.S. banks during the 1980s is told in a brilliant doctoral dissertation by Brent Keltner[19] that ought to be read by all banking executives and by managers in any industry who have become accustomed to viewing technology and simply cutting costs, particularly people, as the road to competitive salvation. Keltner found that the strategy of eliminating people and service in what is, after all, the financial *services* industry was a prescription for losing market share. German banks, and those in the U.S. like Norwest that took a different approach, profited from developing and implementing more people-centered strategies.

The dominant approach of U.S. banks—to compete on the basis of price and convenience rather than on the basis of developing a financial relationship—was at best questionable as a foundation for long-term success.

> Customers attracted to a bank by promises of price discounts or other one-time offers can be expected to be the least loyal and thus constantly in search of a better offer. Product strategies based on continuous customer acquisition require high levels of expenditure on product development and advertising to compensate for customer churn.[20]

Moreover, since other providers had networks of distribution comparable to those of banks, when customers were pushed out of the branch—some banks charge extra to deal with a teller[21]—and the banks stressed convenience, they found it substantially more difficult to cross-sell other products to those customers. The problems with this approach can be seen by contrasting the dominant response of most banks with that of Norwest, a company that sees its branches as stores: "We like customers in our stores. Do you know of a successful retailer that doesn't? We believe we can do a more effective job of understanding our customers' financial needs when we meet them face to face."[22]

With a perspective that saw people as costs, U.S. banks invested heavily in technology and made extensive use of part-time help, minimized training, and used outside recruiting to fill positions that required higher level skills. The consequence of these employment policies was, not surprisingly, high turnover rates. Keltner reported that annual turnover across the commercial banking sector as a whole was 22 percent in the United States compared to 7 percent in Germany, 8.4 percent in Japan, and 10 percent in France.[23] Overall turnover masked much higher levels of turnover in specific positions, such as tellers and new account employees, which had turnover rates between 35 and 40 percent in most U.S. banks. With turnover among commercial credit officers at 33 percent and turnover among consumer credit people at 50 percent, the concept of relationship banking is reduced to a one-night stand; the odds of seeing the same person twice are not too high.[24]

With an undertrained and uncommitted work force and a basic business strategy almost destined to produce customer churn and disloyalty, it was nonetheless the case that some U.S. banks in the 1980s did manage to enjoy a measure of financial success because their cost cutting and consolidation efforts bore fruit even as their market shares in almost every segment declined. But this erosion in market position bodes ill for the future, when the strategy of consolidation and shrink-

Table 1-3   U.S. BANKS' CHANGING MARKET SHARES DURING THE 1980s

Product Segment	Market Share Development
Demand deposits	Decline from 32 to 22 percent of U.S. household assets
Investments	Minor share, with just 17 percent of mutual fund market
Life insurance	Negligible share with few sales of life insurance
Credit cards	Decline from 80 to 60 percent of market; two of three largest credit card companies (Dean Witter and AT&T) are non-banks
Consumer loans	Lost one-quarter of market, with 25 percent of consumer loans now controlled by retailers and finance companies

Source: Copyright © 1995, by The Regents of the University of California. Reprinted from the *California Management Review*, Vol. 37, No. 4. By permission of The Regents.

age will have reached its limit. Table 1-3 illustrates the decline in U.S. banks' overall market share in the consumer or retail banking segment. U.S. banks also lost market share in the wholesale or business market segment. The net result was to change where and how U.S. banks made their money: "By 1992, only 58% of the total revenues of U.S. money-center banks were being generated through interest-earning business, with over 40% of revenues coming from fee-based activities."[25]

By contrast, German banks took a very different approach to their people and a different strategic approach to their customers. For the most part, they invested heavily in human capital and organizational capabilities to pursue strategies founded on relationship banking. Training in the German banking sector was some 250 percent of the level of training in the economy as a whole, and people in banking were twice as likely to attend further training seminars after their apprenticeship programs.[26] German banks built a multi-skilled work force and used those people to sell multiple products to the bank's customer base, a strategy based on economies of scope and customer service rather than economies of scale and customer acquisition. "By offering their customers high levels of financial advising, quality service, and the convenience of consolidating financial service products with one provider, German banks managed to retain their competitive appeal."[27]

Table 1-4 provides evidence on the results of those policies in the retail market segment during the 1980s. Compared to their U.S. counterparts, German banks retained a much higher market share in retail deposits and actually gained market share in credit cards while maintaining a significant share of the consumer loan market and the investment market. In the business market segment, the trend for large firms to rely for financing more on the capital markets than on banks was counterbalanced by the German banks' success in cultivating small and mid-market borrowers. As a result, German banks enjoyed much more stability in how they earned their income. "For the banking sector as a whole . . . the percentage of business generated through lending activities remained at 82% of total revenues in 1991."[28]

Keltner's research provides substantial evidence that these differences in the evolution of banking in the United States and Germany were not simply the result of differences in regulatory or competitive circumstances. Rather, the differences occurred because of differences in strategy and how the banking sector in the two countries treated their people as a result of adopting very different perspectives on what those people could do for the firms. One only needs to consider the strategy and success of Norwest in the United States to see the plausibility of this argument.

How Mismanaging People Creates a Downward Spiral

We saw in the example of U.S. and German banks that a people-centered strategy can be a source of success in the market, as long as leaders can resist the temptation to see their people solely as costs, technology as salvation, and customer service as a burden. A people-centered strategy facilitates higher levels of customer service and enables firms to compete on the basis of knowledge, relationships, and service, not just price. By the same token, inattention to people as a source of competitive advantage and implementing poor, low commitment management practices can contribute to organizational decline. In both the positive and negative cases, important feedback processes create either a virtuous circle of management practices that build high commitment and performance, high levels of skill, motivation, and

Table 1-4 GERMAN BANKS' CHANGING MARKET SHARES DURING THE 1980s

Product Segment	Market Share Development
Demand deposits	Shrinking market share, from 60 to 48 percent of household assets
Investments	Maintained control, holding 66 percent of the share of bond sales to private individuals
Life insurance	Rapid growth from an initial 8 percent market share
Credit cards	Rapid growth from 25 to 80 percent market share
Consumer loans	Virtually the sole provider, with just limited competition from automobile producers

Source: Copyright © 1995, by The Regents of the University of California. Reprinted from the *California Management Review,* Vol. 37, No. 4. By permission of The Regents.

loyalty, and, as a consequence, good results, or alternatively, a downward performance spiral in which the wrong management responses to organizational problems destroy motivation and contribute to the loss of talent, thereby ensuring continued poor performance.

No clearer example of this downward spiral exists than Apple Computer. The Apple story is well known, but most accounts have stressed either strategic mistakes, such as not licensing the Macintosh operating system, or leadership issues, such as the succession to CEO by John Sculley and others. Some data about what happened at Apple, however, illustrate how management responses to performance issues divorced from a people-centered perspective can create a downward spiral and even more severe performance issues. Thus, the Apple story illustrates the negative case of what happens when a firm, the success of which derives fundamentally from its people, fails to put people first.

Founded in 1976 by Stephen Wozniak and Stephen Jobs in Jobs' garage, Apple's vision was to bring the power of the computer to the individual user. The Macintosh operating system, introduced in 1984, was (and many would maintain, still is) a leading technology in terms of ease of use. A column on personal computers in the *New York Times,* for instance, noted, "I have never seen a normal human being compare the Mac OS [operating system], Windows, and Unix systems side by side and come away saying, 'Gee, I really prefer the way Windows and Unix work.'"[29] Apple's laser printers and associated bundled software (from Adobe) launched the desktop publishing movement, and the company's emphasis on networks and connectivity among machines was also ahead of its time.

Apple was a company largely built on a unique culture. The Macintosh design team worked in a separate building with a pirate flag flying over it. The company built a cult-like commitment among its employees. People were recruited to Apple with the idea that they would be helping to change the world. Apple was more than a company, it was a cause. Its strategy of being an innovator in designing user-friendly personal computers that would make people more productive required a highly talented, creative, and innovative work force. When it took actions that resulted in the loss of that work force, its ability to implement its business strategy and to regain market leadership was irreparably harmed.

Obviously, not all of Apple's problems can be traced to how it handled its people. Even though its competitive advantage lay in its unique operating system, employing a mouse and a graphical user interface, the company consistently failed to license the operating system to other manufacturers, thereby limiting its share of the personal computer market. Because its culture emphasized technological innovation and being in the forefront of technology, Apple would occasionally introduce products, such as the Newton, the personal digital assistant, that were either far ahead of their time or had some remaining hardware or software bugs, or both, thus occasionally suffering commercial flops. But, a case can be made that its handling of its people made both its technical and market problems and its recovery from them much worse.

The *Apple Employee Handbook* espoused the importance of people to the firm's success.

> We've managed to succeed—year after year—in leading the personal computer industry largely because of the talent, tenacity, and spirit of our employees; how we work to communicate with each other openly and honestly; and how in the midst of constant change we still treasure our core values such as designing friendly products for people, innovation, quality, and teamwork.[30]

The handbook also spelled out many of the company's cherished cultural traditions, such as management accessibility and open communication, mementos of significant company events, celebrations of important life events of employees, and bagels and cream cheese on Friday mornings. In some sense, this publication, the culture of the company, and its traditions gave it an edge in recruiting talent but also set expectations for what working for Apple would be like. When these expectations were dashed, the resulting letdown was severe.

Apple has always had significant elements of an individualistic culture even as it talked about the importance of teams and teamwork. After the first round of layoffs in 1985, Apple really pioneered in articulating what has come to be called "the new employment contract." Consistently, and with increasing frequency over the years, the company maintained that its responsibility to its employees was not to give them any security or a career with a progression of jobs, but rather simply to provide a series of challenging job assignments that would permit employees to learn and develop so as to be readily employable. In a booming local job market, this encouraged people to develop talent and skills at Apple and then to use them elsewhere. The individualistic culture could also be seen in the language used to talk about people; they were characterized as "A," "B," or "C" players—the idea being that individuals were of varying quality (not that their performance was affected by how they were organized and managed)—and Apple wanted to attract and retain more "A's" and get rid of the "C's."

In 1985, Apple under John Sculley laid off 20 percent of its work force to cut its costs and return to profitability when its sales did not meet expectations. In 1991, another layoff occurred, this time of about 10 percent of the work force. In 1993, Michael Spindler replaced John Sculley, who had been seen as a visionary leader, and continued the cost cutting by laying off 2,500 people, about 14 percent of the company's work force, in July of that year. In 1997, another round of layoffs, this time comprising almost a third of the remaining people, occurred. More damaging than the layoffs themselves was the way they occurred in waves over time, making people unsure of their futures and tempting the best people to leave. Moreover, the layoffs were handled crudely, to detrimental effect in a company that had formerly held up open communication as an important cultural norm. One employee in Information Systems and Technology (the internal management information systems department) reported:

> The dismissal process occurred on a single day. Each employee was told to be at their desk at 9:00 A.M. in the morning. Those that received early calls into their managers' offices were laid off. They were given pink slips, final checks, and severance information. They were then escorted back to their desks by security to gather their things and then to the door. The remaining employees were gathered into a room at around 11:00 A.M. to discuss their new jobs, since restructuring immediately followed.
>
> Very little work was done within the organization from the time that layoffs were rumored, which was approximately two months in advance, and for months afterward. . . . The early word was that subsequent severance packages would not be nearly as sweet. Rumor has it that some of the best employees, including managers and directors, asked to be laid off to take advantage of other opportunities.[31]

The spirit of cost-cutting extended to salaries, which had previously been excellent to attract the best people, and to many of the amenities that had made working at the company special.

Now, all that management worries about is cutting costs. But at what price? For example, they no longer buy bagels and cream cheese on Friday mornings. It's ridiculous. Those bagels brought people together for much needed communication. It also made people get to work earlier than they otherwise would have. The twenty dollars they spent on bagels was easily made up in additional productivity.

Also, management doesn't seem to be concerned about rewarding employees for a job well done any longer. They are not allowed to give us a raise. There is no profit sharing. Offsites are gone. Project completion parties are a thing of the past. And you have to beg for a bonus, if you get one at all.[32]

Other Apple people noted that because of the fear of losing one's job when a project was over, many people slowed their progress substantially to delay finishing. Also, Apple's treatment of its people caused few to want to put in extra effort. Try to imagine turning around an organization facing substantial competitive stress with employees who shared the following perspective:

Overall, employees no longer feel valued here. Before, people were considered the biggest asset of the company. Management still says it, but we don't believe it anymore. In one of his addresses to employees, Michael Spindler made the comment that those employees that didn't like the situation here could go elsewhere. He basically told us that we were expendable.[33]

Although the last chapter of the Apple story has yet to be written, the loss of key technical and marketing personnel over time because of how they were treated has made the firm's prospects even worse than they had been or would otherwise be.

The pathologies at Apple Computer are all too common and result in a downward spiral of performance. One version of this downward spiral is depicted in Figure 1-1. A company, initially having problems with its profits, costs, or share price, takes quick action to raise profits and lower costs. Since employee costs are typically the most quickly and easily changed, the following actions are common: Training is curtailed; pay may be frozen or cut; promotions are held up; the use of part-time or temporary help increases; and people are laid off or forced to work reduced hours. These measures logically and inevitably reduce motivation, satisfaction, loyalty to the company and intentions to remain with it, and focus on the job (as contrasted with discussing rumors and sharing complaints with coworkers). Cutting training cuts skill and knowledge development and dissemination. Attention focused on unhappiness at work can create a climate in which job related accidents and associated worker compensation costs as well as poor customer service flourish. But poor customer service, high accident rates, increased turnover and absenteeism, and the resulting productivity problems adversely affect sales, profits, and costs. So the cycle continues. In the short run, some firms may be able to cut costs and thereby increase profits to a greater extent than the resulting problems cut profits and productivity. In some cases, cuts can be made in ways that do less rather than more damage to the long-run viability of the organization. Nevertheless, the downward spiral just described, while not inevitable, is all

Figure 1-1 DOWNWARD PERFORMANCE SPIRAL

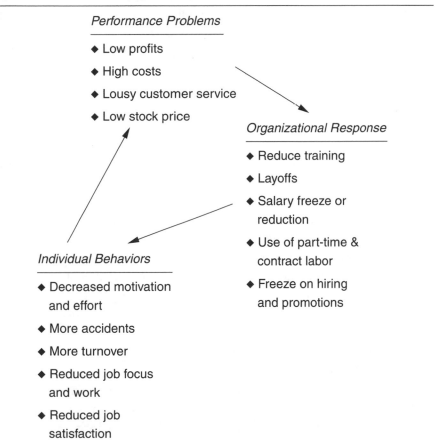

Performance Problems

◆ Low profits

◆ High costs

◆ Lousy customer service

◆ Low stock price

Organizational Response

◆ Reduce training

◆ Layoffs

◆ Salary freeze or reduction

◆ Use of part-time & contract labor

◆ Freeze on hiring and promotions

Individual Behaviors

◆ Decreased motivation and effort

◆ More accidents

◆ More turnover

◆ Reduced job focus and work

◆ Reduced job satisfaction

too common and, in fact, characterized Apple. Clearly, not enough organizations take a people-centered view of the source of their performance and success.

The decimation of the furniture industry in North London, in which a local industry employing about 16,000 people was reduced in less than twenty years to one firm employing fewer than 600, provides another dramatic illustration of this downward spiral in action.

> Faced with increasing competition, the firms sought to maintain market share by cutting prices and costs. They perceived their problem to be excessive wages and competition from neighboring firms, and they reacted by hiring less-skilled workers, automating or increasing the intensity of work, and cutting prices in an effort to drive other firms out of business. These responses, however, left the North London firms with worsening relations with their workers, slimmer margins, and eventually, insufficient financial capacity to survive. They were thus less able to respond to the real problem, which was . . . the emergence of foreign competitors organized around new principles.[34]

CONCLUSION

In this first chapter we have seen that the conventional wisdom about the sources of success—that it's important to be in the right industry, to be large, to be global, to engage in downsizing and cost cutting, and to have some technological or brand equity barrier to competition— turns out not to be consistent with the evidence. Substantial returns are possible even in low technology industries with few barriers to entry and even for relatively small organizations—if they are actually able to implement strategies that provide customer value. Of course, some very successful firms have achieved outstanding technological success. In many instances, this success has been derived from how they manage people, and as we saw in the case of Apple, losing their people advantage can make other problems worse. The management issue is scarcity of time and attention. An emphasis on technological or strategic fixes can divert management action and concern away from the people management practices that develop sustained success. In fact, often, the common response to performance problems creates a downward spiral, as capabilities and motivation are destroyed by short-sighted palliatives.

Seeking success through technology, or strategy, or size, or global positioning somehow seems more complicated or sophisticated. Success achieved by doing the right thing with your people seems simple—but, of course, it does require consistent implementation and a point of view on the sources of success that appears to be in short supply today. Nonetheless, people often ask: If you are about to tell us how to achieve economic success through people, and if, in fact, much if not most of this is well known, how can this be a source of competitive leverage?

My answer is simple: I have come to call it the one-eighth rule. One-half of the people, at most, in spite of the large amount of evidence to be presented both in the next chapter and throughout this book, won't really believe the connection between how organizations manage their people and the profits they earn. Few business schools, management courses, or management books emphasize the importance of people and management practices as contrasted with those that maintain that success comes from strong executive leadership, technological or strategic fixes, or financial engineering. One-half of those who do see the connection will do as many organizations I have seen do—try to make a single change to solve their problems, not realizing that the effective management of people requires a more comprehensive and systemic approach.

Finally, of the half of the firms that will make comprehensive changes to enhance how they manage their people, probably only about one-half of those will persist with their practices long enough to actually derive economic benefits. We live in a world in which long-term thinking is the exception rather than the rule. Managers face demands to make next quarter's numbers, both for the external capital markets and for internal management evaluation and control systems. But it obviously takes time to achieve benefits from training, from reorganized work, and the other practices of high performance management. Not many firms invest the time required. Since one-half times one-half times one-half equals one-eighth, at best a small fraction of organizations will actually do what is required to build profits by putting people first. Those that do will enjoy the benefits. The rest will continue to search for economic success in the wrong places.

The examples, data, and logic presented in this first chapter, although extensive, do not constitute overwhelming evidence for the validity of the claims about the importance of managing people right. We have talked about where success *doesn't* come from, and now it is time to see where it *does*. Managers want hard, scientific evidence about the effects of management practices on organizational performance—the business case for managing people effectively. It so happens that a great deal of such evidence exists, and we will review a substantial portion of it in the next chapter.

2 • The Business Case for Managing People Right

EXECUTIVES FREQUENTLY SAY, "Show me the business case for the effects of management practices that put people first on organizational performance. And, by the way, don't just give me anecdotes specifically selected to make some point. Show me the evidence!" That's just what I will do in this chapter. Most books on management, and this one is no exception, make liberal use of case examples to illustrate points and make them come alive. But, as the old saying goes, "For example is not proof." Managers and other readers should have something more than merely case illustrations, anecdotes, and stories on which to rely when making important business decisions.

Fortunately, there is a substantial and rapidly expanding body of evidence, some of it quite methodologically sophisticated, that speaks to the strong connection between how firms manage their people and the economic results achieved. This chapter reviews that evidence in detail. I believe that in today's competitive world, intelligent executives need to know not just what to do or even how to do it but also the evidence on which these recommendations rest. Those already convinced or not needing extensive data to help convince others can skip this chapter.

It is important to recognize at the outset that effectively managing people is not the *sole* basis for competitive success, nor, obviously, does variation in management practices account by itself for *all* of the variation in organizational performance, even in situations in which it is important. Under some conditions, however, managing people effectively becomes relatively more important in understanding variations in organizational performance.

> Innovative human resource practices are likely to contribute to improved economic performance only when three conditions are met: when employees possess knowledge and skills that managers lack; when employees are motivated to apply this skill and knowledge through discretionary effort; and when the firm's business or production strategy can only be achieved when employees contribute such discretionary effort.[1]

Of course, the amount of discretionary effort people contribute is itself affected by the management practices they experience; obtaining discretionary effort is customarily important; and people typically have some knowledge or skills needed by the organization. These conditions help us to understand, however, when effective people management will be more or less important a determinant of organizational performance.

What the evidence to be presented here shows—drawing from studies of the five-year survival rates of initial public offerings; studies of profitability and stock price in large samples of companies from multiple industries; and detailed research on the automobile, apparel, semiconductor, steel manufacturing, oil refining, and service industries—is this: Substantial gains, on the order of 40 percent or so in most of the studies reviewed, can be obtained by implementing high performance management practices. The available evidence also shows that, in spite of the manifest economic advantages of certain management practices, the diffusion of such practices has been neither quick nor extensive. In fact, some firms are moving away from the use of high commitment management—changes in practice are too often short-lived. Even when implemented, changes in management approach are often introduced in a truncated and partial manner.[2] These findings indicate that simply demonstrating the connection between how people are managed and the results achieved is insufficient to invariably produce change.

How can such substantial benefits in profits, quality, and productivity occur? These tremendous gains come about because high commitment management approaches provide a number of important sources for enhanced organizational performance.

1. People work harder, because of the increased involvement and commitment that comes from having more control over and say in their work.

2. People work smarter; high performance management practices encourage the building of skills and competence and, as importantly, facilitate the efforts of people in actually applying their wisdom and energy to enhancing organizational performance.

3. High commitment management practices, by placing more responsibility in the hands of people farther down in the organization, save on administrative overhead as well as other costs associated with having an alienated work force in an adversarial relationship with management.

Thus, high performance management practices work not because of some mystical process, but because the set of practices is grounded in sound social science principles that have been shown to be effective by a great deal of evidence.

Many, although not all, of the studies to be reviewed in this chapter are studies of single industries, an approach with some powerful advantages. The measures of performance can be more precise and comparability across organizations is enhanced. Operational measures of productivity, for instance, such as the labor hours required to produce some standard output, oil refinery maintenance costs, or the proportion of time a steel finishing line operates, can be computed and meaningfully compared. Cross-industry studies must necessarily rely on outcomes that can be compared across companies operating in different industries, such as growth, profitability, or financial returns, and cannot measure more specific, operations-oriented indicators. Also, in these single-industry studies, other factors that might account for performance differences are either controlled by the very design of the study, for example, industry economic conditions are constant for all firms in the industry, or can be more readily measured and included in the analysis. Consequently, the single-industry studies typically have more detail and specificity than those that cover firms that span industries.

The industries in which high performance management has been shown to have significant economic benefit range from relatively low technology settings such as apparel manufacturing to very high technology manufacturing processes such as semiconductor wafer fabrication. The results seem to hold for both manufacturing and for service firms. Nothing in the available evidence suggests that the results are country-specific and, in fact, the evidence shows that the results generalize quite well cross-nationally. Thus, the evidence outlined below should convince you that the effects of high performance management practices are real, economically significant, and general—and thus should be adopted in your organization.

MANAGEMENT PRACTICES AND ORGANIZATIONAL FINANCIAL PERFORMANCE

Does how a firm manages its people affect profitability and stock price? Yes, according to an award-winning study by Mark Huselid. The research was based on 968 responses to a survey of the senior human resources professional in a sample of 3,452 firms representing all major industries. Huselid used the survey responses to construct two scales. The first, called employee skills and organizational structures, "includes a broad range of practices intended to enhance employees' knowledge, skills and abilities and . . . provide mechanisms through which employees can use those attributes in performing their roles."[3] The second scale, measuring employee motivation, is comprised of practices "designed to recognize and reinforce desired employee behaviors. These practices include using formal performance appraisals, linking those appraisals tightly with employee compensation, and focusing on . . . merit in promotion decisions."[4]

The study assessed the effects of management practices on turnover, sales per employee (a measure of productivity), and the firm's ratio of stock market to book value. In his analysis, Huselid not only included a large number of potential alternative explanations for the results, such as size, capital intensity, concentration ratio of the firm's industry, research and development expenditures as a proportion of sales, and others, he also employed statistical methodology that permitted him to better assess the direction of causality: Was performance driving management practices or were the practices affecting performance? Finally, the study employed statistical procedures to overcome sample selection bias, that is, the possibility that the 28 percent of the surveyed firms that actually responded were somehow systematically different from the nonresponders in ways that could bias the results.

Huselid observed both statistically significant and substantively important results for both of his scales assessing management practices:

> The magnitude of the returns for investment in High Performance Work Practices is substantial. A one standard deviation increase in such practices is associated with a . . . 7.05 percent decrease in turnover and, on a per employee basis, $27,044 more in sales and $18,641 and $3,814 more in market value and profits, respectively.[5]

Yes, you read those results correctly, and they were derived from a number of different estimation procedures. One standard deviation above the mean puts the company in the upper 16 percent of all those in the study in terms of its use of high commitment work practices—so it is in reasonably select company. But the economic returns for those implementing these policies have been enormous—more than an $18,000 increase in stock market value *per employee.*

A subsequent study conducted in 1996 of 702 firms, using a somewhat more comprehensive conception of the human resource management system, found even larger economic benefits: "A one standard deviation improvement in the HR system index was associated with an increase in shareholder wealth of $41,000 per employee."[6] Since the average stock market value per worker for all of the firms in the sample was about $300,000, firms in the upper 16 percent of the distribution in terms of their use of high performance management practices experienced about a 14 percent market value premium—clearly economically substantial.

Are these results unique to firms operating in the United States? No. Similar results were obtained in a study of more than one hundred German companies operating in ten industrial sectors. The study found "a strong link between investing in employees and stock market performance. Companies which place workers at the core of their strategies produce higher long-term returns to shareholders than their industry peers."[7] The research also found that companies that focused on their people not only delivered superior returns to their stockholders but also created more jobs, an important result given the high unemployment rate in much of Europe.

FIVE-YEAR SURVIVAL RATES OF
INITIAL PUBLIC OFFERINGS

One of the clearest demonstrations of the causal effect of management practices on performance comes from a study of the five-year survival rate of 136 non-financial companies that initiated their public offering in the U.S. stock market in 1988.[8] The results are so compelling that prudent investors may want to use these results in evaluating new companies. The firms studied came from numerous industries ranging from biotechnology to food service retailing and varied widely in size, with half employing fewer than 110 people but with 20 percent having 700 or more employees. Five came from foreign countries. By 1993, some five years later, eighty-one firms, or 60 percent of the sample, were still in existence.

Theresa Welbourne and Alice Andrews developed two scales, along with other factors, for explaining company survival. The information used in measuring the firms' management practices came from their offering prospectuses and thus is publicly available. The first scale measured the value the firm placed on human resources and was comprised of five items: (1) whether the company's strategy and mission statements cited employees as constituting a competitive advantage; (2) whether the company's materials mentioned employee training programs; (3) whether a company official was charged with responsibility for human resource management; (4) the degree to which the company used full-time employees rather than temporary or contract workers; and (5) the company's self-rating of its employee relations climate.[9] The second scale measured how the organization rewarded people; it was computed, using a 0-1 code, by summing whether the company had stock options for all employees; stock options only for key employees and management; profit sharing for all employees; profit sharing for key employees and management; and other group-based incentives, such as gain sharing.

The empirical analysis demonstrated that with other factors such as size, industry, and even profits statistically controlled, both the human resource value scale and the rewards scale were significantly related to the probability of survival. Moreover, the results were substantively important. As shown in Figure 2-1, the difference in survival probability for firms one standard deviation above and one standard deviation below the mean (in the upper 16 percent and the lower 16 percent of all firms in the sample) on the human resource value scale was almost 20 percent. The difference in survival depending on where the firm scored on the rewards scale was even more dramatic, with a difference in five-year survival probability of 42 percent between firms in the upper and lower tails of the distribution.[10]

Figure 2-1 PROBABILITY OF AN INITIAL PUBLIC OFFERING FIRM
SURVIVING FIVE YEARS

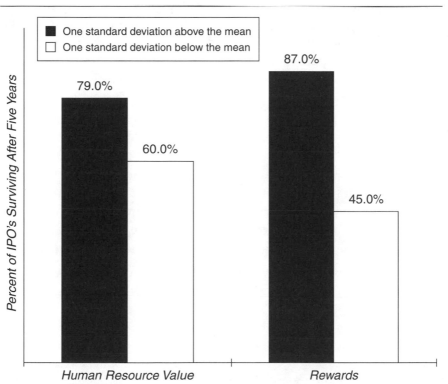

Source: Based on information from Theresa Welbourne and Alice Andrews, "Predicting Performance of Initial Public Offering Firms: Should HRM Be in the Equation?" *Academy of Management Journal* 39 (1996): 910–911.

THE AUTOMOBILE INDUSTRY

The 1980s were a turbulent time for the U.S. automobile industry. The decade began with Ford, Chrysler, and General Motors posting tremendous losses. Chrysler had to rely on government loan guarantees to avoid bankruptcy, and Ford's substantial financial losses drove that company to the brink of disaster. General Motors saw its share of the U.S. market decline by about a quarter, from around 40 percent to 30 percent. Meanwhile, Japanese automobile companies took an increasing proportion of the U.S. and world markets, reaching almost 30 percent in the United States. Faced with substantial distress in an industry important to the economy, the U.S. government negotiated with the Japanese government a set of "voluntary" quotas on automobile imports.

The Japanese auto companies responded in two ways—neither of which, ironically, ultimately contributed to the long-term health of the American manufacturers. First, faced with numerical quotas on the number of cars imported, the Japanese decided to go up-market with larger, more expensive cars that earned higher margins on a per-unit basis. Second, the Japanese, recognizing that the issue of imports was already or soon would bedevil them all over the world, decided to expand their production offshore and to incorporate a higher level of domestic content into their products. In the automobile industry, this resulted in Japanese companies opening numerous assembly plants in the United States. Because the industry had excess capacity, this plant expansion resulted in even more severe competitive pressure.

Because U.S. manufacturers were closing plants while the Japanese were opening new ones, opportunities resulted for the creation of a joint venture between Toyota and General Motors in Fremont, California, near San Francisco. GM had closed its Fremont plant in 1982. At that time, the plant had poor productivity, poor quality, and a history of extensive labor troubles, including strikes, high levels of absenteeism and turnover, and problems with alcoholism and drug abuse. Toyota wanted experience dealing with U.S. workers and suppliers. GM wanted to learn about the famous Toyota Production System (TPS) and how to make cars more efficiently. Their common interests resulted in the formation of a joint venture, New United Motor Manufacturing, Inc. (NUMMI).

When NUMMI began production in the Fremont plant in 1985, 85 percent of the people had been employed in the old plant. The plant was still organized by the United Auto Workers and used the same equipment that had been there in the past. Productivity and quality, however, substantially improved over the results achieved when the plant was run by General Motors. NUMMI provided an important site in which to assess the effects of management practices. Because the personnel, equipment, and location were unchanged, and the only difference was in the production system and management practices, any improvements in conditions at the plant could be attributed to the new management approach. Moreover, to the extent that improvements in NUMMI's operations were documented, the question of whether it was possible to change results in an existing facility was answered in the affirmative.

In 1986, John Krafcik, a GM employee attending graduate school at M.I.T., compiled productivity and quality data for four plants: the GM Fremont plant, using data gathered a few years prior to the plant's closing so that it would not capitalize on a period of particularly poor performance; Framingham, an assembly plant in Massachusetts typical of General Motors' facilities at that time (the plant has subsequently been closed); NUMMI; and Takaoka, a major Toyota assembly plant in Japan. Krafcik gathered data on the raw production figures—the labor hours required to assemble a car—and then adjusted those figures for other things that might affect productivity, such as product design, option content, and other technical considerations. The results of his analysis appear in Table 2-1.

The NUMMI advantage over both Framingham and the old GM Fremont plant was substantial—more than 50 percent fewer labor hours to assemble an automobile even after adjusting for various technical factors. Krafcik's results demonstrated that nothing inherent in the U.S. work force precluded U.S. automobile assembly plants from reaching world-class levels of productivity and, for that matter, quality—NUMMI achieved quality better than did the two GM comparison plants and approached the quality achieved by Toyota in Japan.

Perhaps the most interesting part of the NUMMI story, however, is what happened to John Krafcik. GM had entered into the joint venture with the stated goal of learning about the Toyota Production System. When confronted with evidence that the system could be implemented in the U.S. in a unionized setting with outstanding results, GM reacted defensively. Learning from NUMMI came with difficulty to General Motors, which had bet heavily on automation and capital equipment rather than people. As John Paul MacDuffie noted, "GM did a terrible job of learning from NUMMI."[11] John Krafcik eventually wound up working for Ford, a firm much more open at that time to employee involvement and to achieving productivity and profits through people.

The NUMMI results stimulated researchers at M.I.T. to launch a major comparative study covering virtually every mass-production automobile assembly plant in the world. In 1989, ninety plants were contacted and seventy participated in a study that spanned plants representing twenty-four companies in seventeen different countries, with the data to be reported here coming from sixty-two volume (as contrasted with luxury) plants. The research contrasted two production systems: first, the traditional, mass production system with its Tayloristic, control-oriented approach to managing people, reliance on inventories to maintain production volumes against unanticipated events, and inspection and control to ensure quality; and second, a lean or flexible production system with an emphasis on teams, employee involvement, and reduction of inventories to highlight production problems that could then be remedied. An analysis of these data by John Paul MacDuffie uncovered substantial differences in both quality and productivity attribut-

Table 2-1   PRODUCTIVITY AND QUALITY COMPARISONS AMONG FOUR AUTOMOBILE PLANTS

	Framingham 1986	GM–Fremont 1978	Nummi 1986	Takaoka 1986
Adjusted Productivity (hours required to assemble a car, adjusted for engineering and technical differences)				
Hourly	26.2	24.2	16.3	15.5
Salaried	4.6	4.9	3.3	2.5
Total	30.8	29.1	19.6	18.0
NUMMI's Advantage	57.1%	48.5%	0	–8.2%

Source: Table from "Learning from NUMMI," by John Krafcik, International Motor Vehicle Program, MIT, 1986.

able to the two systems. Table 2-2 presents some of the differences between the two systems. The data in the table reveal two things: first, quality and productivity are much higher in flexible than in mass production systems, and second, the two systems differ substantially in how they manage people—in the amount of training provided, in the use of teams, in the reduction of status differences, and in the use of contingent, performance-dependent compensation.

I have found that many organizations want change, but nobody wants to do anything differently. The automobile assembly plant study demonstrates how profoundly different management practices must be

Table 2-2 PRODUCTIVITY, QUALITY, AND WORK ORGANIZATION IN SIXTY-TWO AUTOMOBILE PLANTS

	Mass Production	Flexible Production	% Difference
Results			
Quality (defects/100 cars)	94.1	49.5	47.4%
Productivity (hours/car)	36.6	20.9	42.9%
Management Practices			
% of Work Force in Teams	5.0	70.2	1,304%
Training of New Hires (0=Low to 3=High)	1.0	2.4	140%
Training Experienced Employees (0=Low to 3=High)	.9	2.1	133%
Job Rotation Index (0=None to 4=Much)	1.2	3.0	150%
Contingent Pay (0=None; 4=Based on Plant Performance)	.72	3.0	317%
Status Differences (0=Extensive to 4=Little)	1.1	3.4	209%

Source: John Paul MacDuffie, "Human Resource Bundles and Manufacturing Performance: Organizational Logic and Flexible Production Systems in the World Auto Industry," *Industrial and Labor Relations Review* 48 (1995): 211, 212.

to achieve the economic benefits of high commitment management. Although these changes are not economically costly in many instances, they do fundamentally challenge how many firms think about managing their people.

The results of the worldwide motor vehicle study appeared in *The Machine that Changed the World,* published in 1990. Within a few years, it was impossible to find executives from the automobile or automotive parts industry that were not familiar with the elements of flexible or lean production. The following list details the characteristics of lean or flexible manufacturing systems—elements similar to those used in the Toyota production system.[12]

◆ Just-in-time inventory systems and lean staffing that minimize production buffers.

◆ Rapid machine setups to permit small production runs by reducing changeover times.

◆ Use of work teams on the production line.

◆ Extensive training to develop multiskilled workers, who can, for example, both operate equipment and do some repairs on it.

◆ Job rotation to facilitate on-the-job learning of multiple tasks and skills.

◆ Off-line problem-solving or quality circle groups that involve employees in continuous improvement activities.

With great economic benefits to be derived and a wide dissemination of this information, did the adoption of flexible production principles follow quickly and universally? Not according to a follow-up study of many of the same plants conducted by Frits Pil and John Paul MacDuffie. A second round of data collection in 1993 and 1994 generated data from forty-three plants that had also participated in the first round. The research used a composite "Work Practices" index to measure the amount of change in the use of high performance management practices between 1989 and 1994. The values of the index ranged from 0 (for the plant with the lowest amount of high commitment work practices) to 100 (for the plant with the greatest implementation of those practices).

Pil and MacDuffie reported that high-involvement work arrangements increased over the five-year period, with the index increasing by about 35 percent. The study also showed, however, substantial variation in the degree to which plants changed. "Some plants undertook only minor change in their use of high-involvement work practices . . . while other plants showed dramatic increases and still others showed modest decreases."[13]

One of the most interesting findings from the analysis of the adoption of flexible production was that the worst performing plants in the earlier period were no more likely than better-performing plants to increase their use of high involvement management practices. In other words, the plants that most needed improvement were not more likely to adopt the flexible manufacturing and high commitment management practices that could actually improve their performance. Performance had no impact on the use of performance-enhancing methods. Another important finding was that the longer-tenured plant managers were more likely to increase their use of high commitment management practices, contrary to the customary assumption that those with less tenure and investment in a system are more likely to change.

The data from the automobile industry also permit us to see to what extent national-level management practices vary and the extent to which such variation persists. In Table 2-3, I reproduce data comparing the adoption of a set of specific, high performance management practices in automobile plants with different ownership in different countries. Although some evidence shows a degree of convergence toward the flexible or lean production model, differences persist. The largest increase in the use of high performance management practices occurred in Europe, with the newly industrializing countries and Australia close behind. The least change occurred in the U.S-owned plants in North America. It is likely that the rapid diffusion of these practices in Europe derived both from the long-time interest of European unions in experimenting with alternative work arrangements and from the strength of the unions, which meant that simply closing plants and shifting production off-shore was less of an option. Consequently, manufacturers had to fix their productivity and quality problems rather than simply trying to run away from them or to overcome them by moving to lower cost sites.[14] These data are significant because they provide evidence for the importance of national institutional factors in affecting the adoption of high performance management practices, and they support the idea that competitive or technological determinism has a limited effect on work practices. In other words, managerial and institutional choices matter, and all is not determined simply by competitive dynamics and some inexorable march of technology.

THE STEEL INDUSTRY

Two major studies have examined management practices and operational performance in the steel industry. One looked at thirty production lines that used a specific type of finishing operation, to ensure comparability in the results. The sample included multiple lines for the major steel producers and one or two lines for smaller producers. The research gathered data on incentive pay, employment security, the actions taken to increase the skills and knowledge of employees, job flexibility, communication and information sharing, grievance rates for

Table 2-3   DIFFUSION OF SOME HIGH PERFORMANCE MANAGEMENT PRACTICES ACROSS DIFFERENT AUTOMOBILE ASSEMBLY PLANTS

Plant Ownership/ Location	% Work Force in Teams		Job Rotation		Suggestions per Employee	
	'89	'93/94	'89	'93/94	'89	'93/94
Japan/Japan	78	70	3.8	4.2	56	48
Japan/North America	71	76	2.7	3.7	1.1	1.9
U.S./North America	10	6	0.9	2.1	0.3	0.2
U.S. & Europe/ Europe	0.4	75	1.8	3.9	0.3	1.0
Newly industrialized countries	2	30	2.2	3.7	2.3	Not available
Australia	0	34	1.7	3.7	0.1	0.2

Source: John Paul MacDuffie, "International Trends in Work Organization in the Auto Industry: National-Level vs. Company-Level Perspectives," in The Comparative Political Economy of Industrial Relations, eds. Kirsten S. Wever and Lowell Turner (Madison, WI: Industrial Relations Research Association, 1995): 90.

unionized plants, and the degree of cooperation between labor and management.[15] The measure of performance was line delays or downtime, which the authors found to be the most important predictor of productivity.

On average, for the sample as a whole, the lines operated 91.9 percent of the time, with the percentage ranging dramatically from a low of 39.8 percent to a high of 99.6 percent. The research found that the various management practices tended to be correlated with each other—human resource environments tended to define distinct systems or employment relation cultures. Using a statistical procedure to categorize management systems into four categories, the study denoted System 1 lines as those with progressive human resource policies, including careful selection, training, and orientation of new employees, extensive formal training for all operators, job rotation and multiskilling of all people, and the use of team problem-solving techniques. By contrast, System 4 lines had a traditional, Tayloristic approach to organizing work, with strict work rules and narrow job responsibilities, minimal employee involvement, incentive pay based on quantity and not quality, little formal training, and little selective screening of new people.[16]

Controlling statistically for numerous factors that might affect the proportion of time a finishing line operates, the use of the various management systems had a statistically significant and economically important effect. The difference in the proportion of time a line operated moving from the traditional System 4 to the most progressive System 1 lines was about 11 percent, or from operating 87 percent of the time to being in operation 98 percent of the time.[17] Using cost data from one specific line as an example, the research estimated that a one percent increase in the amount of time a line operated would increase operating income by about $360,000 per year. Since this line was comparatively small, the profit effects on larger lines would be even more substantial.[18]

The research also gathered data on changes in management practices. The evidence about the effects of changing to a more progressive system indicated significant improvements in productivity. In spite of the substantial economic benefits to be derived from moving to a high commitment management system, the evidence showed a low level of implementation of high performance management systems. Although a great majority of steel mills used at least one or a few of the practices, "only 11 percent of these production units had the full system of innovative work practices that is shown to lead to the highest level of productivity and quality."[19] Because the study found the effects of management practices to be complementary, meaning that a company gets relatively little benefit from adopting them piecemeal, the failure of plants to adopt a comprehensive system of high performance management practices meant that comparatively few enjoyed the productivity gains from managing their people using best practices.

Another study of thirty of the fifty-four existing minimills in the United States contrasted two different management approaches, one characterized as a "control" approach and the other as a "commitment" approach.

> The goal of *control* human resource systems is to reduce labor costs, or improve efficiency by enforcing employee compliance with specified rules and procedures and basing employee rewards on some measurable output criteria. . . . In contrast, *commitment* human resource systems shape desired employee behaviors . . . by forging psychological links between organizational and employee goals. . . . [T]he focus is on developing committed employees who can be trusted to carry out job tasks.[20]

Table 2-4 CONTROL AND COMMITMENT MANAGEMENT PRACTICES IN THIRTY STEEL MINIMILLS

Management Practice	Control	Commitment	% Difference
Wages	$18.07	$21.52	19.1%
Skill (maintenance and craft workers as % of all employees)	14.0%	19.0%	35.7%
% in teams or small problem-solving groups	36.6%	52.4%	43.1%
Decentralization (1=very little to 6=very much)	2.42	3.04	25.6%
General training	1.92	3.35	74.5%

Source: Jeffrey B. Arthur, "Effects of Human Resource Systems on Manufacturing Performance and Turnover," *Academy of Management Journal* 37 (1995): 676.

Table 2-4 shows the differences in management practices across the two systems. Note that commitment systems pay higher wages, use teams more, have a more highly skilled work force, engage in more general training, and have more decentralization and delegation of authority. As we will discuss in the next chapter, high wages, an emphasis on training and skill development, organization of people in teams, and decentralization of decision making are among the key dimensions that constitute high performance management practices and that produce substantial economic gains.

The research measured two dimensions of minimill performance, labor efficiency, or the hours of labor required to make a ton of steel, and the scrap rate. After statistically controlling for the age, size, union status, and business strategy of the mills, the results showed that using a commitment strategy was significantly related to improved performance in terms of labor hours and the scrap rate. Moreover, the differences between the two systems were economically important. Minimills using commitment-oriented management practices required 34 percent fewer labor hours to produce a ton of steel and showed a 63 percent better scrap rate.

APPAREL MANUFACTURING INDUSTRY

The apparel industry is a particularly interesting setting in which to explore the effects of high performance management practices. Unlike some other industries that depend on high levels of skill or that are protected by the relatively high cost of transporting the product, apparel manufacturers truly compete on a worldwide basis, albeit in the United States with still some degree of quota and tariff protection. By 1991, imports of apparel accounted for more than half of U.S. expenditures. Focusing only on wage rates, one might conclude that there should not be an apparel industry at all in the United States or, for that matter, in Italy or any other comparatively high-wage country. For instance, in 1989, average hourly earnings for textile and apparel workers were $2.69 in Hong Kong, $2.19 in Korea, $2.36 in Singapore, and $2.68 in Taiwan, compared to $6.85 in the United States[21] In fact, employment in the industry has shrunk dramatically in the United States over the past several decades. U.S. textile manufacturers have complained bitterly about their labor cost disadvantage, although textile industry wages are substantially lower than for either U.S. manufacturing or U.S. industry overall.

With a disadvantage in direct labor rates, one might think that manufacturers would aggressively seek other sources of competitive advantage, such as reducing labor costs through productivity gains or by offering delivery, quality, and other attributes of service. But, for the most part, "apparel production is still dominated by operators pushing material through sewing machines."[22] In response to the wage rate pressure, the apparel industry has pursued a set of related strategies of outsourcing production to sweatshops (in violation of U.S. labor laws), locating new plants in the South to avoid unionization, emphasizing piecework (paying on the basis of what is sewn in a day), and generally operating using management practices that are throwbacks to times long past and that, among other things, increase occupational injuries substantially.[23]

The industry has also sought salvation in automation rather than by changing management practices, as demonstrated by this quote from an article in the leading apparel magazine:

> Our main hope for the return of production of basic apparel items to the U.S. mainland is automation of the production process. Only with the labor element essentially eliminated through robotic automation can the advantages of the emerging countries be overcome by the U.S. manufacturer.[24]

This emphasis on wage rates may be, in this instance as in many others, highly misplaced. In fact, the direct labor cost component of most garments is trivial—$1.71 for a shirt, $2.24 for pants, $.17 for a T-shirt, and a mere $12.50 for a man's suit.[25] Meanwhile, in an industry based importantly on fashion and with retailers increasingly seeking better inventory management, quality and delivery performance can be more important than wage cost as bases of competitive success. Nevertheless, industry executives have often failed to change their approach to management.

> The faster changes in styles and the greater variety and uncertainty in apparel markets increase the advantages of fast delivery times; thus physical proximity to the U.S. market is now an important competitive advantage for domestic producers, but only if they can produce on short notice. . . . "Manufacturing executives in the sewn products industry have traditionally spent their careers maximizing the output of individual operators."[26]

Most apparel production in the United States still uses a system that predates 1900, a method called the bundle system, or a slightly more modern variant, the progressive bundle system (PBS).

> In PBS, each operation is done by a single worker operating a stationary sewing machine. Each worker receives a bundle of unfinished garments. She . . . then performs a single operation on each garment. . . . Refinement of PBS over time has led to high levels of pace and labor productivity. . . . A major by-product of PBS derives from its dependence on buffers between assembly operations to minimize the downtime of workers given uneven assembly time requirements for different operations. Standard practice is a one-day buffer between operations.[27]

The amount of in-process inventory that results from this system is tremendous. A production executive from Levi Strauss told me that under the bundle system, more than 90 percent of the time nothing was happening to material or work-in-process in the plant. A newer system of production, the modular system, is based on a different set of premises.

> [M]odular production entails grouping tasks . . . and assigning that task to members of a module (i.e., a team of workers). . . . Although most operators in the module still spend the majority of their time on a single assembly task, operators do move to other tasks if work is building up at some other step. . . . Compensation is primarily based on the module's output. . . . Modules are partially self-directed in that operators determine task assignments, pace and output targets. . . . Focusing production at the group level means that modular lines rely on far smaller buffers between assembly steps than under PBS.[28]

A close relationship exists between various management practices, such as compensation and training, and the two production systems. For instance, bundle systems rely almost completely on piece rates, while modular systems rely on group incentives as well as, to a much more limited extent, individual piece rates. People working in modular systems are much more likely to be trained for more than one job than are workers in traditional bundle systems.

A study of 121 business units representing ninety separate companies and accounting for about 28 percent of all U.S. apparel industry production in 1992 revealed that, by almost any measure, performance was substantially better under the modular production system compared to the traditional bundle method. Table 2-5 presents information on some performance indicators and how they varied by the production system and the associated management practices used. The differences are substantial. Modular systems earned a 22 percent higher gross margin as a percent of sales, had substantially less work-in-process inventory, and had almost 50 percent more sales growth between 1988 and 1992.

Modular production reduces worker compensation injuries. Because of the peer pressure that comes from group-based production, it reduces employee absenteeism. In fact, the system is actively recommended or preferred by virtually every constituency in the apparel industry.

> Throughout the 1980s, team-based assembly was heralded for reducing costs and enhancing workforce performance by the garment industry trade press, the major apparel manufacturing association, the major fiber and textile

Table 2-5 BUSINESS UNIT PERFORMANCE FOR MODULAR AND BUNDLE APPAREL MANUFACTURING

Performance Measure	Bundle	Modular	% Difference
Gross margin as % of sales	26.0	31.6	22%
Operating profit as % of sales	7.9	13.0	65%
Sales growth from 1988–1992	29.3	43.8	49%
Average discount to retailers (for products discounted)	14.6	10.2	–30%
Work-in-process inventory (in weeks)	2.9	1.9	–34%
Finished goods inventory turns per year	6.3	7.6	21%
Sewing throughput (days)	9.5	1.8	–81%

Source: John T. Dunlop and David Weil, "Diffusion and Performance of Human Resource Innovations in the U.S. Apparel Industry," Table 4, unpublished paper, Harvard University, Cambridge, MA, December 15, 1994. See also John T. Dunlop and David Weil, "Diffusion and Performance of Modular Production in the U.S. Apparel Industry," Industrial Relations 35, no. 3 (July 1996): 334–355.

producers, the nonprofit Textile Clothing Technology Corporation . . . and the Amalgamated Clothing and Textile Workers Union.[29]

So, here is a production system that is superior in economic performance and advocated by every major entity in the industry, including the relevant unions. What is the record for diffusion? Not too good. In 1992, about 80 percent of all garments were still sewn using the bundle method with its control-oriented, Taylorist approach, and only 9 percent utilized the modular system.[30] The decline in the use of the bundle system since the mid-1980s has been small, and manufacturing plants frequently abandoned the bundle system only to return to it.

Yet, persisting with the bundle system is almost certainly a recipe for going out of business in a modern apparel manufacturing industry increasingly facing worldwide competition with numerous cost-based advantages. Only by better serving the customer—the retailer—by providing superior order fulfillment and less delay in restocking can U.S. firms survive in the long run. But before we harshly criticize the apparel industry for its inertia and myopia, we should recognize that many industries have repeated its mistakes: not recognizing the basis for achieving competitive advantage through customer service, overemphasizing labor rates, and failing to move to more progressive systems of management practices, even when such systems, coupled with related changes in the production system, could produce superior economic performance.

SEMICONDUCTOR MANUFACTURING INDUSTRY

The manufacturing (sometimes called fabrication) of semiconductors involves a process through which a geometric pattern or set of patterns is transformed into an operating integrated system. The industry is extremely high technology and capital intensive, and as a modern manufacturing process, "modern wafer fabrication is probably the most exacting."[31] The industry is facing rapid technological change and a high degree of competition. It also has some strong industry associations, a very highly trained and educated set of people, and a relatively high geographic concentration. Consequently, one might expect relatively complete diffusion of superior management practices and little variation in performance. But a study of fifteen semiconductor fabrication plants (or fabs) found that this was not the case—substantial variation appeared in both management practices and performance.

In this industry, the most important outcomes are defect density, line yield, and cycle time. To measure management practices, the researchers constructed an index of participation based on the scores on four scales: power, information, knowledge, and reward. *Power* represented the extent to which decision-making power was decentralized. *Information* assessed the extent to which performance data were systematically collected and widely shared, to technicians and operators as well as to engineers. *Knowledge* measured the extensiveness and effectiveness of training, particularly on-the-job training programs aimed at developing a more skilled work force. *Reward* measured the use of gain sharing and other forms of group-based, contingent compensation. In Table 2-6, I display the relationship between the scores of the fifteen fabs on the participation index and their effectiveness along the various dimensions of performance. In all three instances, a clear linear relationship exists between performance and participation.

Based on extensive field work, the study concluded that the highest performing semiconductor manufacturing facilities leveraged their people to build competitive capabilities. It concluded: "Work group management practices that lead to high performance include integration of team activities into the reward system, management support for and commitment of resources to team activities, team training, and integration of analysis methodology and analysis tools in team activities."[32]

Table 2-6 PARTICIPATION AND PERFORMANCE RANKING IN
FIFTEEN SEMICONDUCTOR FABS

Participation	Defect Density	Line Yield	Cycle Time
High (6 fabs)	5.83	6.92	5.50
Medium (5 fabs)	7.00	7.00	8.60
Low (4 fabs)	12.50	10.88	11.00

Source: "Workforce Involvement and Wafer Fabrication Efficiency," by Vinay Sohoni, in *The Competitive Semiconductor Manufacturing Human Resources Project: First Interim Report,* ed. Clair Brown, ESRC Report CSM-09, Institute of Industrial Relations, University of California, Berkeley, CA 94720 (September, 1994): 128.

Particularly striking were the results from this performance study showing first, that even in a knowledge-intensive, high technology industry, significant performance variations and limited adoption of more effective management approaches persist; and second, that the factors associated with higher levels of performance—emphasis on training, working in teams, a different role and style for management, sharing information about performance, and the use of contingent, group-based rewards—are similar to those uncovered in studies of less technologically sophisticated industries. These results belie the common assumption that high technology industries have different requirements for the effective development of and derivation of benefits from their people.

OIL REFINING INDUSTRY

Occasionally, research not undertaken to investigate the effects of management practices on organizational performance nonetheless provides data demonstrating the connection between people and profits. One such study was undertaken by Solomon and Associates to explore maintenance costs and operating characteristics in the oil refining industry. The study uncovered that, contrary to the researchers' initial assumptions, refinery age, size, and location had virtually no effect on refinery operations. Moreover, refinery performance was independent of processing complexity, and reliability—the percentage of time the refinery was operating—was *unrelated* to maintenance expenditures. Perhaps most surprising, multirefinery organizations showed little consistency in performance across their separate locations—much larger differences existed across refineries than across companies, providing evidence of little consistency in management philosophy or practices in multi-site operations.[33]

Nor was it the case that refineries had similar operating performance results, which might occur from the universal adoption of best practices. Rather, refineries "in the lowest performance quartile posted twice the resource consumption of those in the highest quartile."[34] By 1992, the difference in profitability between refineries in the lowest and highest performance quartiles was 12 percent.

When Solomon sought to discover what did, in fact, account for the observed performance differences, they uncovered a set of factors remarkably similar to those found in other industry performance studies. One such factor was an emphasis on eliminating failure, similar to the emphasis on improving quality by prevention observed in flexible manufacturing environments. Another factor was the systematic collection and use of performance information. The study highlighted the importance of tapping "the resourcefulness of their process operators to contribute to reliability improvement and maintenance,"[35] accomplished by training the operating staff in multiple skills and by having individuals who could perform both operations and maintenance tasks operate the refineries. Because job rotation encourages the development and maintenance of multiple skills, refineries that used job rotation also invested more in training and development. Building a multi-skilled, trained, and committed work force required paying higher wages, but these practices—investing in training, job rotation, and paying more— paid off in reduced maintenance expenses and higher refinery utilization. The study observed that one refiner "pays its crew 35% more than do other refiners in the region, yet its total maintenance outlay is 25% less than the next best refinery."[36]

The effects of management practices on performance in the oil industry are not limited to refineries. In Texaco's Kern River field, for instance, production rose from 80,000 barrels per day to 91,000 by 1995 and is expected to exceed 100,000 by 1998, as production per worker increased from 150 barrels a day in 1992 to 250 in 1995.[37] These dramatic results were achieved by implementing teams, decentralizing decision making, and sharing performance information with rank-and-file employees.

The oil industry results demonstrate that the same factors associated with high performance management practices in assembly operations are also applicable in a process industry setting.

THE EFFECT OF HIGH COMMITMENT MANAGEMENT PRACTICES IN SERVICE FIRMS

The research reviewed thus far focused for the most part on manufacturing firms. But, as one might imagine, even stronger effects between management practices and organizational performance can be seen in service firms. This relationship is easily explained.

The simultaneous delivery and receipt of service in the face-to-face, for-profit services sector brings employees and customers physically, organizationally, and psychologically close. . . . [C]ustomers often equate services with the employees who render them. . . . [E]mployee and customer perceptions, attitudes, and intentions share a common basis and are related to each other.[38]

A number of studies spanning different organizations operating in various service industries provide evidence for a positive relationship between employee attitudes and customer service and satisfaction and, moreover, a relationship between employee attitudes, customer attitudes, and profits.[39] A study of bank branches found that when *employees* reported that the branch had a high service imperative, assessed by factors such as whether the branch had sufficient numbers and quality of people to perform its tasks, *customers* reported receiving higher levels of service.[40] A subsequent study of bank branches found that customer perceptions and attitudes were affected by what employees experienced. Apparently, organizational practices that are both service-related and human-resources related provide cues that customers use to evaluate service quality.[41]

Research on branches of Ford Motor Credit also uncovered a connection between employee attitudes and customer satisfaction. Attitudes concerning workload, teamwork, training and development, and satisfaction with the job and with the company were all related to customer satisfaction.[42] Research on a security company found that customer satisfaction and perceptions of service quality were significantly related to measures of employee attitudes about the fairness of pay, whether management was concerned about employee welfare and treated people fairly, and whether supervisors encouraged an open and participative work environment.[43]

The relationship between employee attitudes and profits in service firms is somewhat less consistent—for a good reason. Not all businesses or all business strategies depend on outstanding customer service. Some depend on high volumes generated through low prices, regardless of customer service. One of the more successful retailers of computers and software in the San Francisco Bay Area, Fry's, is notorious for poor customer service. But its low prices and large selection attract a sufficient number of computer-literate customers willing to put up with the Fry's experience to make the chain successful. Better service and higher employee satisfaction do, however, frequently produce higher profits. A study of an eye care chain found a significant relationship between employee attitudes and store profits.[44] Finally, numerous firms, such as Singapore Airlines, have succeeded financially by emphasizing employee well-being and customer service.

SHOULD MANAGEMENT PRACTICES BE CONTINGENT ON A FIRM'S STRATEGY?

The conventional wisdom, taught in numerous human resource courses in business schools and frequently stated in articles, holds that management practices need to be contingent on the firm's particular product market strategy. The typical analysis goes like this: Firms pursuing a "high road" strategy based on service, quality, or product differentiation need to follow a high-involvement or high-commitment set of management practices; those firms pursuing a strategy based on cost-minimization should pursue a more control-oriented, Tayloristic strategy. Unfortunately, like much other conventional wisdom in this domain, this is wrong both as a matter of logic and as a matter of empirical results.

Some evidence, for instance from the steel minimill sample, shows an association between the strategy firms actually pursue and their choice of management policies. Jeffrey Arthur did find an empirical association consistent with this precept—minimills pursuing a differentiation strategy were much more likely to use high commitment work practices than were minimills pursuing a competitive strategy based on cost, which generally employed control-oriented management practices.[45] But what exists does not necessarily indicate what is optimal. It is not clear that minimills pursuing a cost-based strategy would not be better off employing high commitment management practices, even if they were empirically less likely to do so.

Also, I do not assert that nothing is contingent—obviously, the particular skills a firm needs from its work force depend on whether it is making automobiles or semiconductors; the amount of training needed will depend on the level of technical complexity involved; the optimal payment systems will depend on how work is organized and the meaningful units of measurement; and so forth. I do maintain that little evidence exists to show that the sensibility of implementing high performance work systems depends on the particular competitive strategy a firm pursues.

Think back to MacDuffie's conditions for the need for high commitment management described at the start of this chapter—when employees have unique knowledge and skills, when they are motivated to apply those skills, and when their skills and knowledge are necessary for a firm's strategy to be executed. But, why wouldn't employee skills be useful in a cost-minimization strategy? How, in fact, can costs be minimized *without* the commitment of the entire work force to reduce waste and come up with the many suggestions for improving the process that result in efficiency gains? It doesn't seem logical that cost minimization can be accomplished without employee commitment. Consider Arthur's own data. If commitment systems produce 34 percent better labor productivity and a 63 percent better scrap rate, with wage costs that are less than 20 percent higher, shouldn't the commitment practices in fact enable minimills to produce lower cost steel? The oil industry study indicated that refinery maintenance *costs* were lower for organizations that paid higher wages and invested in developing people with multiple skills; the semiconductor fabrication plant study indicated that defect density and line yield—important determinants of costs— were superior with greater participation; the study of integrated steel finishing lines showed that uptime was substantially superior, and therefore, costs were lower given the high fixed costs of capital investment, under a more progressive management system. And the list goes on.

Both anecdotal example and systematic empirical evidence is consistent with this position. Not only do Singapore Airlines and Virgin Atlantic, pursing strategies of service differentiation, value their employees: So, too, does Southwest Airlines, with the lowest costs—and the lowest fares—in the domestic airline industry. Southwest emphasizes training, selective recruiting, profit sharing and stock ownership and has never had a layoff or furlough in its history—all elements of high commitment work systems. Not only does Nordstrom, a reasonably upscale department store, emphasize a strong culture of customer service: Wal-Mart and the Men's Wearhouse (a discount retailer of men's suits) do, too. Both have many features consistent with virtually all descriptions of high commitment work systems.

Reviewing the evidence from the worldwide motor vehicle study, MacDuffie concluded:

> This study does shed light on the issue of "fit" between HR strategy and business strategy. . . . A "fit" hypothesis predicts that either mass or flexible production plants with a good fit between their HR and production strategies will perform well. In contrast, these results suggest that, at least for auto assembly plants, the flexible production approach consistently leads to better performance than the mass production approach.[46]

Consider as well Huselid's analysis of a sample of nearly one thousand firms in a variety of industries. Two empirical tests for the existence of a contingent relationship between strategy, the use of different management practices, and financial performance both yielded nonsignificant results. He concluded:

> But despite the . . . theoretical argument that better . . . external fit will increase firm performance, I found . . . little evidence for external fit. These findings are in fact consistent with recent attempts to model fit in the organizational strategy literature . . . and they are perhaps unsurprising. . . . [G]iven the substantial main effects associated with systems of High Performance Work Practices, one might conclude that the simple adoption of such practices is more important than any effort to ensure these policies are internally consistent or aligned with firm competitive strategy.[47]

A recent study of banks also found virtually no empirical support for the idea that the effect of management practices on organizational performance is contingent on the bank's strategy.[48] "Three individual HR practices, profit sharing, results-oriented appraisals, and employment security, had relatively strong universalistic relationships with important accounting measures of performance."[49] Support for contingency arguments has been obtained mostly in manufacturing, where some evidence shows that high performance management practices have more impact on organizational performance when the organization pursues a quality-based strategy. Even in this instance, however, important main effects derive from implementing high performance work systems on operational performance in manufacturing, although these effects are stronger when the organization does other things consistent with implementing quality processes and flexible manufacturing.[50]

I have come to believe that the strategic fit argument is sometimes mustered by managers and organizations that don't want to acknowledge that the way they manage their people is less than optimal and that they should change. They find it easier to say "Even though we aren't doing what some firms have found to be effective, that's all right, because we are pursuing a different strategy." This rationalization should be challenged every time it is made by asking this simple question: Wouldn't our existing strategy, whatever it is, be better implemented and better served if our people were more involved, committed, and better skilled?

CONCLUSION

The research studies described in this chapter represent some of the more comprehensive and well-done, as well as the more current, of the numerous studies investigating the effects of human resource practices on various dimensions of organizational performance. But this evidence is still by no means an exhaustive compilation of the myriad studies examining the connection between people and profits.[51]

A review of more than 130 field studies of organizational change conducted between 1961 and 1991, many of which included changes in management practices, reported that in three-fourths of the cases significant increases in economic performance were observed.[52] A longitudinal study of a unionized paper mill that instituted high commitment work practices—extensive training, reduction in job classifications, guarantees of employment security, and an increase in wages as well as a simplification of the compensation system—found that nonlabor costs declined, production increased, and, as a consequence, the profitability of the mill more than tripled.[53] A study of nearly two hundred banks found that "differences in HR practices are associated with rather large differences in financial performance. . . . [F]inancial performance was estimated to be approximately 30 percent higher for banks one standard deviation above the mean . . . than it was for those banks at the mean."[54] The existing research literature clearly shows that: "prior empirical work has consistently found that use of effective human resource management practices enhances firm performance."[55] Moreover, the effects are large and managerially important.

As I noted at the beginning of this chapter, the positive effects of high commitment management practices derive from a set of predictable and understandable principles. In part, performance increases because people work harder. With the greater involvement and commitment that comes from having more control over the work environment, with contingent compensation that provides an economic payoff from higher organizational performance, and with the peer pressure activated in self-managing teams, effort increases. But these factors probably account for little of the substantial improvements observed. More of the effect undoubtedly comes from individuals "working smarter"—in part by being able to actually implement their wisdom and knowledge in the actual work process and in part because of the training and job rotation practices that enhance the opportunity to learn. A study of individual employees in apparel plants using modular and the traditional bundle system of production found, for instance, no difference in the job satisfaction or commitment of workers in the two types of plants. But in the modular production system nearly 90 percent of the workers reported having learned ways to improve their work through informal training while the corresponding percentage of workers in the bundle system was only 71 percent. The study concluded that "it is the design of work and the communication and learning it promotes that improve performance."[56]

High commitment work practices also save on the both the direct and the indirect costs of employment litigation. Employment disputes in the work place have increased at a rapid rate. Between 1971 and 1991, employment litigation was the fastest growing area of litigation in the federal courts, expanding by about 430 percent while the overall civil caseload increased 110 percent over the same period. When General Motors ran the Fremont automobile assembly plant, the labor law firm that handled its work billed between $50,000 and $70,000 per *month*. Given that the plant had about one hundred grievances per month, very adversarial labor relations, and a climate of mistrust, that amount is not out of line. After NUMMI reopened the plant, however, labor law bills were trivial, on the order of $1,000 per month according to the lawyer who had formerly handled the GM business. Not only did this substantial cost savings immediately flow to the bottom line—money being spent on labor litigation did not design a car, build a car, sell a car, or serve a customer—but tremendous savings accrued in the un-measured cost of management time and attention spent on fruitless conflict and litigation.

But perhaps the biggest effect on performance comes from eliminat-ing positions the primary responsibility of which is to watch people who watch people who watch people who watch people who do the work. At New United Motor (NUMMI), workers manage themselves, layers of management have been eliminated, and supervisors seldom come onto the manufacturing floor to supervise. Administrative over-head is costly—and trained, multiskilled, self-managed, and motivated employees save on a variety of administrative costs, including the cost of management. Clearly, a number of mechanisms create the perfor-mance effects of high commitment work practices. Although we cannot yet specify which are the most important in which circumstances, all collectively contribute to the results we have seen in this chapter.

We have also seen, in the studies of automobile manufacturing, ap-parel, and integrated steel production, that the diffusion of these prac-tices, in U.S.-owned organizations operating in the United States, is not as rapid as one might expect given their performance effects. Data from a comprehensive, random sample survey of establishments showed that "only 16 percent of U.S. businesses have at least one innovative practice in each of the four major HRM policy areas: flexible job design, worker training, pay-for-performance compensation, and employment secu-rity."[57] A study conducted by the National Center on the Educational Quality of the Workforce covering more than 3,300 establishments concluded:

> Despite the considerable attention given to new methods of work organiza-tion, the use of high-performance work systems among employers still re-mains the exception rather than the rule. Only one-quarter of establishments reported using any bench-marking programs to compare practices and per-formances with other organizations, and 37 percent reported that they had adopted a formal Total Quality Management (TQM) program. Very few work-

ers engage in arrangements that have become the hallmarks of high-performance work: 13 percent of non-managerial workers participate in self-managed teams, and 18 percent participate in job rotation.[58]

A similar absence of diffusion of high performance work arrangements characterizes the United Kingdom. "No more than 2% of all establishments with more than 25 workers have quality circles or problem-solving groups. Team work and major alterations in job content are even more rare."[59]

We have seen at least one reason why this is so—the implementation of high performance or high commitment work systems requires more than cosmetic changes: It requires a serious commitment to doing things differently, such as training employees in multiple skills, implementing more contingent compensation, organizing workers in teams, instituting suggestion systems, quality circles, or other mechanisms for soliciting employee ideas, and so forth. Each of these changes challenges existing ways of doing things—particularly if the existing way emphasizes a Tayloristic, control-oriented approach. It is almost impossible to successfully implement high performance or high commitment work practices in the absence of mutual trust and respect. But trust is missing in many employment relationships—and missing in many of the economic theory-based analyses of these relationships. Thus, beyond the specific practices, the atmosphere in the work place is crucial. All work place practices and changes should be evaluated by a simple criterion: Do they convey and create trust, or do they signify distrust and destroy trust and respect among people?

The changes required to implement high performance work arrangements face the customary obstacles confronted by any administrative innovation, regardless of its potential benefit. Many of the practices associated with high commitment work arrangements—such as employment security and working collaboratively with collective bargaining representatives if these exist in the work place—also challenge conventional wisdom and managerial instincts. Consequently, one of the agendas for subsequent chapters will be to confront this conventional wisdom directly to demonstrate how many current beliefs are neither very sensible nor empirically correct.

But first we need to be clear on the dimensions of high performance work practices. Throughout this chapter, I have referred to high performance, high involvement, or high commitment work practices, and each study has used a largely, but not completely, overlapping set of factors to describe these practices. In the next chapter, I extract from these various studies a set of underlying dimensions associated with the term *high performance management practices.*

3 ◆ *Seven Practices of Successful Organizations*

*I*N THE LAST CHAPTER, we reviewed evidence demonstrating that effectively managing people can produce substantially enhanced economic performance. Each of the studies used a slightly different but generally consistent set of factors to measure management approaches, and, indeed, a plethora of terms have been used to describe management practices: high commitment, high performance, high involvement, and so forth. Throughout this book I will use these terms interchangeably, as they all tap similar ideas about how to obtain profits through people.

In this chapter, I extract from the various studies, related literature, and personal observation and experience a set of seven dimensions that seem to characterize most if not all of the systems producing profits through people.

1. Employment security.
2. Selective hiring of new personnel.
3. Self-managed teams and decentralization of decision making as the basic principles of organizational design.
4. Comparatively high compensation contingent on organizational performance.
5. Extensive training.

6. Reduced status distinctions and barriers, including dress, language, office arrangements, and wage differences across levels.

7. Extensive sharing of financial and performance information throughout the organization.

This list is somewhat shorter than my earlier list of sixteen practices describing "what effective firms do with people,"[1] for two reasons. First, this list focuses on basic dimensions, some of which, such as compensation and reduction of status differences, have multiple components that were previously listed separately. Second, some of the items on the previous list have more to do with the ability to implement high performance work practices—such as being able to take a long-term view and to realize the benefits of promoting from within—than with describing dimensions of the practices themselves. It is, however, still the case that several of the dimensions of high performance work arrangements listed, for instance employment security and high pay, appear to fly in the face of conventional wisdom. This chapter outlines these practices, provides examples to illustrate both their implementation and their impact, and explains their underlying logic. In subsequent chapters, I will take on the task of challenging prevailing conventional wisdom about how to manage the employment relationship that is inconsistent with high commitment management practices.

EMPLOYMENT SECURITY

In an era of downsizing and rightsizing—or, as Donald Hastings, CEO of Lincoln Electric, called it in a speech to the Academy of Management in 1996, "dumbsizing"—how can I write about employment security as a critical element of high performance work arrangements? First, because it is simply empirically the case that most research on the effects of high performance management systems have incorporated employment security as one important dimension in their description of these systems. That is because "one of the most widely accepted propositions . . . is that innovations in work practices or other forms of worker-management cooperation or productivity improvement are not likely to be sustained over time when workers fear that by increasing productivity they will work themselves out of their jobs."[2]

This was recognized long ago by Lincoln Electric, the successful arc welding and electric motor manufacturer that has dominated its markets for decades. Years ago, it began offering guaranteed employment to workers after two (and now three) years on the job. It has not had a layoff since 1948. Nor is it the case that this is just because the company has never faced hard times. In the early 1980s, a recession and high interest rates caused Lincoln's domestic sales to fall about 40 percent over an eighteen-month period. Nevertheless, it did not resort to layoffs. One thing the company did to avoid laying off people was to redeploy them. Factory workers who had made Lincoln's products were put in the field with the task of selling them, in the process actually increasing Lincoln's market share and penetration. Over the years, Lincoln has enjoyed gains in productivity that are far above those for manufacturing as a whole, and its managers believe that the assurance workers have that innovations in methods will not cost them or their colleagues their jobs has significantly contributed to these excellent results. Similarly, when General Motors wanted to implement new work arrangements in its innovative Saturn plant in the 1990s, it guaranteed its people job security except in the most extreme circumstances. When New United Motors was formed to operate the Fremont automobile assembly plant, it offered its people job security. How else could it ask for flexibility and cooperation in becoming more efficient and productive?

Many additional benefits follow from employment assurances besides workers' free contribution of knowledge and their efforts to enhance productivity. One advantage to firms is the decreased likelihood that they will lay off employees during downturns. How is this a benefit to the firm? In the absence of some way of building commitment to retaining the work force—either through pledges about employment security or through employment obligations contractually negotiated with a union—firms may lay off employees too quickly and too readily at the first sign of financial difficulty. This constitutes a cost for firms that have done a good job selecting, training, and developing their work force: Layoffs put important strategic assets on the street for the competition to employ. When a colleague and I interviewed the Vice President for People at Southwest Airlines, she noted that the company had never had a layoff or furlough in an industry where such events were common. When we asked why, she replied, "Why would we want to put our best assets, our people, in the arms of the competition?" Seeing its people as strategic assets rather than as costs, Southwest has pursued a careful growth strategy that avoided overexpansion and subsequent cuts in personnel.

Employment security policies will also lead to more careful and leaner hiring, because the firm knows it cannot simply let people go quickly if it has overestimated its labor demand. Leaner staffing can actually make the work force more productive, with fewer people doing more work. The people are often happy to be more productive because they know they are helping to ensure a result that benefits them—having a long-term job and a career. Furthermore, employment security maintained over time helps to build trust between people and their employer, which can lead to more cooperation, forbearance in pressing for wage increases, and better spirit in the company. Herb Kelleher, the CEO of Southwest, has written:

> Our most important tools for building employee partnership are job security and a stimulating work environment. . . . Certainly there were times when we could have made substantially more profits in the short term if we had furloughed people, but we didn't. We were looking at our employees' and our company's longer-term interests. . . . [A]s it turns out, providing job security imposes additional discipline, because if your goal is to avoid layoffs, then you hire very sparingly. So our commitment to job security has actually helped us keep our labor force smaller and more productive than our competitors'.[3]

For organizations without the strategic discipline or vision of Southwest, a guarantee of employment security can help the firm avoid making a costly decision to lay people off that has short-term benefits and long-term costs.

If you want to see just how costly such layoff decisions can be, consider Silicon Valley. Executives from the semiconductor and electronics industries often write newspaper and magazine articles and testify before Congress in favor of permitting immigration of skilled workers. These executives favor immigration because they manage companies that are frequently short of necessary talent. The executives complain about their difficulty in recruiting qualified personnel in their expanding industry.

What you won't see in their articles or testimony, but what you will find if you look at newspapers from a few years ago, is that many of these very same firms laid off engineers, technicians, and other skilled workers in some instances just two or three years—or even less—before subsequently complaining about labor scarcity. Think about it. My friends in the valley have perfected the art of buying high and selling low. When times are tough in the industry, common sense suggests that that is exactly the time to recruit and build your work force. Competition for talented staff will obviously be less, and salaries need not be bid up in attempts to lure people from their existing jobs. By hiring when times are poor and developing a set of policies, including assurance that people will be retained, a firm can become an employer of choice, and the organization will not have to enter the labor market at its very peak to acquire the necessary work force. Instead, many firms do exactly the opposite. They lay people off in cyclical downturns and then, when the entire industry is booming and staff is scarce, they engage in often fruitless bidding contests to rehire the skills that they not that long ago sent packing.

Employment security can confer yet another benefit, in that it encourages people to take a longer-term perspective on their jobs and organizational performance. In a study of the financial performance of 192 banks, John Delery and Harold Doty observed a significant relationship between employment security and the bank's return on assets, an important measure of financial performance: "The greater the employment security given to loan officers, the greater the returns to banks."[4] Why might this be? In a bank that hires and lays off loan officers quickly to match economic fluctuations, the typical loan officer will worry only about booking loans—just what they have typically been rewarded for doing. With employment security and a longer-term perspective on the job, the bank officer may be more inclined to worry as well about the repayment prospects of the loan and about building customer relationships by providing high levels of service. Although a specific loan officer's career may prosper by being a big loan producer and moving quickly from one bank to another, the bank's profitability and performance are undoubtedly enhanced by having people who take both a longer term and a more comprehensive view of their jobs and of the bank's financial performance. This is likely to occur, however, only with the prospect of long-term continuity in the employment relationship.

The idea of employment security does not mean that the organization retains people who don't perform or work effectively with others—that is, performance does matter. Lincoln Electric has very high turnover for employees in their first few months on the job, as those who don't fit the Lincoln culture and work environment leave. Southwest will fire people who don't provide the level of customer service the firm is well-known for delivering and don't want to improve. Employment security means that employees are not quickly put on the street for things, such as economic downturns or the strategic mistakes of senior management, over which they have no control. The policy focuses on maintaining total employment, not on protecting individuals from the consequences of their individual behavior on the job.

The idea of providing employment security in today's competitive world seems somehow anachronistic or impossible and very much at variance with what most firms seem to be doing. But employment security is fundamental to the implementation of most other high performance management practices, such as selective hiring, extensive training, information sharing, and delegation. Companies are unlikely to invest the resources in the careful screening and training of new people if those people are not expected to be with the firm long enough for it to recoup these investments. Similarly, delegation of operating authority and the sharing of sensitive performance and strategic information requires trust, and that trust is much more likely to emerge in a system of mutual, long-term commitments. The issue of employment security is so important that I spend an entire chapter, chapter 6, reviewing the evidence on the effects of downsizing and, most importantly, providing a long list of alternatives to downsizing for those managers who seek to maintain employment even in the face of fluctuating market demand and incessant competition.

SELECTIVE HIRING

Organizations serious about obtaining profits through people will expend the effort needed to ensure that they recruit the right people in the first place. This requires several things. First, the organization needs to have a large applicant pool from which to select. In 1993, for example, Southwest Airlines received about 98,000 job applications, interviewed 16,000 people, and hired 2,700. In 1994, applications increased to more than 125,000 for 4,000 hires. Some organizations see processing this many job inquiries as an unnecessary expense. Southwest sees it as the first step toward ensuring that it has a large applicant pool from which to select its people. Similarly, Singapore Airlines, frequently listed as one of Asia's most admired companies, one of the most profitable airlines in the world, and consistently ranked quite high in ratings of service quality, is extremely careful and selective in its recruiting practices. Flight attendants are an important point of contact with the customer and one way in which Singapore Airlines differentiates its service. Consequently, senior management becomes personally involved in flight attendant selection. Prospective generalist staff, from which the ranks of managers will come, must pass a series of tests and clear two rounds of interviews, including interviews with a panel of senior management. "From an initial pool of candidates, about 10 percent are shortlisted and only 2 percent [one out of 50] are selected."[5]

Nor is such selectivity confined to service organizations. When Subaru-Isuzu opened its automobile assembly plant in the United States in the late 1980s, it received some 30,000 applications for employment. The Japanese automakers have consistently emphasized selecting good people as critical to their success, and they have been willing to expend the resources required on the selection process. It has always fascinated me that some people see selectivity on the part of elite universities or graduate schools as a mark of the school's prestige but see the same selection ratios on the part of companies as a waste of resources. It isn't.

Second, the organization needs to be clear about what are the most critical skills and attributes needed in its applicant pool. The notion of trying to find "good employees" is not very helpful—organizations need to be as specific as possible about the precise attributes they are seeking. At Southwest Airlines, applicants for flight attendant positions are evaluated on the basis of initiative, judgment, adaptability, and their ability to learn. These attributes are assessed in part from interviews employing questions evoking specific instances of these attributes. For instance, to assess adaptability, interviewers ask, "Give an example of working with a difficult co-worker. How did you handle it?"[6] To measure initiative, one question asks, "Describe a time when a co-worker failed to pull their weight and what you did about it."

Third, the skills and abilities hired need to be carefully considered and consistent with the particular job requirements and the organization's approach to its market. Simply hiring the "best and the brightest" may not make sense in all circumstances. Enterprise Rent-A-Car is today the largest car rental company in the United States, with revenues in 1996 of $3 billion, and it has expanded at a rate of between 25 and 30 percent a year for the past eleven years. It has grown by pursuing a high customer service strategy and emphasizing sales of rental car services to repair garage customers. In a low wage, often unionized, and seemingly low employee skill industry, virtually all of Enterprise's people are college graduates. But these people are hired primarily for their sales skills and personality and for their willingness to provide good service, not for their academic performance. Dennis Ross, the chief operating officer commented "We hire from the half of the college class that makes the upper half possible. . . . We want athletes, fraternity types . . . people people." Brian O'Reilly interpolates Enterprise's reasoning:

> The social directors make good sales people, able to chat up service managers and calm down someone who has just been in a car wreck. . . . The Enterprise employees hired from the caboose end of the class have something else going for them . . . a chilling realization of how unforgiving the job market can be.[7]

Fourth, organizations should screen primarily on important attributes that are difficult to change through training and should emphasize qualities that actually differentiate among those in the applicant pool. An important insight on the selection process comes from those organizations that tend to hire more on the basis of basic ability and attitude than on applicants' specific technical skills, which are much more easily acquired. This has been the practice of Japanese organizations for some time. "Japanese recruitment seeks to find the individual with the 'proper character whom it can train.' . . . Instead of searching for applicants with necessary skills for the job, the focus is on social background, temperament, and character references."[8]

Sophisticated managers know that it is much more cost-effective to select on those important attributes that are difficult or impossible to change and to train people in those behaviors or skills that are more readily learned. At Southwest Airlines, a top pilot working for another airline who actually did stunt work for movie studios was rejected because he was rude to a receptionist. Southwest believes that technical skills are easier to acquire than a teamwork and service attitude. Ironically, many firms select for specific, job-relevant skills that, while important, are easily acquired. Meanwhile, they fail to find people with the right attitudes, values, and cultural fit—attributes that are harder to train or change and that are quite predictive of turnover and performance. To avoid having to retrain or resocialize people that have acquired bad habits at their previous employers, companies like Southwest prefer to hire individuals without previous industry experience. Many also prefer to hire at the entry level, obtaining individuals who are eager to prove themselves and who don't know what can't be done.

It is tempting to hire on the basis of ability or intelligence rather than fit with the organization—so tempting that one occasionally observes firms trying to differentiate among a set of individuals who are basically similar in intelligence or ability while failing to try to distinguish those that will be well suited to the organization from those that will not. One of my favorite examples of this is recruitment at Stanford Business School. Stanford has a class of about 370 MBAs, selected from an initial applicant pool that in recent years has exceeded six thousand. These are obviously talented, motivated, and very intelligent individuals. Distinguishing among them on those criteria would be difficult, if not impossible. But many firms seek to do the impossible—they try to get around the school's policy of not releasing grades in an effort to figure out who are the smartest students and to assess differences in ability among a set of applicants through interviewing techniques such as giving them problems or cases to solve. Meanwhile, although many job recruits will leave their first job within the first two years, and such turnover and the requirement to refill those positions are exceedingly expensive, few firms focus primarily on determining fit—something that does vary dramatically.

Two firms that take a more sensible and pragmatic approach to hiring are Hewlett-Packard and PeopleSoft, a producer of human resource management software. For instance, one MBA job applicant reported that in interviews with PeopleSoft, the company asked very little about personal or academic background, except about learning experiences from school and work. Rather, the interviews focused mostly on whether the person saw herself as team oriented or as an individual achiever; what she liked to do outside school and work; and her philosophy on life. The specific question was "Do you have a personal mission statement? If you don't, what would it be if you were to write it today?" Moreover, the people interviewing the applicant presented a consistent picture of PeopleSoft as a company and of the values that were shared among employees. Such a selection process is more likely to produce cultural fit. A great deal of research evidence shows that the degree of cultural fit and value congruence between job applicants and their organizations significantly predicts both subsequent turnover and job performance.[9]

Firms serious about selection put applicants through several rounds of interviews and a rigorous selection procedure. At Subaru-Isuzu's U.S. manufacturing plant, getting hired involved going through multiple screening procedures including written tests and assessment center exercises and could take as long as six months or more. The fastest hire took nine weeks.[10] Such a lengthy selection process has several outcomes. First, it ensures that those who survive it have been carefully scrutinized. Second, it ensures that those eventually hired into the firm develop commitment. Applicants selected become committed as a consequence of having gone through such a lengthy and rigorous process—if they didn't really want the job, why would they go through it? At Subaru-Isuzu, the selection process "demanded perseverance," ensured that those who were hired had "the greatest desire and determination," and, since it required some degree of sacrifice on the part of the people, encouraged self-elimination and built commitment among those who survived.[11] Third, this type of process promotes the feeling on the part of those who are finally selected that they are part of an elite and special group, a feeling that causes them to enter the organization with a high level of motivation and spirit. Laurie Graham's participant observation study of Subaru-Isuzu concluded that "the fact that so much money, time, and effort went into the selection of employees reinforced the belief that the company was willing to go to great lengths to select the best."[12]

Rigorous selection requires a method, refined and developed over time through feedback and learning, to ensure that the firm can identify the skills it is seeking from the applicant pool. At Southwest Airlines, the company tracks who has interviewed job applicants. When someone does especially well or poorly, the organization can actually try to assess what the interviewers saw or missed, and why. It is puzzling that organizations will ensure the quality of their manufacturing or service delivery process by closing the loop on that process through feedback, while almost no organizations attempt to do the same thing with their recruiting process. Sources of applicants, scores on tests or interview ratings, and other selection mechanisms must be validated against the subsequent performance of the people selected if there is to be any hope of improving the effectiveness of the process over time.

The following list summarizes the main points about how to go about selective hiring to build a high performance organization.

- ◆ Have a large number of applicants per opening.
- ◆ Screen for cultural fit and attitude—not for skills that can be readily trained.
- ◆ Be clear about what are the most critical skills, behaviors, or attitudes crucial for success; isolate just a small number of such qualities and be as specific as possible. Simply seeking "the best and brightest" frequently doesn't make sense.
- ◆ Use several rounds of screening to build commitment and to signal that hiring is taken very seriously.
- ◆ To the extent possible, involve senior people as a signal of the importance of the hiring activity.
- ◆ Close the loop by assessing the results and performance of the recruiting process.

SELF-MANAGED TEAMS AND DECENTRALIZATION AS BASIC ELEMENTS OF ORGANIZATIONAL DESIGN

Organizing people into self-managed teams is a critical component of virtually all high performance management systems. Numerous articles and case examples as well as rigorous, systematic studies attest to the effectiveness of teams as a principle of organization design. One researcher concluded that "two decades of research in organizational behavior provides considerable evidence that workers in self-managed teams enjoy greater autonomy and discretion, and this effect translates into intrinsic rewards and job satisfaction; teams also outperform traditionally supervised groups in the majority of . . . empirical studies."[13]

In a manufacturing plant that implemented high performance work teams, for example, a 38 percent reduction in the defect rate and a 20 percent increase in productivity followed the introduction of teams.[14] Honeywell's defense avionics plant credits improved on-time delivery—reaching 99 percent in the first quarter of 1996 as compared to below 40 percent in the late 1980s—to the implementation of teams.[15] A study of the implementation of teams in one regional Bell telephone operating company found that "self-directed groups in customer services reported higher customer service quality and had 15.4% higher monthly sales revenues."[16] In the case of network technicians, the implementation of self-directed work teams saved "an average of $52,000 in indirect labor costs for each self-directed team initiated."[17] Moreover, membership in self-directed work teams positively affected employee job satisfaction, with other factors that might also affect satisfaction statistically controlled. "More than 75% of surveyed workers who are currently in traditional work groups say they would volunteer for teams if given the opportunity. By contrast, less than 10% who are now in teams say they would like to return to traditional supervision."[18]

Teams offer several advantages. First, teams substitute peer-based for hierarchical control of work. "Instead of management devoting time and energy to controlling the workforce directly, workers control themselves."[19] Peer control is frequently more effective than hierarchical supervision. Someone may disappoint his or her supervisor, but the individual is much less likely to let down his or her work mates. At New United Motor Manufacturing (NUMMI), the work process is organized on a team basis with virtually no buffers of either in-process inventories or employees. As a consequence, "all the difficulties of one person's absence fall on those in daily contact with the absentee—the co-workers and immediate supervisor—producing enormous peer pressure against absenteeism."[20] Team-based organizations also are largely successful in having all of the people in the firm feel accountable and responsible for the operation and success of the enterprise, not just a few people in senior management positions. This increased sense of responsibility stimulates more initiative and effort on the part of everyone involved.

The tremendously successful natural foods grocery store chain, Whole Foods Markets, organized on the basis of teams, attributes much of its success to that arrangement. Between 1991 and 1996, the company enjoyed sales growth of 864 percent and net income growth of 438 percent as it expanded, in part through acquisitions as well as internal growth, from ten to sixty-eight stores. In its 1995 annual report, the company's team-oriented philosophy is clearly stated.

> Our growing Information Systems capability is fully aligned with our goal of creating a more intelligent organization—one which is less bureaucratic, elitist, hierarchical, and authoritarian and more communicative, participatory, and empowered. The ultimate goal is to have all Team Members contributing their full intelligence, creativity, and skills to continuously improving the company. . . .
>
> Everyone who works at Whole Foods Market is a Team Member. This reflects our philosophy that we are all partners in the shared mission of giving our customers the very best in products and services. We invest in and believe in the collective wisdom of our Team members. The stores are organized into self-managing work teams that are responsible and accountable for their own performance.[21]

Each store is a profit center and has about ten self-managed teams in it, with team leaders and clear performance targets. Moreover, "the team leaders in each store are a team, store leaders in each region are a team, and the company's six regional presidents are a team."[22] Although store leaders recommend new hires, teams must approve hires for full-time jobs, and it takes a two-thirds vote of the team members to do so, normally after a thirty-day trial period. Through an elaborate system of peer store reviews, Whole Foods encourages people to learn from each other. By sharing performance information widely, the company encourages peer competition. "At Whole Foods, pressure for performance comes from peers rather than from headquarters, and it comes in the form of internal competition."[23]

Second, teams permit employees to pool their ideas to come up with better and more creative solutions to problems. The idea, similar to brainstorming or group problem solving, involves pooling ideas and expertise to increase the likelihood that at least one member of the group will come up with a way of addressing the problem. In the group setting, each participant can build on the others' ideas, particularly if the members are trained in effective group process and problem solving. Teams at Saturn and at the Chrysler Corporation's Jefferson North plant "provide a framework in which workers more readily help one another and more freely share their production knowledge—the innumerable 'tricks of the trade' that are vital in any manufacturing process."[24]

Third, and perhaps most importantly, by substituting peer for hierarchical control, teams permit removal of layers of hierarchy and absorption of administrative tasks previously performed by specialists, avoiding the enormous costs of having people whose sole job it is to watch people watch people who watch other people do the work. Administrative overhead is costly because management is typically well-paid. Eliminating layers of management by instituting self-managing teams saves money. Self-managed teams can also take on tasks previously done by specialized staff, thus eliminating excess personnel and, just as important, putting critical decisions in the hands of individuals who may be closer to the relevant information.

The AES Corporation is an immensely successful global developer and operator of electric power and steam plants, with sales of more than $835 million and six thousand employees in 1996. A 1982 investment in the company of $10,000 would be worth more than $10 million in 1996. The company "has never formed corporate departments or assigned officers to oversee project finance, operations, purchasing, human resources, or public relations. Instead, such functions are handled at the plant level, where plant managers assign them to volunteer teams."[25] Front-line people develop expertise in these various task domains, including finance, and receive responsibility and authority for carrying them out. They do so effectively. Of course, mistakes get made, but learning follows. The AES structure saves on the costs of management—the organization has only five levels—and it economizes on specialized staff. The company developed a $400 million plant in Cumberland, Maryland, with a team of just ten people who obtained more than thirty-six separate permit approvals and negotiated the complex financing, including tax-exempt bonds and ten lenders. Normally, projects of this size require "hundreds of workers, each with small specific tasks to perform within large corporations."[26] The savings and increased speed and flexibility of the AES team-based approach are clear and constitute an important source of the firm's competitive advantage.

At Vancom Zuid-Limburg, a joint venture in the Netherlands that operates a public bus company, the organization has enjoyed very rapid growth in ridership and has been able to win transport concessions by offering more services at the same price as its competitors. The key to this success lies in its use of self-managed teams and the consequent savings in management overhead.

> Vancom is able to [win transport contracts] mainly because of its very low overhead costs. . . . [O]ne manager supervises around forty bus drivers. . . . This management-driver ratio of 1 in 40 substantially differs from the norm in this sector. At best, competitors achieve a ratio of 1 in 8. Most of this difference can be attributed to the self-managed teams. Vancom . . . has two teams of around twenty drivers. Each team has its own bus lines and budgeting responsibilities. . . . Vancom also expects each individual driver to assume more responsibilities when on the road. This includes customer service (e.g., helping elderly persons board the bus); identifying problems (e.g., reporting damage to a bus stop), and active contributions (e.g., making suggestions for improvement of the services).[27]

How can moving to self-managed teams, possibly eliminating layers of administration and even specialized staff, be consistent with the earlier discussion of employment security? Eliminating positions need not entail the elimination of the people doing these jobs—those individuals can be redeployed to other tasks that add more value to the organization. In the case of Lincoln Electric, recall that, at least temporarily, factory workers became salespeople, something that Mazda Motors also did when it faced a production employee surplus because of low sales in the 1980s. At SAS Airlines, staff that formerly did market research and planning were moved to positions where they had a more direct effect on customer service and operations. At Solectron, a contract manufacturer of electronics, institution of self-managed teams meant that managers, who typically had engineering degrees, could spend more time rethinking the overall production system and worrying about the technology strategy of the company—activities that added a lot more value than directly supervising $7 per hour direct labor. Often many tasks, such as the development of new products and new markets and the evaluation and introduction of new production technologies, require the time and strategic talents of managers, and these activities and decisions add much more value to the organization by using the knowledge and capabilities of the people. Consequently, a move to self-managed teams is consistent with maintaining employment when other, often more important, things are found for supervisors and specialized staff to do.

Even organizations for which working in formal teams is not sensible or feasible can benefit from one of the sources of team success: decentralization of decision making to front-line people, who have the knowledge and ability to take effective action. The Ritz-Carlton Hotel chain, winner of the Malcolm Baldrige National Quality Award in 1992, provides each of its people with discretion to spend up to $2,500, without any approval, in order to respond to guest complaints. Hampton Inn Hotel, a low-priced hotel chain, instituted a 100 percent Satisfaction Guarantee policy for its guests and permitted employees to do whatever was required to make the guests happy.

> A few years ago while working as a guest services representative at a Hampton Inn Hotel, I overheard a guest at our complimentary continental breakfast complaining quite loudly that his favorite cereal was not available. Rather than dismiss the person as just another disgruntled guest, I looked at the situation and saw an opportunity to make this guest happy. I gave him his money back—not for the continental breakfast, but for the cost of one night's stay at our hotel. And I did it on the spot, without checking with my supervisor or the general manager of the hotel.[28]

These policies may seem wasteful, but they're not. Ritz-Carlton managers will tell you that a satisfied customer will talk to ten people and an unhappy customer to one hundred. Spending money to keep clients satisfied is a small price to pay for good advertising and encouraging guests to return. Similarly, at the Hampton Inn, "company research suggests that the guarantee strongly influences customer satisfaction and loyalty to Hampton Inn, and that guests who have experienced the guarantee are more likely to stay with Hampton Inn again in the future."[29] It is important to realize that successful implementation of guest satisfaction programs or, for that matter, programs to use the ideas and knowledge of the work force require decentralizing decision making and permitting people at all levels to exercise substantial influence over organizational decisions and processes. All of this requires trust, a commodity in short supply in many organizations that have become accustomed to operating with an emphasis on hierarchical control.

HIGH COMPENSATION CONTINGENT ON ORGANIZATIONAL PERFORMANCE

Although labor markets are far from perfectly efficient, it is nonetheless the case that some relationship exists between what a firm pays and the quality of the work force it attracts. It is amusing to see firms announce simultaneously that first, they compete on the basis of their people and that their goal is to have the very best work force in their industry, and second, that they intend to pay at (or sometimes slightly below) the median wage for comparable people in the industry. The level of salaries sends a message to the firm's work force—they are truly valued or they are not. After all, talk is cheap and many organizations can and do claim that people are their most important asset even as they behave differently.

I sometimes hear the statement that high compensation is a consequence of organizational success, rather than its progenitor, and a related comment that high compensation (compared to the average) is possible only in certain industries that either face less competition or have particularly highly educated employees. But neither of these statements is correct. Obviously, successful firms can afford to pay more and frequently do so, but high pay can also produce economic success.

When John Whitney assumed the leadership of Pathmark, a large grocery store chain in the Eastern United States in 1972, the company had about ninety days to live according to its banks and was in desperate financial shape. Whitney looked at the situation and discovered that 120 store managers in the chain were paid terribly. Many of them made less than the butchers, who were unionized. He decided that the store managers were vital to the chain's success and its ability to accomplish a turnaround. Consequently, one of the first things he did was to give the store managers a substantial raise—about 40 to 50 percent. The subsequent success of the chain was, according to Whitney, because the store managers could now focus on improving performance instead of worrying and complaining about their pay. Furthermore, in a difficult financial situation, the substantial raise ensured that talent would not be leaving for better jobs elsewhere, thereby making a turnaround more difficult. Whitney has consistently tried to pay a 15 percent wage premium in the many turnaround situations he has managed, and he argues that this wage premium and the resulting reduced turnover *facilitates* the organization's performance.

The idea that only certain jobs or industries can or should pay high wages is belied by the example of many firms including Home Depot, the largest home improvement and building supply company in the United States, with about 8 percent of the market and approximately 100,000 employees. The company has been successful and profitable, and its stock price has shown exceptional returns. Even though the chain emphasizes everyday low pricing as an important part of its business strategy and operates in a highly competitive environment, it pays its staff comparatively well for the retail industry, hires more experienced people with building industry experience, and expects its sales associates to provide a higher level of individual customer service.

> At Home Depot, clients can expect to get detailed instruction and advice concerning their building, renovation, and hardware needs. This requires a higher level of knowledge than is typical of a retail sales worker. Management considers the sales associates in each department as a team, with wide discretion over department operations. Associates also receive above average pay for this retail segment.[30]

Contingent compensation also figures importantly in most high performance work systems. Such compensation can take a number of different forms, including gain sharing, profit sharing, stock ownership, pay for skill, or various forms of individual or team incentives. Wal-Mart, AES Corporation, Southwest Airlines, Whole Foods Markets, Microsoft, and many other successful organizations encourage share ownership. When employees are owners, they act and think like owners. Moreover, conflict between capital and labor can be reduced by linking them through employee ownership. Since 1989, Pepsico has offered a broad-based stock option plan available to 100,000 people, virtually its entire full-time labor force. Publix, a supermarket chain with 478 stores in the Southeastern United States, earned 2.75 percent on net sales in 1995 in an industry where the average is 1 percent. The company has enjoyed rapid expansion. It is important to note that the sixty-four-year-old company "has always been owned entirely by its employees and management, and the family of its late founder. . . . Employees become eligible for stock after working one year and one thousand hours. . . . [E]mployees . . . wear name badges proclaiming that each is a stockholder."[31] Home Depot, the number one rated *Fortune 500* service company for profit growth, makes sure its managers own stock in the company. At Starbucks, the rapidly growing coffee outlet chain, 100 percent of the employees, even those working part-time, receive stock options in the company.[32] But such wide-spread encouragement of stock ownership remains quite rare. Hewitt Associates, a compensation consulting firm, estimated that in 1993 "only 30 large companies now have stock option plans available to a broad range of employees. Instead, most companies simply give stock options to employees once they reach a certain level in the corporation. Many workers then exercise the options and sell the stock in a single transaction. . . . They do not acquire a stake in the company."[33]

As various schemes for encouraging employee stock ownership have become increasingly trendy, in part because they frequently have tax advantages and, more importantly, are relatively straightforward to implement, it is critical to keep two things in mind. First, little evidence suggests that employee ownership, by itself, affects organizational performance. Rather, employee ownership works best as part of a broader philosophy or culture that incorporates other practices as well.

> An employee ownership culture is . . . a high-performance workplace in which each employee becomes an owner who is afforded certain rights in exchange for assuming new responsibilities. Such a culture is achieved by following the "working for yourself" thrust of employee ownership in conjunction with a battery of practices intended to create a non-bureaucratic, less hierarchical organization focused on performance.[34]

Merely putting in ownership schemes without providing training, information sharing, and delegation of responsibility will have little effect on performance because even if people are more motivated by their share ownership, they don't necessarily have the skills, information, or power to do anything with that motivation.

Second, many organizations treat stock options and share ownership as psychologically equivalent, but they are not. An option is just that— the potential or option to acquire shares at some subsequent point in time, at a given price. If the stock price falls below the option price, the option has no value. As Bill Gurley, one of Wall Street's premier technology analysts, has argued, "The main problem with stock options is that they do not represent true ownership." Gurley goes on to describe the two potential negative effects that follow from the option holder's being given the upside but protected from the downside:

> There is a huge incentive for option holders to take undue risk [and] there is an incentive for [people] to roam around. Try your luck at one job, and if it doesn't pan out, move on to the next one. . . . [A]n aggressive stock-option program has many of the same characteristics as leverage. When times are good, they are doubly good . . . when times turn bad, the effects of stock-option compensation can be quite devastating.[35]

If, by contrast, someone purchases stock, even at a slightly discounted price, that person has made a behavioral commitment with much more powerful psychological consequences. The person remains an owner, with psychological investment in the company, even when the stock price falls. Consequently, share ownership builds much more powerful commitments and psychologically binds people to their organizations more than do options, even when the economic consequences of the two schemes are largely similar.

One worry I sometimes hear voiced about share ownership concerns inevitable declines in stock price. When I asked AES people working at the power plant in Thames, Connecticut, specifically about this issue, I was told that people do watch the stock price, but when it goes down, most employees want to buy more. One person stated, "We feel we're part of the entrepreneurs. The fluctuations in stock price reinforces the fact that we're responsible. If there were only upside, we're taking a free ride. The fact that the stock price fluctuates and that people gain and lose accordingly makes people feel like they are more of an owner of the company."

A number of organizations use profit sharing to great effect, particularly when it extends throughout the organization. At Southwest Airlines, profit sharing causes its people to focus on costs and profits because they receive a percentage of those profits. At Hewlett-Packard, quarterly profit-sharing payments are greeted with anticipation and excitement. The enthusiasm of vice presidents and secretaries alike, the excited talk pervading the organization, makes it clear that when profit sharing covers all employees the social pressure to continue producing good results becomes both powerful and widespread.

Profit sharing also makes compensation more variable, permitting adjustments in the labor bill without layoffs. At Lincoln Electric, profit sharing averages around 70 percent of individual employee salaries. When business falls, profit-sharing payments fall and labor expenses decrease—without having to break the firm's commitment to employment security. This variable component of wage costs, achieved through profit sharing, has permitted Lincoln to ride out a substantial sales decrease without laying off anyone covered by its guaranteed employment policy.

Paying for skill acquisition encourages people to learn different jobs and thereby to become more flexible. Gain sharing differs from profit sharing in that it is based on incremental improvements in the performance of a specific unit. Levi Strauss, for instance, has used gainsharing in its U.S. manufacturing plants. If a plant becomes more efficient in its use of labor and materials, the people share in the economic gains thereby achieved. They share in these gains even if profits in the firm as a whole are down. Why should employees in a plant in which they have achieved efficiency gains be penalized for problems in the general economy that have adversely affected sales or, for that matter, by the performance of other parts of the organization over which they have no control?

For a number of reasons, contingent compensation is important. First, simply, it is a matter of equity and fairness. If an organization produces greater returns by unharnessing the power of its people, justice suggests that some proportion of those gains should accrue to those who have produced the results as opposed to going solely to the shareholders or management. If people expend more effort and ingenuity, observe better results as a consequence of that effort, but then receive nothing, they are likely to become cynical and disillusioned and to stop trying.

Second, contingent compensation helps to motivate effort, because people know they will share in the results of their work. At Whole Foods, a gainsharing program "ties bonuses directly to team performance—specifically, sales per hour, the most important productivity measurement."[36] Teams, stores, and regions compete on the basis of quality, service, and profitability, with the results translating into bonuses. At Solectron, the implementation of self-managed teams positively affected quality and productivity. But when bonuses based on team performance were instituted, productivity and quality improved yet again.

Managers sometimes ask how to prevent employment security from turning into something resembling the civil service, with people just marking time. The answer is by coupling employment security with some form of group-based incentive, such as profit or gainsharing or share ownership. The organization thus unleashes the power of the team, whose economic interests are aligned with high levels of economic performance. Explaining Whole Foods' exceptional performance record, their CEO, John Mackey, stated the following:

> Whole Foods is a social system. . . . It's not a hierarchy. We don't have lots of rules handed down from headquarters in Austin. We have lots of self-examination going on. Peer pressure substitutes for bureaucracy. Peer pressure enlists loyalty in ways that bureaucracy doesn't.[37]

Peer pressure is stimulated by profit sharing and stock ownership that encourages team members to identify with the organization and to work hard on its behalf.

TRAINING

Virtually all descriptions of high performance management practices emphasize training, and the amount of training provided by commitment as opposed to control-oriented management systems is substantial. Training in steel minimills, for example, was almost 75 percent higher in mills relying on commitment as opposed to those relying on control. The previously cited study of automobile assembly plants showed that training was substantially higher in flexible or lean compared to mass production systems. Training is an essential component of high performance work systems because these systems rely on frontline employee skill and initiative to identify and resolve problems, to initiate changes in work methods, and to take responsibility for quality. All of this requires a skilled and motivated work force that has the knowledge and capability to perform the requisite tasks.

> [H]aving a work force that is multiskilled, adaptable to rapidly changing circumstances, and with broad conceptual knowledge about the production system is critical to the operation of a flexible production system. The learn-

ing process that generates these human capabilities is an integral part of how the production system functions, not a separate training activity.[38]

Training is often seen as a frill in many U.S. organizations, something to be reduced to make profit goals in times of economic stringency. Data from the worldwide automobile assembly plant study, in this instance, from fifty-seven plants, are particularly instructive in illustrating the extent to which U.S. firms, at least in this industry, underinvest in training compared to competitors based in other countries. Table 3-1 presents information on the amount of training provided in automobile assembly plants operating in various countries and with different ownership.

The data in the table are startling. In terms of the amount of training provided to newly hired production workers, U.S. firms operating either in the U.S. or in Europe provide by far the least. Japanese plants in North America provide about 700 percent more training, and plants in newly industrialized countries such as Korea, Taiwan, and Brazil provided more than 750 percent more training than do U.S. plants. Only the amount of training provided in Australia compares with U.S. levels. Similar, although not as dramatic, differences exist in the training provided for experienced production workers. Once again, the United

Table 3-1   AMOUNT OF TRAINING FOR PRODUCTION WORKERS IN AUTOMOBILE ASSEMBLY PLANTS

Ownership/Location	Hours of Training in the First Six Months for New Workers	Hours per Year for Those with > 1 Year Experience
Japanese/Japan	364	76
Japanese/North America	225	52
U.S./North America	42	31
U.S./Europe	43	34
European/Europe	178	52
Newly industrialized countries	260	46
Australia	40	15

Source: John Paul MacDuffie and Thomas A. Kochan, "Do U.S. Firms Invest Less in Human Resources? Training in the World Auto Industry," *Industrial Relations* 34 (1995): 156.

States and Australia lag, with Japanese firms operating in Japan providing more than twice as much training to experienced workers. It is, of course, possible that U.S. firms' training is so much better and so much more efficient that it accomplishes just as much with a small fraction of the effort. This explanation cannot be definitively ruled out because the study did not measure (which would be almost impossible in any event) the consequences or the effectiveness of training. Although this explanation for the differences is possible, it is not very plausible. Rather, the differences in training reflect the different views of people held by the different firms and their corresponding production systems. "The Japanese-owned plants appear to train a lot because they rely heavily on flexible production, while the U.S.-owned plants in Europe and the Australian plants appear to train very little because they follow traditional mass production practices and philosophies."[39] U.S. automobile plants serious about pursuing profits through people show substantially larger training expenditures. Workers coming to Saturn initially "receive between 300 and 600 hours of training and then at least 5 percent of their annual work time (92 hours)" goes to training.[40]

The differences in training levels also reflect differences in time horizon—the Japanese firms and Saturn, with their policies of employment security, intend to keep their people longer, so it makes more sense for them to invest more in developing them. This illustrates a more general point—that the returns from any single high performance management practice depend importantly on the entire set of practices that have been implemented. A firm that invests a lot in training but considers its people to be expendable costs to be quickly shed in times of economic difficulty will probably see little return from its training investment.

Studies of firms in the United States and the United Kingdom consistently provide evidence of inadequate levels of training and training focused on the wrong things: specialist skills rather than generalist competence and organizational culture. For instance, a case study of eight large organizations operating in the United Kingdom found one, W. H. Smith, a retailing and distribution organization, in which less than half of the people received *any* training at all in the past year. Furthermore, in only two of the organizations "did more than half the respondents indicate that they thought they received the training they needed to do their jobs well,"[41] and less than half of the organizations had a majority of employees who felt they were encouraged to develop new skills. What training is provided frequently focuses narrowly on specific job skills. "One Lloyds Bank senior manager said, 'People's perceptions of development would be that it is inadequate. But of course they are looking at being developed as generalists and I want them to be specialists more and more.'"[42] And all of this is occurring in a world in which we are constantly told that knowledge and intellectual capital are critical for success. Knowledge and skill *are* critical—and too few organizations act on this insight.

Training can be a source of competitive advantage in numerous industries for firms with the wisdom to use it. Consider, for instance, the Men's Wearhouse, an off-price specialty retailer of men's tailored business attire and accessories. Because four of the ten occupations expected to generate the most job growth through 2005 are in the retail trade sector, and in 1994, 17.9 percent of all American workers were employed in retail trade, this industry has some importance to the U.S. economy.[43] Yet the management of people in retailing is frequently abysmal. Turnover is typically high, as is the use of part-time employees, many of whom work part-time involuntarily. Employees are often treated poorly and subjected to arbitrary discipline and dismissals. Wages in retailing are comparatively low and are falling compared to other industries, and skill and career development and training are rare. The industry is characterized by both intense and increasing competition, with numerous bankruptcies of major retailing chains occurring in the last decade.

The Men's Wearhouse went public in 1991 and in its 1995 annual report noted that since that time it had achieved compounded annual growth rates in revenues and net earnings of 32 and 41 percent respectively. The value of its stock increased by approximately 400 percent over this period. In 1995, the company operated 278 stores with a total revenue of $406 million. The key to its success has been how it treats its people and particularly the emphasis it has placed on training, an approach that separates it from many of its competitors. The company built a 35,000 square-foot training center in Fremont, California, its headquarters. In 1994, some 600 "clothing consultants" went through Suits University, and that year the company added "Suits High and Selling Accessories U to complement our core program."[44] "New employees spend about four days in one of about thirty sessions held every year, at a cost to the company of about $1 million."[45] During the winter, experienced store personnel come back to headquarters in groups of about thirty for a three- or four-day retraining program.

The Men's Wearhouse has invested far more heavily in training than have most of its competitors, but it has prospered by doing so.

> Our shrink is 0.6 percent, only about a third of the industry average. And we spend zero on monitors in our stores. We have no electronic tagging and we spend nothing on security. . . . We feel that if you create a culture and an environment that is supportive of employees, you don't have to spend money on security devices. . . . My sense is that our rate of turnover is significantly lower than elsewhere.[46]

Not only does the typical U.S. firm not train as much, but because training budgets often fluctuate with company economic fortunes, a perverse, procyclical training schedule typically develops: Training funds are most plentiful when the firm is doing well. But, when the firm is doing well, its people are the busiest and have the most to do, and consequently, can least afford to be away for training. By contrast, when the firm is less busy, individuals have more time to develop their skills and undertake training activities. But that is exactly when training is least likely to be made available.

Training is an investment in the organization's staff, and in the current business milieu, it virtually begs for some sort of return-on-investment calculations. But such analyses are difficult, if not impossible, to carry out. Successful firms that emphasize training do so almost as a matter of faith and because of their belief in the connection between people and profits. Taco Inc., for instance, a privately-owned manufacturer of pumps and valves, with annual sales of under $100 million, offers its 450 employees "astonishing educational opportunities—more than six dozen courses in all,"[47] in an on-site learning center. It cost the company $250,000 to build the center and annual direct expenses and lost production cost about $300,000. Asked to put a monetary value on the return from operating the center, however, the company's chief executive, John Hazen White, said "It comes back in the form of attitude. People feel they're playing in the game, not being kicked around in it. You step to the plate and improve your work skills; we'll provide the tools to do that."[48]

Even Motorola does a poor job of measuring its return on training. Although the company has been mentioned as reporting a $3 return for every $1 invested in training, an official from Motorola's training group said that she did not know where these numbers came from and that the company is notoriously poor at evaluating their $170 million investment in training. The firm mandates forty hours of training per employee per year, and believes that the effects of training are both difficult to measure and expensive to evaluate. Training is part and parcel of an overall management process and is evaluated in that light.

REDUCTION OF STATUS DIFFERENCES

The fundamental premise of high performance management systems is that organizations perform at a higher level when they are able to tap the ideas, skill, and effort of all of their people. One way in which they do this is by organizing people in work teams, a topic already briefly covered in this chapter. But neither individuals nor teams will feel comfortable or encouraged to contribute their minds as well as their physical energy to the organization if it has sent signals that they are not both valuable and valued. In order to help make all organizational members feel important and committed to enhancing organizational operations, therefore, most high commitment management systems attempt to reduce the status distinctions that separate individuals and groups and cause some to feel less valued.

This is accomplished in two principal ways—symbolically, through the use of language and labels, physical space, and dress, and substantively, in the reduction of the organization's degree of wage inequality, particularly across levels. At Subaru-Isuzu, everyone from the company president on down was called an Associate. The company's literature stated, "SIA is not hiring workers. It is hiring Associates . . . who work as a team to accomplish a task."[49] It is easy to downplay the importance of titles and language in affecting how people relate to their organization—but it is a mistake to do so.

> The title "secretary" seems subservient, Wilson [a consultant at Miss Paige Personnel agency in Sherman Oaks, California] said, "whereas administrative assistant sounds more career-oriented, and they like that." . . . Paul Flores . . . said employees at the Prudential Insurance Co. of America treat him better because of his new title. . . . When he moved to the supply unit, he became a SIMS (supply inventory management system) technician. . . .

[I]nstead of people saying, "I want it now," they say, "Get it to me when you can."[50]

At NUMMI, everyone wears the same colored smock; executive dining rooms and reserved parking don't exist. Lincoln Electric also eschews special dining rooms—management eats with the employees—as well as reserved parking and other fancy perquisites. Anyone who has worked in a manufacturing plant has probably heard the expression, "The suits are coming." Differences in dress distinguish groups from each other and, consequently, help to inhibit communication across internal organizational boundaries. At Kingston Technology, a private firm manufacturing add-on memory modules for personal computers, with 1994 sales of $2.7 million per each of its three hundred people (a higher level of revenue per employee than Exxon, Intel, or Microsoft), the two co-founders sit in open cubicles and do not have private secretaries.[51] Solectron, too, has no special dining rooms and the chief executive, Ko Nishimura, does not have a private office or a reserved parking space. Parking has become quite tight as the company has expanded, and shuttle buses ferry employees in from more distant parking lots. Ko Nishimura rides these same shuttles and has said that he learns more riding in with the employees than from almost anything else he does. The reduction of status differences encourages open communication, necessary in an organization in which learning and adaptation are encouraged.

Status differences are reduced and a sense of common fate developed by limiting the difference in compensation between senior management and other employees. Whole Foods Markets, whose sales in 1996 were over $800 million and which has enjoyed substantial growth and stock price appreciation, has a policy limiting executive compensation. "The Company's publicly stated policy is to limit annual compensation paid to any executive officer to eight times the average full-time salary of all Team Members."[52] In 1995, the CEO, John Mackey, earned $130,000 in salary and a bonus of $20,000. Nor does Whole Foods circumvent this restriction on executive compensation through grants of stock options or by giving executives shares in the company. In 1995, Mr. Mackey received options at the market price on four thousand shares of stock.

Herb Kelleher, the CEO of Southwest Airlines who has been on the cover of *Fortune* magazine with the text, "Is he America's best CEO?" earns about $500,000 per year including base and bonus. Moreover, when in 1995 Southwest negotiated a five-year wage freeze with its pilots in exchange for stock options and occasional profitability bonuses, Kelleher agreed to freeze his base salary at $395,000 for four years.

> Southwest's compensation committee said the freeze, which leaves Mr. Kelleher's salary unchanged from his 1992 contract, "is pursuant to a voluntary commitment made by Mr. Kelleher to the Southwest Airlines Pilots' Association." . . . The . . . compensation committee said the number of options granted Mr. Kelleher, at his recommendation, was "significantly below" the number recommended by an independent consultant as necessary to make Mr. Kelleher's contract competitive with pay packages for rival airline chief executives.[53]

Sam Walton, the founder and chairman of Wal-Mart, was typically on Graef Crystal's list of one of the most underpaid CEOs. These individuals are, of course, not poor. Each of them owns stock in the companies they manage. But stock ownership is encouraged for employees in these companies. Having an executive's fortune rise and fall together with those of the other employees differs dramatically from providing them large bonuses and substantial salaries even as the stock price languishes and people are being laid off.

Clearly, practices that reduce status differences are consistent with rewards contingent on performance—as long as these contingent rewards are applied on a group or organizational level so that the benefits of the performance of the many are not awarded to the few. Reducing status differences by reducing wage inequality does limit the organization's ability to use individual incentives to the extent that the application of individual rewards increases the dispersion of wages. But, as we will explore in more detail in chapter 7, this is not necessarily a bad thing. Many managers and human resource executives mistakenly believe that placing *individual* pay at risk increases overall motivation and performance, when it is actually the contingency of the reward itself, not the level at which it is applied (individual, group, or organizational) that has the impact. In chapter 7 we will see evidence that contingent rewards provided at the group or organizational level are at least as effective, if not more so, than individual incentives and that, moreover, they avoid many of the problems inherent in individual merit or incentive pay.

SHARING INFORMATION

Information sharing is an essential component of high performance work systems for two reasons. First, the sharing of information on things such as financial performance, strategy, and operational measures conveys to the organization's people that they are trusted. John Mackey, the chief executive of Whole Foods Markets, has stated, "If you're trying to create a high-trust organization, . . . an organization where people are all-for-one and one-for all, you can't have secrets."[54] Whole Foods shares detailed financial and performance information with every employee—things such as sales by team, sales results for the same day last year, sales by store, operating profits by store, and even information from its annual employee morale survey—so much information, in fact, that "the SEC has designated all 6,500 employees 'insiders' for stock-trading purposes."[55] AES Corporation also shares detailed operational and financial information with its employees to the extent that they are all insiders for purposes of securities regulation. But Whole Foods goes even further, sharing individual salary information with every employee who is interested.

> The first prerequisite of effective teamwork is trust. . . . How better to promote trust (both among team members and between members and leaders) than to eliminate a major source of distrust—misinformed conjecture about who makes what? So every Whole Foods store has a book that lists the previous year's salary and bonus for all 6,500 employees—by name.[56]

This idea may at first seem strange. But think about your organization. If it is anything like mine, where salaries are secret, when it's time for raises people spend time and effort attempting to figure out what others got and how their raise (and salary) stacks up. This subtle attempt to find out where you stand takes time away from useful activities. Moreover, individuals frequently assume the worst—that they are doing worse than they actually are—and in any event, they don't have enough information to trust the salary system or, for that matter, the management that administers it. John Mackey of Whole Foods instituted the open salary disclosure process to signal that, at least this company had nothing to hide, nothing that couldn't be seen—and questioned—by any team member.

Contrast that organization with *Fortune* magazine, where a now-retired senior editor told me that after the Time-Warner merger when the company was saddled with debt senior personnel were called together and told to "cut expenses by 10 percent." When the editor asked to see the expense budget and how it was allocated, he was told he could not. He resigned soon after. What message does an organization send if it says "Cut expenses, but, by the way, I don't trust you (even at senior levels) enough to share expense information with you?"

A second reason for sharing information is this: Even motivated and trained people cannot contribute to enhancing organizational performance if they don't have information on important dimensions of performance and, in addition, training on how to use and interpret that information. The now famous case of Springfield ReManufacturing beautifully illustrates this point. On February 1, 1983, Springfield Re-Manufacturing Corporation (SRC) was created when the plant's management and employees purchased an old International Harvester plant in a financial transaction that consisted of about $100,000 equity and $8.9 million debt, an 89–1 debt to equity ratio that has to make this one of the most leveraged of all leveraged buy-outs. Jack Stack, the former plant manager and now chief executive, knew that if the plant was to succeed, everyone had to do their best and to share all of her or his wisdom and ideas for enhancing the plant's performance. Stack came up with a system called "open-book management" that has since become a quite popular object of study—so popular that SRC now makes money by running seminars on it. Although the method may be popular as a seminar topic, fewer organizations are actually willing to implement it.

The system has a straightforward underlying philosophy, articulated by Stack:

> Don't use information to intimidate, control or manipulate people. Use it to teach people how to work together to achieve common goals and thereby gain control over their lives. . . . Cost control happens (or doesn't happen) on the level of the individual. You don't become the least-cost producer by issuing edicts from an office. . . . [T]he best way to control costs is to enlist everyone in the effort. That means providing people with the tools that allow them to make the right decisions.[57]

Implementing the system involved first making sure that all of the company's people generated daily numbers reflecting their work performance and production costs. Second, it involved sharing this information, aggregated once a week, with all of the company's people, everyone from secretaries to top management. Third, it involved extensive training in how to use and interpret the numbers—how to understand balance sheets and cash flow and income statements. "Understanding the financials came to be part of everyone's job."[58]

Springfield ReManufacturing has enjoyed tremendous financial success. In 1983, its first year of operation, sales were about $13 million. By 1992, sales had increased to $70 million, the number of employees had grown from 119 at the time of the buy-out to 700, and the original equity investment of $100,000 was worth more than $23 million by 1993.[59] No one who knows the company, and certainly not Jack Stack or the other managers, believes this economic performance could have been achieved without a set of practices that enlisted the cooperation and ingenuity of all of the firm's people. The system and philosophy of open-book management took a failing International Harvester plant and transformed it into a highly successful, growing business. Similarly impressive results have been reported in case studies of Manco, a Cleveland-based distributor of duct tape, weather stripping, and mailing materials; Phelps County Bank, located in Rolla, Missouri; Mid-States Technical Staffing Services, located in Iowa; Chesapeake Manufacturing Company, a packaging materials manufacturer; Allstate Insurance; Macromedia, a software company; and Pace Industries, a manufacturer of die cast metal parts.[60]

If sharing information makes simple, common sense, you might wonder why sharing information about operations and financial performance is not more widespread. One reason is that information is power, and sharing information diffuses that power. At an International Harvester plant, "the plant manager's whole theory of management was 'Numbers are power, and the numbers are mine.'"[61] If holding performance information is the critical source of the power of a firm's leaders, however, let me suggest that the organization badly needs to find some different leaders.

Another rationale for not sharing information more widely with the work force is managers' fears that the information will leak out to competitors, creating a disadvantage for the organization. When Bob

Beck, now running human resources at Gateway 2000, a manufacturer of personal computers sold largely by mail order, was the Executive Vice President of Human Resources at the Bank of America in the early 1980s, he told his colleagues that the organization could never improve customer service or retention until it shared its basic business strategy, plans, and measures of performance with its entire work force. When his colleagues on the executive committee noted that this information would almost certainly leak out to the competition, Beck demonstrated to them what ought to be common knowledge—in most instances, the competition already knows.

When organizations keep secrets, they keep secrets from their own people. I find it almost ludicrous that many companies in the electronics industry in the Silicon Valley go to enormous lengths to try to keep secrets internally, when all you have to do to penetrate them is to go to one of the popular bars or restaurants in the area and listen in as people from different companies talk quite openly with each other. When people don't know what is going on and don't understand the basic principles and theory of the business, they cannot be expected to positively affect performance. Sharing information and providing training in understanding and using it to make better business decisions works.

CONCLUSION

Firms often attempt to implement organizational innovations such as those described in this chapter piecemeal. This tendency is understandable—after all, it is difficult enough to change some aspect of the compensation system without also having to be concerned about training, recruitment and selection, and how work is organized. Implementing practices in isolation may not have much effect, however, and, under some circumstances, it could actually be counterproductive. For instance, increasing the firm's commitment to training activities won't accomplish much unless changes in work organization permit these more skilled people to actually implement their knowledge. If wages are comparatively low and incentives are lacking that recognize enhanced economic success, the better trained people may simply depart for the competition. Employment security, too, can be counterproductive unless the firm hires people who will fit the culture and unless incentives reward outstanding performance. Implementing work teams will probably not, by itself, accomplish as much as if the teams received training both in specific technical skills and team processes, and it will have less effect still if the teams aren't given financial and operating performance goals and information. "Whatever the bundles or configurations of practices implemented in a particular firm, the individual practices must be aligned with one another and be consistent with the [organizational] architecture if they are ultimately to have an effect on firm performance."[62] It is important to have some overall philosophy or strategic vision of achieving profits through people, because an overall framework increases the likelihood of taking a systematic as contrasted with a piecemeal approach to implementing high commitment organizational arrangements.

Clearly, it requires time to implement and see results from many of these practices. For instance, it takes time to train and upgrade the skills of an existing work force and even more time to see the economic benefits of this training in reduced turnover and enhanced performance. It takes time not only to share operating and financial information with people but also to be sure that they know how to understand and use it in decision making; even more time is needed before the suggestions and insights implemented can provide business results. It certainly requires time for employees to believe in employment security and for that belief to generate the trust that then produces higher levels of innovation and effort. Consequently, taking a long-term view of a company's development and growth becomes at least useful if not absolutely essential to implementation of high performance organizational arrangements. One way of thinking about various institutional and organizational barriers and aids to implementing high performance management practices is, therefore, to consider each in terms of its effects on the time horizon that characterizes organizational decisions. This theme appears throughout this book as we consider the various barriers and beliefs that have impeded the implementation of these ideas.

Although the management practices described in this chapter come directly from a number of systematic studies that have examined the effects of the management of the employment relationship on economic performance, are supported by numerous case examples, and seem to be logical and based on straightforward common sense, in fact a number of them are at some substantial variance both from dominant practice and conventional wisdom. Employment security is out of fashion; compensation systems are returning, in some instances, to the piecework characteristic of Frederick Taylor and scientific management; training is talked about more often than done; and arguments have been offered that executive compensation and associated status differences are too low, particularly in countries other than the United States. It is not possible to take on and debunk all of the misinformation in discussions about managing the employment relation, but a few important issues warrant further exploration simply because they are both so deeply ingrained and so fundamental to enhancing organizational performance. This I do later in the book. But first I offer a diagnostic framework and some tools for implementing these ideas.

4 ◆ *Aligning Business Strategy and Management Practices*

ALL RIGHT. After all the data in chapter 2 and the examples in chapter 3, you are convinced that implementing high performance management practices is important for your firm's competitive success and believe the connection between how you manage people and your organization's profits. What do you do? As already noted, "if there is a best practice effect it is more likely to be in the 'architecture' of a system."[1] But the design of a high performance work system must ultimately get beyond issues of philosophy, architecture, and mind set—even though these are absolutely critical and fundamental—to questions of specifically what must be done and how to do it. A relatively straightforward diagnostic process, outlined here, can be used to address this question of implementation. The diagnostic framework is premised on the idea of alignment, that is, that an organization does specific things to manage the employment relationship and these practices need to be first, internally consistent or aligned with one another, and second, externally consistent, in the sense that the organization's procedures produce the behaviors and competencies required for it to compete successfully given its chosen marketplace and way of differentiating itself in that marketplace.

Such alignment is easier described than accomplished, because few organizations have developed a set of consistent practices. Moreover, when firms uncover examples of misalignment, they are often unwilling to make any (or very many or significant) changes. Of all the many organizations that talk about implementing teams, for example, only a small fraction implement team-based compensation, moving away from predominantly individual assessments and rewards. Only a few permit teams to hire members, to schedule their own work, to make budget and investment decisions, and to use peer evaluations as part of the performance management process. Firms that hire, reward, allocate tasks and resources, and train solely on an individual basis, however, are unlikely to build a team culture or effectively self-managing teams. As another example, although many organizations talk about trust, empowerment, and delegation of responsibility, only a small subset evaluate *all* of their practices in terms of whether they are consistent with these ideas or are willing to change whatever they discover is not.

One organization that consistently behaves in ways congruent with its espoused values and its culture is AES, described in the last chapter. In 1992, the AES Corporation faced a severe test of a culture that emphasized trust, decentralization, and delegation of responsibility. Some employees at its Shady Point, Oklahoma, plant falsified some of the tests required by the Environmental Protection Administration concerning the facility's waste-water discharge. Following the announcement of this problem, the price of AES stock fell from $26.50 to $16.50, wiping out some $400 million of shareholder value. Since the company has integrity as one of its core values and concern for the environment as another, this violation of law was also a violation of the AES culture. In response, the people at Shady Point decided to reorganize the plant in some ways that were different from the rest of AES in an effort to prevent a recurrence. They added supervisory levels and specific functions and departments to ensure EPA compliance—in short, they began to look more like a typical utility plant. These solutions were not consistent with the CEO Dennis Bakke's beliefs about how such a problem should be handled. AES culture firmly holds that systems that affect 100 percent of the people are not changed or implemented to deal with the 2 percent of employees or situations that cause problems.

What would Bakke do? He had forcefully advocated decentralization of the corporation and the autonomy of each plant. But now, people at a plant had decided to manage in a way inconsistent with Bakke's beliefs about eliminating bureaucracy and using systems that imply and encourage trust.

When we got in trouble back in '92, the people at the plant decided to chuck the entire system. They went back to shift supervisors, an environmental department, a super environmental group, and a deputy plant manager. I mean, they just went for a total control kind of mentality, because they were scared to death. The lawyers were all over them like crazy, and they basically fired me. They said, "Please do not come back to the plant." I felt a little hurt, you know. I own this company (or at least part of it). The fact that I almost lost my overall AES job made me worry less about just being fired by one plant. But it was a real test of whether we were going backwards toward centralization or whether we would be decentralized. And we went along with it. I wouldn't go there for a whole year, until they finally called back and said, "We'd like you to come back again, we'd like to rejoin the company."

That was an amazing time. But it illustrated a couple of things. One was that we did mean it when we were talking about decentralization and autonomy. And second, it proved me wrong when I said the principles were pretty fragile.[2]

But because it is difficult, companies do not always behave consistently with their espoused values. Think about how you would react if some employees caused a problem that, at least temporarily, cost your firm $400 million of market value in about a week. Would you remain faithful to core values, culture, and a set of management practices even when they seemingly had failed? Many senior executives believe that decentralization and participation are fine for those further down in the organization, but not for them. Many managers believe that delegation and putting people first is fine as long as things are going smoothly, but then centralize control and react harshly when in crisis. It is important to be aligned and consistent at a point in time. It is possibly just as important to maintain that consistency over time.

Consider another example, also drawn from AES. The world of electric power production is rapidly changing. In many states in the United States, this formerly regulated industry faces increased competition, potentially disrupting the practice of selling power on long-term contracts. Many countries are privatizing power systems and building plants, sometimes by joint ventures. The technology of electric power production also continues to evolve, as do the financial markets and the skills required to be successful in the business. In short, this is a dynamic business facing rapid change, not unlike many businesses in today's world. In such an environment, entrepreneurial, responsive organizations will have a comparative advantage, particularly if their people are motivated and multiskilled.

Thus, many organizations, including AES, talk about building an entrepreneurial culture, reducing the time needed to make and implement decisions, and so forth. The difference is not in the talk but in the ability to actually implement practices that accomplish these high-sounding goals. At AES, several specific things the organization does (or doesn't do) help it to actually achieve entrepreneurial, quick, and skilled behavior. First, it has almost no centralized staff functions—no formal purchasing department, for instance, and no human resources department. When I asked AES executives about this, and about the potential cost in terms of the loss of specialization, I was told that specialization comes with a price. After you have negotiated coal contracts repeatedly, for instance, one becomes habituated to the process and tends to do things and think about things pretty much the same way. But this is costly in an environment that is itself changing all the time. Sure, it takes more time for people to continually learn how to do new things that they have never done before—a process that, at AES, involves a lot of asking questions and talking to others within the organization. But the result of this apparently inefficient process is that more people can do more things—an outcome consistent with Dennis Bakke's goal of having all of the employees think like business people. In addition, by getting new people to take on new tasks, these individuals have the opportunity to figure out innovative approaches, which an individual doing the same thing for the hundredth time is much less likely to do. Also, the absence of large, specialized staffs permits AES to be leaner and faster in responding to market opportunities.

Second, the corporation does not do a lot of formal planning or strategic analysis and does not require prior approvals from senior management before an action can be taken. Even in its highly regulated, lawyer-ridden, capital-intensive business of developing and operating electric power plants, AES encourages individual initiative. For instance, an individual who saw an opportunity for the company in South America spent a year, on his own initiative, attempting to negotiate a deal. Finally, his manager at headquarters called him in and asked if maybe it wasn't time to give up. The person said, "Give me two more months, and if nothing happens, I'll come home." Within that period he was finally able to negotiate the purchase of a power plant for AES to operate. Nor is this example unique, as this passage from the AES 1996 annual report illustrates:

> Maybe the most surprising development of the year came when Scott Gardner, who came to us from Dartmouth College a few years ago, spent his summer before leaving to [sic] graduate school preparing, submitting, and then winning the bid for a 288-megawatt peaking facility (Mt. Stuart, Australia). This project reinforces our belief in how much difference one dedicated, creative, responsible person can make.[3]

How many organizations do you know that would permit someone to go off on his own, still being paid by the company and using its resources, on the basis of a belief or hunch about a commercial opportunity to be exploited? How many organizations would have the patience to wait more than a year for the fruition of the project? And how many companies would do this for a relatively junior person and without a lot of prior review, planning, and approval? More to the point, would the organization you manage operate this way? AES's track record suggests that it has made the right decision by favoring decentralization and encouraging initiative, but not very many organizations would implement the practices just described or other similar practices that can produce innovative, creative, behavior and learning. Many firms talk about initiative and competence even as they implement procedures that destroy wisdom and entrepreneurship.

Moreover, simply knowing what to do to achieve profits through people is insufficient. I have seen many managers, when confronted with instances in which practices were clearly not consistent with what was required to produce the behavior necessary, nevertheless come up with all sorts of reasons to keep on doing what they had been doing. Sometimes an established faction opposes change, and senior leadership cannot or will not take it on. Sometimes firm practices that should be changed have become institutionalized, so much taken for granted that doing things differently seems impossible. Sometimes change requires too much effort, effort that takes time and attention away from other, more pressing organizational issues and problems.

Out of my experiences with companies facing these situations, I have developed what I have come to call "the religious theory of management." An organization that wants to achieve skill in doing some activity and yet is unwilling to recruit, select, compensate, evaluate, or measure very much or at all on the basis of that activity will achieve its performance goals only through some form of divine intervention. Many organizations hope or wish for improvement without facing the necessity to change the systems that direct and affect behavior—this myopia is widespread. Policies and practices have lives of their own, and powerful constituencies support the status quo. Many managers want things to change, but only if they need not themselves do very much very differently. So, be forewarned. Going through the exercise outlined below for seeing the extent to which your company's management practices align with what it requires to succeed will have results on performance if and only if you implement the insights gained. Insight without action will have no effect at all.

And you should be forewarned about something else: Not only will changing practices be difficult, not all managers—particularly senior human resource professionals—will be very aware or forthcoming about the extent of misalignment. Very often, managers talk a great deal about alignment but do not analyze behavior. Consider the following data. As part of a project for the U.S. Army about changing its procurement practices, Beth Benjamin and some of her colleagues from the RAND Corporation interviewed a number of major business firms about what they had learned about accomplishing change and what they had done to become more efficient and productive. Here is what they found:

> In every firm we visited, the human resource folks went to great lengths to explain to us the importance of alignment. They then proceeded to tell us about all their practices, which even in the interview we could tell were not aligned. When this issue of misalignment was raised, they often provided elaborate explanations for why practices were the way they were. In some cases, they just didn't acknowledge the misalignment. In others, they admitted there were problems but said they couldn't change the practices because of organizational culture or tradition. In most cases, there were "practical, administrative issues" that blocked the change. . . . Managers think because they recognize the need for alignment and state the concept on paper and make one or two changes—at one point in time—that everything is suddenly in alignment.[4]

It is as if the wish for and belief in alignment magically made practices internally consistent and consistent with what would be necessary to produce the behaviors crucial to implementation of the firm's strategy. Unfortunately, wishful thinking does not substitute for reality, and one must actually make the changes required in order to produce differences in how the firm operates.

When things go wrong and performance suffers, firms sometimes do recognize the importance of their people and the need to align their management practices. Failures to implement strategy and problems with quality, customer service, and productivity are more visible when a company is struggling than when it is growing and apparently prospering. But, in fact, attention to the alignment of management practices with one another and with the organization's basic strategy is at least as necessary during times of growth as when facing tough competitive challenges. Otherwise, organizations risk developing problems that can come back to cause problems later.

Consider, for instance, one of the big six accounting firms. In the 1990s, this particular firm changed its culture and some of its incentives with a goal of building a high sales growth mentality. With booking business more important in promotion and compensation decisions, sales increased rapidly. But the firm failed to do anything about its people infrastructure. In a high-growth mode where merely doing the work that had been sold was a major challenge, little or no attention was paid to the development of the firm's intellectual capital and of new knowledge and new products. Worse than that, little systematic attention was given to recruiting, training, and governance—there simply wasn't time.

The results of this inattention were predictable. People became overworked and turnover soared. The compensation system was increasingly seen as inequitable. The increased workload made people more sensitive to their tasks and compensation and, moreover, the increased profits from the higher sales that went mostly to the partners, not to the many minions who actually did much of the work. Worst of all, the job market in accounting and consulting was tight because competing firms were also doing well. This meant that leaving the firm was easy—other opportunities were plentiful. As this is being written, the results of this experiment in ignoring people issues and trying to manage in a misaligned system are not yet fully in. But the negative consequences have already begun to appear and the firm's ability to correct its problems is limited by habits of attention that do not include a focus on people issues.

This example illustrates an important point: Aligning management practices is often overlooked in the early stages of a plan for growth. As a result, problems arise that severely constrain the organization's subsequent ability to achieve its real potential. It is much easier and less costly to try to prevent these sorts of problems than to fix them once they have become pressing.

THE ALIGNMENT DIAGNOSIS

The diagnostic process begins by considering the organization's particular strategy and the distinctive competencies it intends to develop. Most organizations have a reasonable sense of their environment and what will be required to succeed in that environment. The next step entails specifying the few key competencies or behaviors that are necessary to actually implement the strategy and succeed in the organization's environment. Then, the diagnostic asks managers to consider in some detail the various management practices. The final step is a simple logic check to assess the extent to which these practices are internally consistent—logically related to each other—and externally consistent, in order to ensure that they produce the critical skills and behaviors necessary for effective implementation of the organization's strategy.

Determine the Organization's Strategy or Strategic Intent

The first step in aligning management practices with the firm's business strategy is to understand what the business strategy is. This sounds simple, but it isn't. In many organizations, when I do this exercise and ask people to work in groups, much of the groups' allotted time is spent trying to figure out the company's strategy. This difficulty occurs even with groups of senior managers, although the problem worsens if groups consist of a random sample of organizational employees. In part, this problem arises because some firms see their strategy as a competitive weapon and are reluctant to share it too widely, an instance of the fear of disclosing information to the work force discussed in chapter 3.

In addition, more than a few firms don't think very strategically about their businesses, so what little strategy has been developed has not been discussed and refined enough to be widely known. Finally, some organizations have confused a strategy with a financial forecast or financial plan. It isn't.

A firm's strategy is simply a blueprint as to how it will compete in its marketplace—that is, a statement of what value proposition the firm will offer that will cause customers to prefer it over the competition. The value proposition may be based on price, technological leadership, customer service, or some combination of these with other factors. A good strategy successfully differentiates a firm from its competition and is difficult to copy. A bad strategy is easily copied, or basically makes the value proposition worse.

An example can help make the point. Many of the U.S. airlines decided a while ago that they would compete on the basis of price and that they would do this by taking away "amenities" (like meals) and by putting in more seats. They thus followed the successful model of Southwest Airlines, believing that the key to Southwest's success was its no frills service—no assigned seats, no meals, and so forth. The problem with this thinking is that anyone can eliminate meals. In fact, the whole concept of airline food is an oxymoron, even though American Airlines is now apparently selling (or giving away) the recipes it uses to prepare its airline meals. Price cutting, too, is easy to copy. Cutting costs was, of course, another matter. Finally, duplicating Southwest's lack of on-board amenities without duplicating its on-time performance and outstanding record of baggage handling and care for the customer by motivated and dedicated staff was just an invitation for customers to defect. On international routes, this strategy of offering less opened up the opportunity for Virgin Atlantic to offer more in every price category of service—larger seats, more amenities, better customer care—and thereby to build its business. In the domestic market, Alaska Airlines was successful with a policy and advertising campaign based on the premise "you just get more."

This book is not about strategy, so I will stop here. But it is important, in thinking about your organization's strategy, to keep firmly in mind what your customers want, what your firm wants, and what it can cost-efficiently deliver. It is also important to remember that finding some way of delivering value that is not readily duplicated by others is likely to provide a more enduring source of success than doing something that is easily copied.

What Skills and Behaviors Are Necessary to Implement the Strategy?

The second step in the diagnostic process requires answering the following question: Given our particular strategy and approach to the market, what skills and behaviors do we need from our people to successfully implement the strategy? A strategy premised on fast cycle time and being the first to market with new products or services requires from employees a sense of time urgency and the ability to innovate. If the strategy has a customer service component, people who are knowledgeable—you can't deliver service otherwise—interested, and committed to service would seem to be critical. When costs and prices form the basis of the strategy, productivity and an absence of wasted effort and resources becomes essential. List the specific required behaviors and skills across the top of as many sheets of paper as necessary; these will constitute the columns in a matrix or chart.

Focus on at most six or seven critical behaviors or competencies initially, because it is difficult to focus on more. Reduce the longer list of desirable attributes produced by the above question and search for the basic, underlying dimensions that cut across behaviors and skills. Be willing to prioritize: What are the most critical skills and behaviors required for the organization to succeed, given its strategy? It is important to note that the skills and behaviors depend on the strategy. A service as opposed to a price strategy requires different behaviors and skills—just fly Singapore Airlines and United and see the difference. Success can have different bases. What this part of the diagnostic exercise should produce is not some generic wish list of employee qualities, but specific behaviors and competencies crucial for implementing the firm's strategy.

Returning to an earlier example, AES, which develops and operates electric power plants all over the world, in common with most electric utility companies in the United States, faces a business increasingly run by lawyers.[5] AES's competitive advantage lies in its decentralized structure and minimal corporate staff, which, in combination, imbue the corporation with a sense of entrepreneurship. CEO Dennis Bakke has as one of his goals getting every person to think like a business person. Hiring in the company is very important—about the most important thing they do, many people inside the company say. AES is quite clear about what makes a good employee—and what makes a bad one. A bad hire would be "someone who is a chronic complainer, who is not happy, who blames others, who doesn't take responsibility, who is not honest, who doesn't trust. A poor hire would be someone who needs specific direction and waits to be told what to do. Someone who wasn't flexible and who says, 'it's not my job.'"[6] Note that these behaviors are in direct relation to the company's style and strategy and would not necessarily be the same at companies with other ways of approaching the electric power market.

List the Organization's Management Practices

To develop the rows of the matrix, it is necessary to describe what your organization presently does with respect to managing people. You might want to use a separate page for each of the categories below, or, if you want to do the analysis in a more aggregated fashion, to combine the categories with less detail on a single page. Down the page (or pages as required), list, in some detail, what your organization does with respect to the following:

1. How it recruits, including the sources it uses, and what it promises prospective employees.
2. How it selects from among its recruits, including the use of tests and interviews and particular questions asked, and how it decides whom to hire.
3. How it pays people, including (a) the level of pay, and (b) any incentive compensation or bonus programs in place.
4. What training activities it directly or indirectly sponsors.
5. What career paths and career development activities exist and how people are identified and prepared to assume more responsibility.
6. The degree of specialization and division of labor.
7. What basic organizational structure is used for organizing work: how many levels it has and the nature of the basic organizing units.

8. The physical layout and amenities provided.

9. What is measured in the performance management and appraisal process, how often this is done, and by whom.

10. What is measured and talked about more generally in the organization.

It should be clear that these are guidelines only and that you should feel free to include any additional dimensions of importance to your organization. (See Table 4-3 for an illustration of one such matrix for one particular organization.)

This part of the exercise is often as illuminating as the discussion of the organization's strategy. In many firms, even senior managers either don't know or don't agree on how the organization manages its people. I have listened to lively disagreements about an organization's policies with respect to salary levels and whether it pays well or poorly, to disputes about whether teams are being used, and to people who are unaware of some of the incentive schemes used by their firms. Uncertainty about a firm's people handling policies is not a good sign—if people don't know what is going on, it is unlikely that the policies and practices are having as much impact on behavior as they might or should.

Assess External Congruence and Internal Consistency

The next and final step of the alignment exercise requires those doing the task to ask themselves a simple question: For each of the things the firm is doing to manage the employment relation, to what extent would one logically expect that practice or program to produce or fail to produce each of the skills and behaviors previously identified as critical? One can use a simple rating scheme for this: For example, 1–0 could indicate that the practice did or did not produce the behavior or skill; +1, 0, or −1 could be used to indicate that the practice promotes the skill or behavior, is neutral in its effect, or, in fact, produces the opposite of what the organization has said it needs. A more refined scale could also be used. The objective of this part of the alignment exercise is to think logically about whether or to what extent the specific things being done to manage people actually generate the competencies and performance that the organization has already determined are critical to its success.

Many firms will uncover substantial misalignments, and below I will provide two specific examples of how this diagnostic process can help highlight what an organization needs to change for better strategy implementation. For the moment, let me note that some problems occur so often that they are almost generic. One is the link between training activities and required skills and behaviors. Training in many organizations focuses on developing individual skills and knowledge— knowledge and competence that, without doubt, is in some general sense useful and that might enhance organizational performance, but is not necessarily tightly linked to the organization's most critical objectives. Does your organization offer generic courses in time management, negotiation, leadership, and computer skills? Without question, all of these things are interesting and worthwhile—but the question is, are they key skills and behaviors required to implement your firm's particular strategy? Time and attention are limited, and often critical behaviors and skills are neglected in favor of more general training. Another notorious example of misalignment is compensation. In many firms, the particular compensation and incentive schemes in use bear little or no connection to the critical skills and behaviors identified as being critical for success. Many firms, for example, reward making the budget numbers even as they stress the importance of innovation, being fast, and customer focus. Although many firms talk about the importance of managing people, comparatively few include measures of people management, such as attitudes or success in getting people ready for promotions, as part of the performance appraisal process. I have seen compensation practices in firms that have virtually no positive effect on developing or reinforcing critical skills and behaviors, and this condition is all too common.

A second part of the exercise entails having the group list the same practices as both rows and columns and ask to what extent the practices are consistent with one another. To what extent, for instance, is the performance appraisal and management process, in terms of when and how it is done, the questions asked, and so forth, consistent with the firm's training programs and career development efforts? In many firms, training is one thing, appraisal is another. But if the firm emphasizes key behaviors and competencies in its training activities, then surely these should be highlighted in performance management activities. Or, to what extent does the compensation system reward and measure in a way consistent with the firm's training and organization of work? In many places, training covers quality processes and teamwork and employees are organized in self-managing teams, but the compensation system continues to focus on the individual and fails to highlight the behaviors and outcomes featured in the quality management process. The point is not that a particular process (such as total quality management) is good or bad, but simply that if an organization emphasizes a process in training and then does not reinforce it in the measurement and pay system, it sends very mixed messages to employees and the effectiveness of both its training and its compensation practices are correspondingly reduced.

EXAMPLES OF MISALIGNMENT AND ITS CONSEQUENCES

To make this process concrete, let me give you two examples of organizations that went through this exercise and what they learned from it. The first was a Silicon Valley defense contractor with considerable expertise in hardware and particularly software useful for signal detection and pattern recognition, determining whether, for example, a blip on a radar screen was or was not an enemy missile. The organization had real technological strength. But its business came almost exclusively from the military, and after the fall of the Berlin Wall (a phrase often heard in the organization), its people generally recognized that, if the organization was to remain viable, let alone grow, it needed to use its expertise to develop commercial applications. The company of which it was a division had commercial businesses and encouraged this endeavor. Moreover, I was told by numerous people both inside and outside the company that it did actually have expertise that would find many commercial outlets, particularly if it could continue to develop its technology and could get ideas and products to the marketplace quickly.

When I encountered the company, however, in spite of many talks and much exhortation from senior management, little progress had been made. New structural arrangements had been implemented, but, nevertheless, the old culture, oriented toward Department of Defense requirements and methods, persisted, despite what I was assured were tremendous efforts to change things.

I went through the diagnostic process with a group of general managers to examine the alignment between strategy and management practices, area by area, beginning with training. In Table 4-1, I present the list of their most important courses and the extent to which each made a contribution to one of their key business priorities. Similar analyses were done for other aspects of their management practices, including recruiting and selection and compensation with similar results. Table 4-1 clearly illustrates why the company had problems diversifying.

Notice that the column under business diversification is empty—none of the courses, regardless of their other merits, was judged by senior management to be relevant to the task of commercializing the company's technologies in non-defense markets. A similar absence of marks under this column occurred in all the other charts the group made. Suddenly it became clear to everyone why business diversifica-

Table 4-1   CONNECTION BETWEEN TRAINING AND BUSINESS
REQUIREMENTS IN ONE ORGANIZATION

Training Courses	Priorities						
	Shared understanding	Changing employee and manager role	Performance management	Business diversification	Specific skills	Compliance	Diversity
Eight-hour all-employee course	X	X	X			X	X
Concurrent engineering	X	X	X		X		
Performance management		X	X			X	X
Leadership through facilitation	X	X			X		
Program management					X		
Systems engineering					X		
Compliance courses	X		X				X

tion was not proceeding smoothly—nothing the firm did in its day-to-day management practices was linked to the task of diversifying the organization's business base. Since nothing was linked to that activity, progress was inevitably slow.

Although this diagnostic exercise was illuminating and worthwhile to the company, their approach was not perfect. Specifically, the "priorities" listed are couched in quite general terms. If, rather than using terms such as "shared understanding," "specific skills," and "performance management," the company managers had devised a list of more specific skills and behaviors, they would have gained even more from the exercise. The more specific you are, the more readily you and your colleagues can assess the extent to which various processes build the requisite organizational competencies and the more accurate the assessment of alignment will be.

Table 4-1 also illustrates another point. Consider the course "systems engineering." Although this was an undoubtedly excellent course, very well delivered and with sophisticated content, it links to almost none of the firm's core business priorities, but, rather, simply imparts some specific skills. One way of evaluating training courses or any other set of activities is to see how many important skills and behaviors each affects. A course that receives excellent evaluations, has good content, and is well delivered but that does not have much effect on the firm's core competencies is a luxury, particularly if the necessary behaviors and skills are not being developed elsewhere. Go to Motorola University and do this same diagnosis, and you will observe a very different result. Motorola is committed to a total quality management process, and its various course offerings are virtually all designed to impart training relevant and necessary for doing the various aspects of total quality management.

As I've already noted, the problem in this particular case was not just with the training activities. The company's recruiting and selection strategies had not changed as its business strategy altered. They still tended, for example, to recruit individuals who had top secret security clearances. This practice made eminent sense when the firm did all of its business with the Defense Department, because hiring someone without a top secret security clearance meant paying that individual's salary for the time required to obtain the clearance even though the person could not perform his or her job. But this practice no longer made sense when the firm needed individuals who could commercialize technology and build products and markets for non-governmental users. The company's people had simply overlooked—forgotten—the need to revisit and adjust their criteria to reflect the company's new orientation.

The organization's compensation practices also presented problems. As a defense contractor, the firm had come to resemble the government in many of its policies. This was partly because of the close and frequent contact and partly because, as a defense contractor, the firm was subject to oversight and audit by its customers, who wanted the firm to operate as they did. Rewards were thus achieved primarily through promotion up the hierarchy; very little pay was at risk; performance evaluation focused heavily on individual outcomes and behavior; rewards were little differentiated; and employees had very much an entitlement mentality, expecting that pay increases would reflect cost of living increases and that everyone deserved and would receive some raise every year. These policies, for the most part, do not encourage entrepreneurial behavior. With little or no variable pay, employees had little incentive or encouragement to take commercial risks: the upside was limited and, if things didn't work out, the person risked his or her job. Individual performance rewards did not orient individuals toward teamwork and left them with little compelling interest in the total organization's success. This detachment was intensified by the company's Silicon Valley location, with its individualistic culture and numerous competitors nearby, which gave employees the sense that if things didn't work out where they were, they could always move on. Given this poor alignment between compensation and what the company now needed, a set of recommendations emerged, outlined in Table 4-2.

Unfortunately, by the time the misalignment was recognized and after some delay in taking remedial actions, it was too late for this organization to recover, and it first shrank substantially before being consolidated with another division of its parent corporation. Was it the case that it was simply impossible to commercialize the technology? Evidence to the contrary exists, as the company did spawn a number of successful new businesses that either opened independently or were sold and developed by other companies.

As another example, consider the case of a large, successful health maintenance organization providing prepaid medical services and dominating the health-care market in California. The health-care marketplace in the United States has become increasingly competitive, and competition in the HMO industry has intensified substantially with many new entrants and a great many mergers and consolidations. This particular organization could sense the erosion of its competitive edge, and it sought to implement a number of remedies. It changed its marketing and distribution, agreeing to sell through insurance brokers as well as through its direct sales force. It intensified the training of that sales force to ensure that its salespeople had the most up-to-date negotiating and sales skills. It reorganized a number of times, changing lines of authority and, presumably, accountability in the hope that more direct lines of responsibility would enhance performance. It cut expenses, and in a health-care organization, expenses often mean people. It was particularly hard on administrative and headquarters people. It even closed facilities and began to duplicate what many of its competitors did: It contracted out for hospital and other services, something it had never done in the past. But none of this seemed to bring much

Table 4-2 DIFFERENCES BETWEEN CURRENT REWARD
PRACTICES AND THOSE NECESSARY TO ACHIEVE
BUSINESS OBJECTIVES

Former Rewards	Future Rewards
Based on promotion	Based on lateral development
Mostly base pay, determined by the market	Variable pay based on business success
Viewed as a result of behavior	Used as a means of communicating values
Based on individual performance	Based on team (unit) and company performance
Evenly distributed among everyone	Differentiated
Based on cost of living and the labor market	Based on business performance
Correlated with seniority	Based on performance

relief, even temporary, from its troubles, reflected in the loss of market share and an inability to grow.

At an in-company executive program, a number of high-level managers from the organization undertook the alignment diagnosis described in this chapter. Their results are displayed in Table 4-3. The table clearly shows the organization's problems: Its human resources system and the values and competencies its people believe are necessary to succeed in the health-care marketplace show almost no alignment. Moreover, none of the actions just described—upgrading its sales and marketing, reorganizing, cutting staff, and so forth—address the basic problems of misalignment between how it recruits, trains, pays, and organizes and the skills and behaviors required to execute its intended strategy.

This operationalization of the alignment exercise has some advantages and disadvantages over the previous example. The required skills

Table 4-3 ALIGNMENT IN A HEALTH-CARE ORGANIZATION

Practices	Teamwork	Customer focus	Skills/Training	Commitment	Problem solving	Caring	Hard work	Flexibility	Values (social mission)
Recruitment	L	O	L	L	O	L	O	O	O
Selection	O	O	L	O	O	O	O	O	O
Compensation	O/L	O	H-L	O	O	O	L	O	O
Training	O-L	O-L	L	O	O	O	O	O	O
Career development	L-O	O	L	O	L	O	L	L	O
Use of contractual help	O	O	O	O	O	O	O-L	L-O	O
Governance	D*	O	O	L-O	O	O	O	O	O
Management	L-H	L-O	O-L	L-H	H-L	L	L-O	O	O

H = High
L = Low
O = Don't Do
D* = Dysfunctional

and behaviors are somewhat more specific; the managers named things like "customer focus" and "service orientation," which have more specific behavioral referents and implications. But, as might be expected for something done under severe time constraints, little detail is provided in the list of practices. Whatever problems may plague the hiring process, they do not emerge with any specificity here. Without painstakingly detailed documentation of specifically what the organization does and how it does it, it is hard to know precisely what to change or how.

Unlike our first example, where the firm took action but was basically too late, this organization has, for the most part, failed to act on the implications of the misalignment between its management practices and the behaviors and competencies it seeks to produce. Rather, it has pursued a series of layoffs and reorganizations. Note that merely laying people off, thereby reducing the cost base of the organization, will not produce the skills and behaviors necessary for competitive success. Nor will rearranging the boxes in the organization chart. Almost none of the organization's "solutions" focus on its core problems—a set of practices that fail to produce what it needs to be successful given its strategic approach to the health-care marketplace.

Don't be surprised or, for that matter, depressed by these examples of insight without decisive action. Recall that in the first chapter I noted that one of the reasons why it is possible to achieve profits through people is that few firms either recognize the connection or, even when it is recognized, act on it. If every organization had perfectly aligned management practices, this would no longer be a potential—and significant—source of competitive leverage. Since they don't, great returns are possible for those organizations that develop the specific insight and make the requisite changes.

IS ALIGNMENT REALLY A GOOD THING?

Some executives express concern about alignment. After all, if the organization's practices are so internally congruent, doesn't that very congruence and the interconnectedness among the elements make change difficult? Much of the advantage of aligning management practices lies in the consequent greater effectiveness in implementing the firm's strategic intent. But what if the strategy is incorrect or must be changed due to changes in the competitive environment? Wouldn't the internal consistency of the various aspects of the organization make such change more difficult?

I have two responses to this concern. First, I haven't observed that fundamental organizational change to meet new market demands occurs without friction or delay even in firms that have poorly aligned people management practices. The empirical case has yet to be made that firms with internally and externally inconsistent management practices are more flexible or adaptive than firms with a greater degree of alignment.

Second, the premise of the question seems to confuse chaos with change. An organization that has training in teamwork but no team-based incentives, little implementation of self-managed teams, and little sharing of the information necessary to utilize the teamwork training is not necessarily better able to change. Such an organization simply has many processes operating at cross purposes and in ways inconsistent with obtaining profits through people. Disorganization, inconsistency, and sending mixed messages about what the organization values and how it will operate will not necessarily make change easier, even as it makes getting anything done, including transformation, both more difficult and less likely.

MEASURING ALIGNMENT AND PUTTING PEOPLE FIRST

Several reasons make it useful to figure out how to measure organizational alignment and the extent to which an organization has people-centered management approaches. First, this information allows managers to gauge how their organization is doing and whether it is making progress toward better congruence between its management practices and what it needs to be successful. Second, organizations that are better at doing the things described in this book outperform those that aren't, so over the long term, an organization would be very well served by investing in doing them. In fact, a senior executive at U.S. Trust, an individual responsible for running one of their mutual funds and overseeing a number of large portfolios—someone who has been in the upper quartile of professional money managers for a long time—told me just that. He was wise enough to try to find firms that did the things described in this book, but the process entailed a lot of detective work and travel. He wondered if he could somehow find a way to discern what organizations were doing along these dimensions by looking at standardized financial information.

Unfortunately, the answer to that question, at least at this time, is no. I say "at this time" because the accounting profession is interested in capturing data on people management practices to provide investors with better disclosure about this important aspect of organizational management. That effort is ongoing and has not yet reached fruition. It is currently necessary to make up one's own indicators and then measure them.

How might one assess the extent to which an organization is putting people first? If you believe in the usefulness of the seven dimensions described in the last chapter, why not try a survey that asks people at all levels questions that assess the extent to which they think these practices characterize the organization? If information sharing is important, ask people if they know the organization's strategy, how well it is doing financially, its performance on key indicators of operational effectiveness, and so forth. If employment security is important, ask people if they think the organization is committed to providing long-term employment opportunities. Ask them if they work on a team, if the team meets, and if they have been trained in team processes.

But one can also use non-survey based measures. Motorola, with a commitment to training, actually monitors whether its people receive the prescribed minimum amount of training per year. Singapore Airlines, which is also committed to training, organizes its training under a Management Development Centre and has core programs that "are mandatory and sequentially planned—courses which staff have to attend during the various stages of their career with the company."[7] Another measure of people-centered management is turnover, and particularly turnover among full-time employees at key career stages. Gordon Bethune, the CEO of Continental Airlines and the person who restored its service culture, finds useful data on employee purchases at the company store of items marked with the firm's logo. Particularly informative, he says, are changes in the levels of those purchases. He is right. Employees at firms where loyalty is building are, other things being equal, more likely to want to identify with the firm by wearing company-logo T-shirts or using company-logo coffee mugs or pens. The number of suggestions for improvements made can be a useful indicator, as is the number of job applicants referred by employees. An organization that puts its people first will find that its people put the organization first, as a place to work that they feel they can recommend to their friends and colleagues. The assessment measures that you will find useful obviously depend on your specific circumstances—not all firms sell items with their insignia on it. The effort expended to determine and follow through on such measures pays off by providing means for assessing organizational improvement and for judging the success of various initiatives designed to implement systems for producing profits through people.

How might one know that an organization is effectively aligned? Or, put another way, what are the empirical consequences of alignment? One way is obviously to do the exercise already described in this chapter and to examine the resulting matrix. Particularly if you and your team do this regularly, you can chart progress or its absence through the proportion of the entries that are consistent with required skills and behaviors.

After the fact, the operation of an aligned system is easy to assess. If a system links the various aspects of the organization's operations, organizational performance should be relatively constant over time and invariant over executive succession. The organizational arrangements, with an internal logic and consistency, guarantee persistent levels of performance regardless of who is in charge and across varying competitive conditions. This illustrates what is meant by having a system in the first place: A system is a set of arrangements independent of particular executive leadership or luck that produces results almost inevitably simply from the operation of the management practices.

For an empirical illustration of this effect, consider a study of productivity differences in the automobile industry, done by Marvin Lieberman and some colleagues using data from the early 1950s through the late 1980s. The study defines productivity as "the efficiency with which physical inputs are converted to physical outputs."[8] Using publicly available data and standard econometric techniques for estimating labor, capital, and total factor productivity growth, Lieberman and his colleagues statistically estimated the sources of productivity growth as well as the effects on productivity of chief executive succession at the various automobile companies. The results indicated that productivity improvement over time, which was substantial for the automobile industry, "has been attained primarily through more efficient utilization of labor; long-term growth in capital productivity was close to zero for most firms."[9]

Moreover, most firms showed no simple trend over time, but rather, differences in productivity depended importantly on the particular executive in charge. At Ford Motor Company, for instance, the productivity level in the "initial year of Petersen's [the CEO] regime was 21% above the average initial year productivity level of all Ford executives over the sample period," while other results indicate that "his annual rate of productivity growth was 3.1% above the average of all Ford executives."[10] Although some executives had positive effects and others negative, significant differences in firm performance, as assessed by productivity, existed under top management regimes at all of the firms *except Toyota*.[11] What does this mean? It means simply that the Toyota Production System (TPS) described in chapter 2 is, in fact, just what its name implies—a system. As a system, it works, in this case, to produce superior economic performance (Toyota's labor productivity growth over the 1950 to 1987 period was about twice that of any of the U.S. automobile firms) regardless of who is in charge, changes in consumer tastes, and varying economic and competitive conditions.

Now we have another insight into the downside, at least from the point of view of senior managers, of aligned organizational practices. Such systems, because of their internal logic and alignment with what is required to implement the organization's strategy, do not depend on the heroic actions or decisions of one or a few senior managers. This is the system's strength: It does not rely on a few "big brains" or great ideas, but rather on the effective performance and ideas of the entire organization, mobilized through a coherent set of high performance work arrangements. But, it is also the system's "weakness." In a culture that venerates leadership, in a world in which saving organizations from crises and performing turnarounds gets a lot of press and a lot of pay, who wants to set up and then oversee an aligned system that reduces the need for heroics and, in fact, makes them all but impossible? From an investment point of view, of course, an aligned system means that one does not need to worry about the health or age of the senior executive: the system will survive because it is, in fact, a system. Leaders who actually want to build an organization that can sustain its competitive success over time, however, would be well served to learn from the Toyota example. It seems to me that one of the essential tasks of organizational leadership is to build a system that can learn, develop, and produce superior results over time and is robust against changes in the competition or even in the face of succession.

After the fact, then, evaluating the existence of an aligned system is a matter of estimating the existence or absence of "executive succession" effects on productivity. An aligned system should exhibit virtually no effects from executive change. Before the fact, one can do a thought experiment, basically asking the same question: To what extent are our operations dependent on the decisions and behavior of a few senior executives? Or, alternatively, to what extent would what we do continue pretty much the same regardless of change in our leadership or competition? An aligned system is robust—and it is robust simply because its various pieces, from how people are hired to how they are trained, compensated, and organized are all designed to ensure that the management practices in place produce the skills and behaviors needed, thus making strategic execution crisp. This would seem to me to be a recipe for success and even for successful change, not a prescription for problems.

BUILDING HIGH PERFORMANCE WORK ARRANGEMENTS

A chapter on alignment and change must also consider the practicalities of implementation. Once an organization discovers a misalignment, the task arises of changing things. Once a firm has decided to pursue the connection between people and profits, the issue arises of doing what is necessary to build organizational competence and effectiveness through the management of the employment relation. It is easier to do things the right way from the beginning than to change behavior later on. Southwest, AES, Virgin Atlantic, ServiceMaster, Singapore Airlines, and many other companies cited in this book got it right from the start. So, to many executives, the task of change looks daunting—and in some respects it is. This assertion may, however, lead to the temptation to say "we can't do it"—and that is not true. This book contains many examples of organizations that have made profound changes—firms such as

Magma Copper, the New Zealand Post, and Norwest. Such change mostly entails the willingness to be serious about change followed by its sensible implementation.

Three principles appear common to most of the successful transformations to high performance work practices that I have observed:

1. Build trust.

2. Encourage change.

3. Measure the right things and align incentive systems with new practices.

Below I consider these in order.

The first and most fundamental principle—and, I might add, the most often violated—is to build trust. The essence of high performance work arrangements is reliance on *all* organizational members for their ideas, intelligence, and commitment to making the organization successful. Such efforts will not be forthcoming in the absence of trust. One occasionally hears that incentives or surveillance and control (or some combination of the two) can substitute for trust by affecting the environment in such a way that people do the right thing. But this view is naive, for incentives and controls work only for behaviors that can be specified in advance. Moreover, these techniques for producing behavior are invariably more costly than those built on trust and respect.

So, the first question that leaders should ask about any proposed practice is whether it is likely to build and maintain trusting relationships. If the answer is no, the practice shouldn't be instituted—period. One way to build trust is by sharing information, including business and strategic plans, with all employees. This isn't always done because one of the incentives senior managers seem to enjoy is knowing things that others don't—knowledge is power and holding secrets can become a source of status. Let me suggest that this is a very costly incentive, however. By keeping things secret, the organization conveys that it really doesn't trust its members. Conversely, sharing business plans, strategies, and, of course, operating information conveys the idea that all members are partners in the task of improving performance and that all have an important role in these efforts.

Part of building and maintaining trust is dealing fairly with those who can't or won't change or who are redundant because of changes in technology or business conditions. At Rockwell Automotive's Heavy Vehicle Systems division, the president of the division, Larry Yost, spent some two years explaining and then explaining again the need for change in the business processes at the division to the division managers. People invariably described him as "patient" during this effort. But for a long-tenured work force, many of whom had spent their entire working lives at Rockwell, patience earned Yost acceptance as leader, even though he had come from outside the division. As several managers told me, "we have been given ample opportunity to understand and accept the new way of doing things." This time to change was appreciated by the organization's members. At the Siemens Corporation's Communications division, redundant employees were given generous severance and the opportunity to say goodbye to their coworkers. Bonnie Hathcock, their human resources manager, commented, "We treated the employees with respect. None of this security guards escorting them out of the building stuff."

Why do firms use security guards to rapidly escort laidoff employees out the door? Companies are afraid that laidoff employees will take proprietary information with them—customer lists, technical specifications, product plans, and so on—or, worse yet, in their anger, sabotage things such as computer databases. Guards and a rapid exit may not prevent these behaviors: In these days of the Internet, sabotage can occur from off-site. In fact, treating employees with so little respect or regard may actually increase their anger as well as that of their coworkers left behind, thereby encouraging more acts of hostility directed at the company. Moreover, this way of treating people signals profound distrust and disrespect, and it makes it difficult to build commitment or motivation among those who remain in the organization.

Building trust also requires that senior management meet with employees, preferably in small groups, both to explain what is going on and to listen. Elmar Toime, the CEO of the New Zealand Post, an organization that went from a typical government bureaucracy to a profitable state-owned enterprise and the most efficient post office in the world, made (and makes) a particular effort to meet with small groups of people from throughout the organization. This more personalized communication signifies that management sees employees as important. Simply putting out a newsletter or a video does not convey the same sense of respect and caring. At Southwest Airlines, employees have the home phone numbers of all of the senior corporate officers. At Virgin Atlantic Airways, employees have Richard Branson's home phone number. I doubt if many call—and those that do probably do so only about issues of such importance that the leaders would want to hear about them anyway—but this gesture of making senior leadership accessible sends the message that all people are valued and trusted to use this access appropriately.

Finally, building trust entails working cooperatively with employee representatives, for example, with union leaders where a work place is organized. What does it say to the work force if the first thing that occurs during a change is that their representatives are ignored or challenged? How can an organization build a high commitment, participatory work environment if its actions signal that senior leadership does not trust or expect employee representatives to behave responsibly or to understand the work practice changes?

The second principle that seems to help in implementing high commitment work arrangements is to do various things to encourage change. It is easier to obtain changes in work practices if other changes occur simultaneously, thereby unfreezing the system. For instance, when NUMMI took over the General Motors Fremont plant, in addition to changing the relationship with the employees, the firm changed the production system, implementing lean principles. It also painted the plant. A new, fresh look encouraged people to see the organization differently, and a nice looking work place facilitated caring about the quality of the product. At the New Zealand Post, the company instituted its own version of "lean" manufacturing—the "clean floor policy." This meant simply that mail arriving either at a sorting center or at a substation at the start of a work shift all had to be processed during that shift, with none held over. Work places were redesigned physically to make it easier to spot inventories of mail left at the end of a work shift. When the international mail processing center moved from downtown Auckland to a site near the airport, Bill Osborne, the head of that division, took the opportunity to redesign the work facility in a way that signaled a change in work practices as well. He later noted that the change of the physical setting had acted as a lever for change because it unfroze the operation's processes.[12] Physical changes—in the look and feel of the work place, in how things are arranged—provide a tangible, ever-present reminder that the organization is changing, and this facilitates change in work arrangements and the employment relationship as well.

Another way to encourage change in how people are treated in a firm is to change titles and forms of address, both of which can either limit or exacerbate status differences among organizational members. Eliminating titles and other status distinctions in the language used in everyday conversation encourages informality and collegiality. "Many major corporations—including Mars, Corning, Walt Disney, General Electric, UPS, Electronic Data Systems, Hewlett-Packard, and Xerox—have adopted formal policies of 'universal first naming,' meaning that all employees of the firm are explicitly on a first-name basis."[13]

Changing job titles can also be useful. Although it takes more than calling everyone an "associate" or "team member" to create a collegial, team environment, language does have profound effects on employees' perceptions about their jobs. Substituting "work team leader" for "supervisor" helps to establish expectations for what that individual's role and behavior should be, expectations that can have a self-fulfilling and powerful effect on behavior. Bill Osborne of the New Zealand Post is dedicated to working in a new way and to making the international mail operation, with its 160 people, a model for the rest of the organization. One of the things he did was to change the title "Mail Center Manager" to "Operations and Development (of People) Manager."

Change can also be encouraged by changing the organizational structure. Eliminating layers of hierarchy makes close supervision impossible and encourages participation. Bill Osborne reduced the number of layers in the international mail operation of the New Zealand Post from five to three. NUMMI took out a layer of management. At AES, additional levels are added only after substantial scrutiny, and this corporation, involved in the highly regulated and technically demanding business of electric power generation, has only five levels in a firm with more than $800 million in sales. At the New Zealand Post, since its creation as a state-owned enterprise in 1987, there have been numerous reorganizations—on a product line basis, a functional basis, and a matrix basis. When I inquired as to why these various structures were implemented—what the underlying rationale was—I was consistently told by a number of senior managers that the principal objective in the reorganizations was to shake things up. Putting people in new roles with different reporting relationships and responsibilities made it much more likely that other changes—such as changes in how they managed—would also occur. It was impossible to do the same things in the same way because the reorganizations didn't permit it.

It is important in implementing high performance management practices that all departments and all leaders model the desired behaviors. In one organization, for instance, the human resources department itself had five levels of hierarchy, a situation that made less credible its arguments in favor of removing hierarchical layers. By contrast, Whole Foods consistently implements its team culture throughout the organization—senior management is a team, regional managers are a team, each department in each store is a team, and so forth. At the New Zealand Post, Bill Osborne of international mail operations runs the management team at the facility as a self-directed work team. An organization's leaders must adopt whatever practices are to be generally implemented if the change is to have any hope of taking.

In addition to building trust and encouraging change, the third overriding principle that I have seen to be useful in implementing high performance work practices is aligning measurement practices and incentives with the desired behaviors and culture. Many measurement practices and systems signal distrust through their emphasis on monitoring and control. Many measurements target a level of observation different from that being advocated (for instance, measuring individual performance even though the basic principle of organizational design is the team). It is crucial to measure what actually matters and not just what can be easily measured or what appears to be a "hard" measure. I don't care for the distinction between "hard" and "soft" measures. Costs, which are so-called hard measures, are frequently misleading because of issues of allocation, and in the end they often don't reveal much about whether the organization is actually pleasing its customers, developing new products or services, and attracting and retaining talent. Measures of employee attitudes, customer satisfaction, or operational performance may all be much more meaningful in charting how well the organization is actually doing and where improvement is necessary. It is all too easy to talk about implementing high performance management practices and then to do nothing. Charting progress along each dimension, and updating these measures periodically, is one of the best ways of ensuring that the objective of implementing high involvement management is taken seriously.

II. BARRIERS TO IMPLEMENTING PERFORMANCE KNOWLEDGE: HOW CONVENTIONAL WISDOM IS WRONG

5 ◆ Ten Reasons Why Smart Organizations Sometimes Do Dumb Things

*I*T ALL SEEMS SO EASY. How difficult could it be to increase the level of training, to share information and plans with people, to reorganize work into teams, to upgrade hiring practices, and to do all the other things described in chapter 3? To not only talk about alignment, but actually to do it? At one level, it is easy—no rocket science is involved in the *ideas* that form the foundation for people-centered management. But, if it were actually so easy to *do*, other airlines would have been able to copy Southwest or, for that matter, Singapore or Virgin Atlantic. Other grocery stores would be as successful as Whole Foods Markets. Other power producers would be as profitable and efficient as AES. Other financial service organizations would have the same growth record as Norwest. Other janitorial and home service firms would have earned the same returns as ServiceMaster. Other retailers would have achieved the same record of growth and profitability as the Men's Wearhouse. The list goes on and on. Examples of organizations that put people first are not unknown, but implementing these ideas in a systematic, consistent fashion remains rare enough to be an important source of competitive advantage for firms in a number of industries. How can this be?

I have identified ten factors that seem to cause trouble for companies trying to implement the tremendous wisdom and insight embodied in the numerous studies reviewed in chapter 2, studies that make the business case for managing people right. I should add that this list is no doubt not comprehensive and that you will think of sources of resistance that I have overlooked.

- The desire to do what everyone else is doing and to follow the crowd—a problem if the conventional wisdom is incorrect.
- Managerial career pressures, derived from the need to "make the numbers" and to have a track record that makes one "mobile," pressures that create an emphasis on short-term, financial results.
- A belief in leadership and a tendency to overvalue things we have helped produce, making delegation difficult.
- Demands for accountability and reproducibility in results and decisions that destroy the benefits of expertise, which is inevitably dependent on *tacit* knowledge.
- Career trajectories—who gets promoted—that seemingly reward financial rather than human resource or people management.
- Excessive focus on measuring costs—often short-term costs, at that—and neglecting to assess the returns to those costs and investments.
- Press and management education veneration of or obsession with "mean" or "tough" management.
- A management education and training focus on finance and accounting rather than on human resources or organizational behavior.
- The normative and economic value placed on being a skilled analyst—on knowing—compared to the value placed on being able to manage people.
- Capital market primacy over other stakeholders and demands for short-term performance that make long-term investments in people more difficult.

To see an instance in which at least some of these forces operated, consider the following example. The British Land Rover Company, a leading manufacturer of four-wheel drive vehicles, was, for many years, notorious for its poor manufacturing practices. Its costs were high, its labor relations terrible, and the quality of its products left much to be desired. Mired in a downward spiral of poor performance, the company finally adopted an entirely new approach to managing its work force. Individual employees received a £100 allowance for training, to be used however they wanted—even, for instance, on cooking classes. The company believed that if it could get its work force interested in learning and training, it would be on its way to building a learning organization even if, at least initially, some of the learning was of little or no direct use to the company's operations. The company itself instituted more extensive training of its work force, in the process becoming an "Investors in People UK" designee. This national standard recognizes "organisations that have placed the involvement and development of people at the heart of their business strategy."[1] Rover instituted a "Total Quality Leadership" program to develop managers' skills in listening, coaching, and goal setting. As part of that program, Quality Action Teams were implemented and British Land Rover soon had one of the largest quality circle movements in Europe.

The results of this new approach to managing the work force were quite positive. Between 1991 and 1993, the Quality Action Teams saved the company some £16 million, and employee suggestions produced savings of £2 million. The labor hours required to produce a vehicle decreased by 25 percent, while the number of vehicles manufactured increased by a third.[2] Product quality got better, helping to improve sales. Employee relations improved significantly, and the company soon became a destination for United Kingdom executives who wanted to see the implementation of flexible or lean manufacturing techniques and the benefits from efforts to achieve profits through people.

Then BMW bought the company. In spite of the overwhelming evidence of the effectiveness of the new management methods and the changed organizational culture, BMW soon began to dictate further changes—changes that at once undid the cultural transformation and altered industrial relations and, unfortunately, also reversed the improvements in quality and efficiency. Training was recentralized—after all, why should the firm pay for outside interests? The power of shop-floor teams and employees was drastically curtailed, and, in the process, the old system of adversarial labor relations was recreated. In an emphasis on control, the participatory culture that had only recently been created was largely lost. Instead of being a stunning success story, British Land Rover soon became a favorite illustration among British executives and academics of organizational folly.

Although perhaps somewhat more striking than some other cases, the British Land Rover story is all too common—that of management instituting practices counter to the evidence on how best to achieve profits through people and, on occasion, doing things that they know are not necessarily in the best long-term interests of the company, but doing them anyway. Many possible explanations offer themselves, and we will explore some of them in this chapter; then, in subsequent chapters, we will see how much of what passes for conventional wisdom about some important management practices is almost certainly wrong. Although this material will be helpful for those leaders seeking to overcome barriers to implementing high commitment management practices, I am increasingly convinced that merely knowing how organizations make unwise choices will not necessarily prevent those decisions from occurring. Nonetheless, executives who seek to achieve profits through people need to be aware of at least some of the pitfalls along the way and of some possible ways for attempting to circumvent those pitfalls.

In this chapter, I consider some of the reasons, from the list above, why seemingly smart organizations and smart managers sometimes seem to do dumb things with respect to managing their people. The first set of factors includes orientation and emphasis. If executives focus primarily on costs and have a short-term time horizon, if they don't focus on human assets as a critical source of competitive advantage, and if they don't take a strategic approach to managing the work force, then simply through oversight and lack of attention they may create problems with their companies' efforts to change and to manage the employment relationship effectively. The second set of factors concerns how organizations do things that have the unintended consequence of destroying the ability of those with expertise to actually use that knowledge in their decisions. A third set of problems concerns the concepts of trust and of participation in decision making, both of which are important elements of high performance work arrangements. Because of some potent social psychological processes that lead to an emphasis on control, decentralization and delegation of real decision-making responsibility are often difficult. Finally, there are normative pressures about what constitutes "good management" and associated values and beliefs about people that seem to make achieving profits through people more difficult to the extent that one succumbs to these socially-shared beliefs about effective behavior.

If there is one theme that runs throughout these problems in implementing high performance management practices it is the need to make one's own path to ignore or overcome a set of norms, beliefs and values, measures, and social psychological forces that all seem to push behavior in nonproductive directions. It is this requirement for the courage to be different, apparently useful if not essential to achieving profits through people, that makes managing people effectively so difficult to duplicate and consequently such an important source of competitive leverage.

MANAGERIAL FOCUS AND EMPHASIS

If achieving profits through people takes time to accomplish, which it does, an emphasis on short-term financial results will not be helpful in getting organizations to do the right thing—and short-term financial pressures and measurements abound. Many organizations provide raises and bonuses based on annual results—a time horizon of one year. Ask senior managers how long it takes to change an organization's culture, and I doubt if you will frequently hear, "a year or less." But that is the time horizon of the evaluation process. It is difficult and risky to take actions with payoffs that will occur beyond the time for which you will be measured on your performance. Consistent with this idea of the importance of time horizon, a study of 152 organizations found that firms "relying more on long-term compensation incentives for managers exhibited less employment variability."[3] In other words, these firms were better able to maintain a policy of employment security, a critical foundation for implementing high commitment management practices.

A second pressure comes from organizations seeking to create shareholder value by increasing stock price. This is fine, but the time horizon for evaluating stock market returns is again often quite short, often a year or even much less. Mutual fund and other institutional money managers are themselves frequently evaluated on a quarterly or at most an annual basis; they often invest in stocks for only a short time and have high portfolio turnover, so it is little surprise that they, in turn, put pressure on organizations for short-term, quick results.

A third pressure can be seen in the observation that everyone who has ever tried to do any long-term planning recognizes that the immediate drives out the long-term. Today's pressing problems make it difficult to focus on actions aimed at building a better organization for the future. Fourth, managerial career processes contribute to this short-term pressure. When and where managers are hired for an indefinite period and careers are embedded in a single organization, it makes sense for those individuals to take a long-term view. Currently, managerial mobility—moving across organizations—is up dramatically at virtually all organizational levels. Under these circumstances, individuals logically try to build a resume and track record that will look good on the external labor market, and this pressure to be mobile in the managerial marketplace is largely inconsistent with taking a longer-term view of building organizational competence and capabilities. Stephen Smith has argued that the typical career system facing managers today encourages "'managerial opportunism': managers are rewarded . . . for appropriating the ideas of their subordinates or for improving the bottom line in the short run and then moving on to other positions before the long-term implications of the strategies they have adopted make themselves felt."[4]

Evidence shows that problems arising from a short-term, crisis orientation make it difficult to implement high performance work arrangements. The Laborforce 2000 Survey of 406 very large U.S. firms provided some information about executives' perceptions of the most significant barriers to making changes in the management of the employment relation. Three categories of barriers emerged from that survey: an efficiency or crisis orientation, a lack of support from employee constituencies, and a corporate culture and management that fails to give proper weight or attention to human resource issues. Concerning the relative importance of these barriers, the data in Table 5-1 indicate that "a company's orientation to efficiency and crises results in the most significant barrier to desirable strategic HR [human resources] change."[5] This short term, cost-based orientation was a bigger barrier than a lack of support from various employee constituencies or even the problems from having a corporate culture that failed to emphasize human resource management issues.

The absence of a human resource focus and the emphasis on cost cutting and responding to crises is not surprising given the background and training of most senior management of U.S. business organizations. Although executives with financial backgrounds and, to a lesser extent, legal backgrounds have come to the fore in senior management positions, this was not historically the case. As documented by Neil Fligstein, executives originally came from operations and manufacturing after which marketing produced many of the largest corporations' chief executives. In 1929, thirty-four of the largest one hundred firms in the United States had presidents with a manufacturing background, while only seven were run by individuals with a background in finance.[6] Although "sales and marketing . . . came to dominate the largest firms after World War II,"[7] by the 1950s a finance conception of control of the large corporation began a rise to the prominence that it still enjoys. Between 1919 and 1979, the proportion of company presidents with finance backgrounds rose from 7.6 percent to 27.5 percent.[8] "The finance conception . . . stressed the use of financial tools to evaluate product lines and divisions. . . . The pioneers of this new strategy were

Table 5-1   BARRIERS TO ADOPTING HIGH COMMITMENT HUMAN RESOURCE MANAGEMENT PRACTICES

Barrier	% Saying a Major Barrier	% Saying a Barrier
Cost of making changes	32%	82%
Need to address crises	29%	73%
Focus on short-term change	14%	47%
Lack of support from middle management	16%	69%
Corporate culture that does not emphasize human resource issues	20%	56%
Getting top management's attention	14%	47%

Source: Edward E. Lawler III, Susan G. Cohen, and Lei Chang, "Strategic Human Resource Management" in Building the Competitive Workforce, ed. Philip H. Mirvis (New York: John Wiley, 1993), 44. Copyright © 1993 John Wiley & Sons, Inc. Reprinted by permission of John Wiley & Sons, Inc.

trained in finance and accounting. Their views were not shaped by the necessities of production or the desire to sell more products. Instead, they focused on the corporation as a collection of assets that could and should be manipulated to increase short-run profits."[9]

The particular background and orientation of management varies not only over time in the United States but also over culture and context. Most senior Japanese executives, for instance, were at one time in their careers members of their organizations' labor unions. Many have spent some time in personnel, a common rotation for Japanese managers because of the importance accorded this function in Japanese firms. Most Japanese executives also have at least some experience in operations or manufacturing. Many German firms, too, emphasize backgrounds in both manufacturing and engineering for their executives. In fact, the dominance of finance and law experience is a particularly U.S. phenomenon. This is undoubtedly related to the comparative importance of MBA (Master of Business Administration) degrees in the U.S. business context. Each year in the United States more than 75,000 students graduate with advanced degrees in business or management. Although the prestige of the MBA degree is spreading to other countries, both Japan and Western Europe for quite some time had almost no business schools and the study of business was not a high status activity. MBA programs, with their emphasis, since the mid-1950s reform movement, on analytical methods, have curricula that emphasize finance, economics and decision analysis, and accounting, particularly as core subjects. Although business schools all require at least one course in organizational behavior, there are virtually no schools in the top tier, other than Stanford, that in 1996 required that all students take a course in human resource management. Background and training are not necessarily destiny—Herb Kelleher, the CEO of Southwest Airlines, is a lawyer by training. But clearly, background and education help to shape what people focus on and what they see as important. Consequently, the neglect of human resource issues in considering how to achieve exceptional economic performance is not surprising given the backgrounds of most of those doing the considering.

If I seem to treat harshly a financial emphasis on management issues, particularly the likelihood of achieving profits through the effective management of people, it is only because accumulating evidence shows how deleterious such an orientation is, even as it increases in prominence. As one vivid example, consider a recent study of innovation in a sample of about 250 firms that nicely illustrates the problem of adhering to a strictly financial emphasis. At the outset, it is necessary to recognize that "innovation is an important outcome of firm processes and has been shown to be critical for firm performance, particularly in industries with global competition."[10] Innovation obviously results from actions and decisions as well as from a particular organization's culture, and decisions and culture are affected by managerial emphasis and how managers spend their time. This study measured internal innovation in two ways, research and development expenditures per $1,000 of sales and the number of new product announcements divided by the total sales of the firm. The study statistically controlled for average research and development intensity in the firm's industry as well as for the level of diversification and for financial performance. The research demonstrated that "an active acquisition strategy has direct, negative effects on the internal development of firm innovation. . . . [M]anagers have little time left to manage other important projects and target firm managers in particular become strongly risk averse."[11]

The study also showed indirect negative effects on innovation through the use of financial rather than strategic controls, because the financial controls were used more in firms that were pursuing active acquisition strategies. The study demonstrated that "strategic controls have a positive effect on internal innovation, but financial controls have a negative effect on it. Financial controls establish financial targets whereby division managers become increasingly oriented toward the short term and reduce investments . . . that will not pay off except in the long term."[12] By contrast, "strategic controls entail the use of long-term and strategically relevant criteria for the evaluation of business-level managers' actions and performance. Strategic controls emphasize largely subjective and sometimes intuitive criteria for evaluation . . . and requires that corporate managers have a deep understanding of business-level operations and markets."[13]

A financial orientation and emphasis views the firm as a collection of assets, as a portfolio of activities to be bought and sold to maximize shareholder value. But the study of innovation found that "the least innovative firms are . . . those following a portfolio strategy. . . . Thus, a portfolio strategy is likely to be successful only in industries in which innovation is unimportant."[14] The results from this comprehensive and sophisticated study are quite consistent with the argument made here that managerial emphasis and orientation are important and that a financial control, portfolio approach is unlikely to be useful in encouraging either innovation or the achievement of profits through people.

But the problem of neglecting the importance of human resources and focusing excessively on short-term, financial issues is not just the fault of senior line management. Evidence shows that, although senior human resource executives have a different focus and bring different information to the decision-making process, for the most part these individuals, as well, do not take a very strategic view of the role that the management of people can play in producing profits. The Laborforce 2000 Survey asked the top human resource executive in each of the 406 companies to "identify the best strategic HR decision that their company made to prepare itself for the mid-90s."[15] The results were striking.

> Over 20% identified changes and improvements to benefit and compensation plans as their best decision. . . . Other frequently cited decisions were investments in training and development. . . . Based on these findings, we can conclude only that most HR departments have a long way to go before they become business partners in the enterprise. Clearly, many do not see productivity, customer satisfaction, and quality improvements as major responsibilities. Nor is there a strong strategic coherence to human resource programs and initiatives in many firms.[16]

Other questions explored the most important competitive issues facing the corporation, as perceived by senior management, and the responsibilities of the human resources department. Again, the response of senior human resource executives at major corporations—well-paid, very senior people—are instructive. Some "21% see no relationship between the priorities of top executives and the work of the HR department, and another 6% are not sure where the HR function fits into company strategy. This means that over one out of every four HR departments says that *none* of their company's business strategies are a major responsibility of their department."[17] If senior human resource executives aren't of great help in implementing high performance work practices because of their focus on benefits costs and plans as contrasted with a more strategic, business orientation, then organizations are un-likely to move readily to change the management of the employment relation. Who will advocate such a change at the senior management level?

The problem lies, moreover, not simply in the backgrounds and focus of both senior management and human resource executives, although these are both serious issues. The focus on short-term costs is very much affected by organizational measurement practices that quantify in great precision and detail the costs of change and investment in human resources but fail to capture well (if at all) any potential returns from these investments. What is salient becomes focal, and what is salient is very much a consequence of what is measured. Costs are typically emphasized in many organizational financial reporting systems and reports. Thus, for instance, salaries paid to employees are costs, as is money spent on training in either skills or decision making, on recruit-ment and selection, and, of course, on keeping people on the payroll during cyclical fluctuations in demand when they may not be needed. Because cutting any or all of these expenditures cuts costs, such actions seem to increase profits. Since profits are revenues minus expenses, anything that reduces expenses seems to increase profits.

I use the word "seems" because many of these profit gains are, in fact, illusory when considered over a longer time horizon. To the extent that, by cutting recruiting and selection efforts, wages, training, and attempts to retain the work force during downturns, the organization winds up with a less committed, skilled, and motivated work force, it is virtually certain that a consequence of such actions will be poorer customer service, diminished productivity and innovation, and other adverse effects that impact the organizational top line of revenues. But it is almost impossible to trace the consequences of these decisions to sub-sequent operating problems, and few organizations even try. Corpora-tions face a strong temptation, therefore, because of the way things are measured, to cut expenses even when doing so does not make much sense in terms of actually increasing the organization's profits.

HOW ORGANIZATIONS DESTROY COMPETENCE

The problems and issues enumerated above, however, would not, by themselves, be that bad. Although some managers may not have a perspective that values achieving profits through people, others do. Although some will be tempted to cut costs, others will see the importance of developing and maintaining a work force that can effectively serve customers, develop products, and get things done. Although some human resource managers and senior management will focus on short-term actions and solving immediate crises, surely others will take a longer-term view.

What really cause organizations difficulty are the things they do inadvertently that either destroy wisdom and competency or, equivalently, make it impossible for that wisdom, knowledge, and experience to be employed to the benefit of the firm. This occurs in a number of ways, but probably the worst are those management practices that require the explanation and review of decision processes—including exercises in formal planning, that is, requiring programs and ideas to be explained and reviewed in groups—in short, anything that requires a formal presentation and accounting of what a given individual is doing and why.

The argument about why formal planning and evaluation and particularly the use of financial criteria destroys competence is fairly easy to make and is quite consistent with the results of the study of innovation cited above. First, consider the nature of expert knowledge: What distinguishes experts from novices in any domain of activity or decision making, including organizational management? Experts have acquired, through their experience in some activity, the ability to see and understand things that are not evident to novices. An expert advertising executive moves quickly and creatively to come up with a good advertising campaign; an expert in production management understands the dynamics of both the human and mechanical elements of the production system and can accurately and quickly diagnose problems and figure out appropriate action; an expert in management or leadership has a good grasp of the principles of human motivation, great intuition, and the ability to read people and situations. But, in any domain of expertise, by definition, some portion of the expert's knowledge and competence must be tacit, not readily articulated or explainable, irreducible to a formula or recipe. If that were not the case, then the expert knowledge would be codified and novices could do about as well as experts at the task in question, given access to the same formulas or insights.

But, if expert knowledge has some component—probably a substantial component—of tacit knowledge, it will be impossible for those with the expertise to present the real basis of their judgments and decisions when called upon to do so. How can you describe to others insights and intuitions based on judgment and experience? What is likely to occur is simply this: When those with expertise are called on to explain their decision processes or to account for their decisions, they are likely to rely not on the tacit knowledge and judgment, which cannot be articulated, but rather on those factors and evidence available and accessible to all. In doing so, the expert loses virtually all the benefits of his or her expertise. Forced to account for and explain decision making in ways legitimate and comprehensible to a wider audience, the expert will have to forgo any insight or intuition that can't be articulated and will be forced to rely, instead, on the same data and decision processes as anyone else. Thus, the organization will have created a decision process in which its experts behave like novices, and the organization will have lost the benefits of their wisdom and competence.

Note that the problem occurs primarily in demanding accountability for a decision or judgment "process" rather than the outcome of the decision—but that is just what goes on in many organizations, for some good and not so good reasons. A good reason to avoid evaluating people just on outcomes is that performance outcomes may depend on a number of factors, including chance, over which the person has no control, and thus an evaluation just on results would be unfair. Second, because of this chance element in results, being judged on outcomes involves risk, and individuals will want to be compensated for bearing that risk. Additionally, in organizations with a great deal of interdependence among individuals, attributing outcomes to the actions or decisions of any specific individual, or even a small group of individuals, may be difficult if not impossible. Further, because results may be known only with some delay, as in a research and development project, for instance, firms may not be comfortable with waiting to make evaluations and judgments. This leads to probably the worst but also the most common reason for reviewing the decision making and judgments of experts: Managers and firms have a desire to maintain control that causes them to intervene and exercise monitoring and oversight.

This is far from being a hypothetical argument. Consider the following two case examples and the data below derived from a set of social psychological experiments. The first case illustration comes from Bob Scott, associate director of the Center for Advanced Study in the Behavioral Sciences at Stanford. Each year at the Center about fifty social scientists from various disciplines arrive to spend a year doing their work and interacting with one another, thereby refreshing and broadening their outlooks. The Center tries to stimulate interesting and important research and to provide a setting in which such work is encouraged. This is not a process easily amenable to a formula or, perhaps, even to explanation. At lunch one day Bob Scott told me that, as he is often requested to do, he had to give a talk about the "management" of the Center to an outside group interested in the general process of establishing an interdisciplinary, social-science research center. As he was giving the talk, he recalled thinking, "If we actually managed the Center this way, it would be a disaster." It was not possible for him to access or articulate his expertise, to explain his tacit knowledge. Fortunately, this was no problem on this occasion, as he and his colleagues could continue to run the organization using that tacit knowledge. But suppose that instead of a presentation made to a group of curious outsiders, the presentation was to a governing board or oversight body that would then hold Scott and his colleagues accountable for actually following and implementing the ideas they had expressed? In that case, they would be forced to manage in ways that would ignore their tacit knowledge and in ways that would seriously degrade the organization's operations.

Dave Spence, formerly a plant manager at a Boise Cascade paper-making facility, related a similar story. The chemical process that transforms wood pulp into paper of varying quality, weight, and surface characteristics is quite complex. Yields and quality are both important outcomes, and it is also important to keep the tremendously expensive equipment running, which may involve decisions about shutting down for preventive maintenance to avoid bigger problems later. The operators—the front-line people—in these plants may not have a lot of formal scientific education, but they have a great deal of tacit knowledge developed through years of experience working in a particular site with the same equipment. "But surely," I said, "there must be gauges and measures that permit one to monitor the process and even to control it." Spence smiled and replied that managing paper-making operations by the book, using only the measures and formulas, was likely to result in not very good performance and possibly much worse than that.

Thus, this operation required both management and operators with experience operating the technology. It was also useful, if not essential, to have individuals who trusted and respected each other's knowledge and judgment, because sometimes decisions were made that, although correct, could not be explained simply by recourse to numbers, dials, or formulas.

The experimental data come from a study conducted with Stanford MBA students in which a colleague, Robert Cialdini, and I set out to see if we could get experts to behave like novices by following procedures typical in organizations—presenting misleading information in a "scientistic" format so that it looks precise and valid (using fancy color charts, for instance) and making individuals explain and justify their decision-making processes. The task involved allocating funds in a portfolio to several stocks, one of which had some misleading analytical information presented in formats that varied in terms of their sophistication from a hand-written note describing a new analytical method and its results to the same information presented with color charts and graphs. The subjects were also asked in one condition to explain their rationale for the decisions they made and were told that these explanations would be reviewed; under the second, no-scrutiny condition participants were not told that their decision process would be reviewed. The preliminary evidence from this study indicates that the same data tends to influence decisions more when presented in a fancy format than when presented simply. Of greatest interest to the present discussion, the study indicated that scrutiny of the decision process tends to make those with more stock market experience behave like novices. In the absence of scrutiny, experts allocated less money to the stock with the misleading analysis favoring its purchase, while under scrutiny, they allocated about the same amount as did the novices. These data suggest that the need to explain and justify one's decisions can cause experts to rely on misleading information, particularly when presented in a fancy, reliable-looking, format. Called upon to explain their decision process, they apparently feel compelled to actually use irrelevant but available and focal information to a greater extent.

It is fascinating to consider that organizations, on the one hand, frequently try to encourage the development of firm-specific expertise and the wisdom that comes only through experience and that such information invariably involves a component of tacit knowledge. On the other hand, those same organizations often institute procedures and processes that, by requiring people to explain and justify their decisions, make it almost impossible for them to employ the tacit knowledge derived from their experience that makes them valuable to the organization in the first place. As in many other examples we have encountered in this book, a principle of first, do no harm, is useful.

WHY MANAGERS DON'T DELEGATE ENOUGH

Relying on the tacit knowledge and expertise of others requires trust and the willingness to let them do what they know how to do. Using self-managing teams as an organizing principle requires permitting the teams to actually be, in fact, self-managing. The difference between the General Motors Van Nuys, California, plant and the New United Motor Manufacturing, Inc. (NUMMI), was not that one used teams and the other didn't; in many respects, the formal aspects of the two plants' processes were similar. At NUMMI, however, the teams were given real responsibility and were listened to, while at Van Nuys, a culture of hierarchical control meant that team members were frequently told to be quiet and supervisors exercised the same control they had before the institution of teams—only now they did so during supposedly participatory team meetings.

Even though participation is associated with enhanced economic performance, organizations frequently fail to introduce it, and it remains fragile even when it is implemented. Consequently, firms implementing high commitment management practices must confront the resistance to participation and figure out what to do about it. Evidence exists showing that at least some of this resistance to participation derives from two social psychological processes: first, belief in the efficacy of leadership, that is, the "faith in supervision" effect; and second, a self-enhancement bias that leads individuals to evaluate more positively the work output they have been involved in creating, for instance, by closely overseeing its production.

The faith in supervision effect means that observers tend to believe that the greater the degree of supervisor involvement and control, the better the work produced. In one study, for instance, *identical* company performance was evaluated more positively when leadership factors accounting for the performance were made more salient.[18] Belief in the efficacy of supervision or leadership has numerous rational bases. First, it is reasonable to assume that someone who has been given responsibility for overseeing some set of tasks received that assignment because of relevant skill and experience; that is, after all, the premise of merit-based promotion in a hierarchical system. Furthermore, observers can reasonably assume that supervisors will be motivated to assure high quality performance in tasks for which they are accountable. They will be responsible for the success or failure of those tasks, and furthermore, accountability normally stimulates people to do more and better work.[19]

Self-enhancement is a pervasive social psychological phenomenon.

> One of the most widely documented effects in social psychology is the preference of most people to see themselves in a self-enhancing fashion. As a consequence, they regard themselves as more intelligent, skilled, ethical, honest, persistent, original, friendly, reliable, attractive, and fair-minded than their peers or the average person. . . . On the job, approximately 90% of managers and workers rate their performances as superior to their peers.[20]

The logical implication of the self-enhancement bias is that the more an individual is identified with and invested in activities or results, the more positively the person will perceive those activities or results in order to enhance the perception of the self. In a work context, this means that the more someone engages in oversight and control of a work process, the more invested and identified with that work he or she will be and, consequently, the more favorably the person will view the work.

Both the belief in supervision and the self-enhancement effect contribute to the same prediction: Work performed under more oversight and control will be perceived as better than the identical work performed with less oversight. Moreover, the self-enhancement bias suggests that this effect will be particularly strong for the person doing the supervision as opposed to observers. An experimental study conducted with Stanford MBA students found strong support for these predictions. People involved in supervising a person producing an advertisement evaluated the identical advertisement more positively than did those who merely observed the process. The more control and involvement the supervisor had, the more positively she or he evaluated the advertisement, the person doing the advertisement, and his or her own managerial competence. Moreover, the effects, even under fairly weak experimental manipulations, were substantial in their magnitude. Compared to evaluations of the same advertisement made by others not involved in the study, participants in the most control-oriented and self-involved experimental condition thought the advertisement was more than 100 percent better in terms of ratings on a seven point scale. This study demonstrates the plausibility that potent social psychological biases cause resistance to delegation and empowerment. "If, when engaging in more intervention and supervision, one thinks the work is better, one's subordinates are better, and one's management efforts are better, it is scarcely surprising that the simple prescription 'delegate more' is likely to have limited behavioral impact."[21]

In a real work setting, these social psychological biases would, of course, be counterbalanced by pressures to achieve results and by the knowledge that participation and empowerment may be helpful in improving performance. Nonetheless, particularly for work output difficult to evaluate unambiguously—and much work is of this type— the effects of a belief in the efficacy of supervision and a tendency to see processes with more self-involvement as being better may be significant factors hindering the use of high performance work practices and the participation and delegation they imply.

PERVERSE NORMS ABOUT WHAT CONSTITUTES "GOOD MANAGEMENT"

Perhaps the most substantial barrier to building high performance work systems is a set of norms and social influences, particularly prevalent in the United States, that define "good management" and excellent managerial practice in ways that make unlikely the implementation of high commitment systems. Social influence and the normative environment are important, for in an uncertain world, we look to others and their beliefs for guidance about what to do and how to evaluate elements of the world we experience. Social influence and the normative environment are also important because of the desire of most high-achieving people for status and recognition. Status and recognition are socially constructed and socially granted. If everyone, or almost everyone, believes that someone is an excellent and effective manager, that person receives status and approval, regardless of the actual results achieved by the organization being managed. If the world believes that laying off employees by the carload is good management and confers status on those that do so with the most vigor, it will be difficult for executives to resist the temptation to conform to the normative definition of "good" management and thereby achieve approval.

Two norms about what constitutes good management seem to be both simultaneously growing in acceptance and enormously perverse in their implications, particularly for achieving profits through the effective management of people. First is the idea that good managers are mean or tough, able to make the difficult choices such as laying off thousands of people and acting decisively. The second is that good management is mostly a matter of good analysis, a confusion between "math" and "management." The two views about what constitutes effective management are actually related because an emphasis on analysis takes one into the numbers and away from the so-called "softer" issues such as motivation, commitment, morale, and so forth, making it more likely that one can and will act in a tough fashion because of lack of consideration for the people side of the business.

Is being a "tough" or "mean" boss really normatively valued? Anecdotal evidence certainly suggests that it is. An article in *Newsweek* noted the following:

> Firing people has gotten to be trendy in corporate America, in the same way that building new plants and being considered a good corporate citizen gave you bragging rights 25 years ago. Now you fire workers—especially white-collar workers—to make your corporate bones. . . . Wall Street and Big Business have been in perfect harmony about how in-your-face capitalism is making America great.[22]

Fortune magazine about every four years runs an article entitled "America's Toughest Bosses." Should one want to appear on that list? That is hard to say, since many of those who made the list did not last very long in their jobs, having been "fired—in part, for being too mean."[23] Furthermore, little evidence exists that being a mean or tough boss is necessarily associated with business success. "Financial results from these bosses' companies vary from superb to pathetic. The median return on shareholder's equity over the past five years for the seven of the ten companies for which data are available ranged from 7.3 percent . . . to 18.1 percent. . . . That compares with the median for the *Fortune* 500 of 13.8 percent."[24] But, *Fortune* itself presciently foresaw the trend toward normatively valuing toughness.

> Toughness . . . will probably become more prevalent. Most nominees for this list rose to prominence in industries shaken by rapid change. . . . As global competition heats up and turmoil rocks more industries, tough management should spread. So look for more bosses who are steely, superdemanding, unrelenting, sometimes abusive, sometimes unreasonable, impatient, driven, stubborn, and combative.[25]

The current exemplar of mean and tough management is Albert Dunlap. In 1994, the *Journal of Business Strategy* selected him as a "Strategist to Watch,"[26] a designation that would seem to indicate social approval and validation of his management approach. Peter Cappelli, chairman of the management department at the Wharton School at the University of Pennsylvania, has argued that Dunlap is "helping change the norms of acceptable corporate behavior . . . He is persuading others that shareholder value is the be-all and end-all."[27] As CEO of Scott Paper, Dunlap laid off 11,200 people in about a year. "This was a third of the total work force. It was 71% of the headquarters staff, 50% of management, and 20% of the hourly employees."[28] Although the employees may not have been happy with all of this, the shareholders and Al Dunlap most certainly were. Within a year Dunlap sold Scott Paper to rival Kimberly-Clark for $6.8 billion. "Scott shareholders saw their investments nearly triple in value, and some became very rich—particularly Dunlap himself, whose compensation in salary and stock after one year approached $100 million."[29]

Based on that track record, when Dunlap took over as CEO of Sunbeam, the manufacturer of small household appliances, his next job after Scott Paper, the response of the stock market was, to put it mildly, overwhelming. On the day his appointment was announced, Sunbeam's stock went up 49 percent.[30] In the quarter in which he was appointed, Sunbeam Corporation stock "surged almost 63%."[31] This movement of the stock, based just on Dunlap's appointment, provides further convincing evidence that at least the securities markets value and respect his management approach.

And what is that approach? At Sunbeam, Dunlap has begun to do what he did at Scott Paper, on even a more massive scale. After a mere four months on the job, Dunlap announced a reduction of 6,000 employees, one-half of Sunbeam's work force, through layoffs or the sale of divisions. "One industry expert said that in percentage terms, it is believed to be the largest work force reduction of its kind ever to be announced."[32]

Without question the Dunlap style and approach are increasingly in vogue. But is this a sensible way to manage a firm? Here the answer is more equivocal. Some analysts argue that Dunlap is, in fact, not a manager at all, because of the eight companies Dunlap claims to have rescued, six are gone. His actual management methods support the conclusion that he is not really a manager.

> After reading the advance proofs of "Mean Business" and chatting with Mr. Dunlap, I am relieved to report that he signals no new trend in management. In fact . . . he isn't even a manager, at least not in my book. . . . So what does that make Al Dunlap? Someone who primps companies for eventual conversion to cash—an '80s style liquidator.[33]

Another article reviewing what Dunlap accomplished at Scott Paper argued that his actions enhanced short-term results at the expense of the long-term health of the company. Research and development expenditures and staff training were both cut. Scott lost "U.S. market share in its three major product fields: paper towels, bathroom tissue, and facial tissue. . . . In Britain, an important overseas market, Scott's share in toilet paper has fallen from 31.5% to 26.4% in the past two years."[34] Ample evidence suggests that many of the things for which Dunlap took (or received) credit at Scott Paper were in the works long before his arrival—including the sale of a large division, the opening of a new, modern tissue mill, and even some of the layoffs.

But business results are not the issue. Anyone who can increase a company's value by almost 50 percent merely by taking over the CEO job, who has received wide press coverage and notoriety, who is invited to speak at leading business schools and directors' forums, and who is able to negotiate huge compensation packages for him or herself will influence the perceived norms about good management practices. This normative climate, favoring layoffs and "meanness," is most certainly inconsistent with what would be required to achieve profits through people.

The "meanness" value derives, in part, from commonly held views about those who are the objects of the mean behavior. Unfortunately, some managers see people who work in organizations at lower than senior management levels in an extremely unflattering light, as this example from a Harvard MBA classroom vividly illustrates.

> A few years ago, Gary Aronson, a fellow Au Bon Pain [a chain of bakery cafes] store manager . . . spoke to a classroom of Harvard Business School students about a new bonus system Boston-based Au Bon Pain Co. planned for its low-level managers. Mr. Aronson recalls one of the students asking: "Why should we reward you people with bonuses? You're like gerbils, running around in a wheel in a cage. Why should we give you more pellets?"[35]

If one sees those who work in an organization not as employees or people but as "gerbils," it is little wonder that downsizing is so casually done. Too often the people who, incidentally, actually make the organization run are viewed with contempt, either subtle or open, and this contempt creates a distance between those making the decisions and those subject to them that precludes empathy or understanding. It is little wonder that downsizing and being a "mean" manager is a particularly American phenomenon: U.S. companies are most likely to have senior management that has not worked in front-line positions and who, therefore, have little appreciation for or understanding of the work life of rank-and-file people or concern for their welfare. The "lifetime employment" system that has traditionally characterized Japan is not just the product of a set of cultural values and institutional norms and practices. It and its counterparts in Europe are natural outgrowths of having senior managers who, at some point in their careers, have done the work of those now subject to their edicts. It is much harder to be tough or to lay people off when one has once been there oneself.

The other normative value—the good manager as skilled analyst— also has both questionable value and validity. Analysis as a value arose in the post–World War II era with the emergence of Robert McNamara and systems analysis in the Defense Department first and then the spread of operations research and mathematical analysis to business schools, for instance, Carnegie Mellon, and to businesses, such as Ford Motor Company. The emphasis on mathematical elegance and analysis as cornerstones for effective management creates two problems. First, such an emphasis implicitly derogates the importance of emotion, leadership, building a vision, and other, similar managerial tasks. Moreover, the emphasis on analysis represents an attempt to substitute data and analytical methods for judgment and common sense. But analysis can get one only so far. When Lyndon Johnson inherited John Kennedy's cabinet, he was almost in awe of the intellectual horsepower it contained. He discussed the cabinet with his mentor and friend, Speaker of the House Sam Rayburn.

> Stunned by their glamour and intellect, he [Johnson] had rushed back to tell Rayburn his great and crafty mentor, about them, about how brilliant each was, that fellow Bundy from Harvard, Rusk from Rockefeller, McNamara from Ford. On he went, naming them all. "Well, Lyndon, you may be right and they may be every bit as intelligent as you say," said Rayburn, "but I'd feel a whole lot better about them if just one of them had run for sheriff once."[36]

Rayburn understood that analysis could take one some distance, but only so far. Experience—in this case, in actually practicing politics and winning an election—and the insight and intuition gained from such experience were also important in making individuals effective. This is as true in business as it is in politics or any other arena. Analysis is useful, but it is far from everything. The problem is not analysis, per se, but the tendency to confuse analytical rigor with management skill. The two are not at all equivalent. Overemphasizing analytical skills to the exclusion of other skills, such as interpersonal, negotiating, political, and leadership skills, inevitably leads to errors in selection, development, and emphasis in what is important to an organization.

As evidence in support of this position, consider the following. The dominant content of most business school curricula has been and continues to be analytical methods—decision science, economics, accounting and finance, strategic analysis (frequently based on industrial organization economics), and similar subjects. Although grades in business school do not perfectly measure a student's mastery of this analytical material, they are certainly highly related to such mastery. If analysis and analytical skills were determinative factors in managerial success, one might expect to see some relationship between grades, particularly in the core business courses in which analytical methods are especially emphasized, and subsequent career success. But, studies of the subsequent careers of business school graduates have consistently found *no* relationship between grades and career attainment, measured either in terms of salary or attainment of general management positions. In other words, business school core curricula emphasize analytical methods, and grades measure at least to some extent mastery of those methods; but grades in business school are uncorrelated (and, in some studies, are even negatively correlated) with career success. Clearly, one must question the relevance of analytical methods for managers.

Understanding the normative value placed on both math and meanness will not, in and of itself, permit organizations or their leaders to overcome these normative pressures. Social influences are potent and the status conferred through social approval and respect is valuable to virtually everyone. Nonetheless, it is important to be cognizant of the normative climate and to be aware that the normative valuation of some particular skill or behavior need not be related to the actual relevance or consequence of the practice or skill for either managerial or organizational effectiveness, more objectively assessed. That realization can help organizations resist the temptation merely to follow the crowd, assuming that the crowd or the dominant trends must certainly be right.

WHAT ORGANIZATIONS MIGHT DO DIFFERENTLY

How can organizations overcome these various forces that result not only in a failure to implement "best" practices but, in many instances, in a tendency to implement "dumb" practices? Certainly no easy or guaranteed answers present themselves. If they did, the competitive advantage that accrues to those organizations that implement high performance work systems would no longer exist, simply because most organizations, including their competitors, could also readily implement the same practices. Competitive advantage comes, we should recall, from being different and from being able to do something not readily copied or duplicated by others that has economic value. The suggestions that follow, although reasonable, based as they are on the previous discussion, will themselves frequently be difficult to implement. Nonetheless, they do represent a starting point for thinking about some of the implementation issues and gaps highlighted throughout this chapter. The suggestions follow logically and directly from an analysis of the sources of the problem.

If one issue is managerial orientation and time horizon, then one set of solutions must deal with these factors. In my earlier book about how to achieve competitive advantage through the effective management of people, I listed as one important factor promotion from within.[37] I based this recommendation on the observation that many, although not all, of the organizations associated with the implementation of high performance work arrangements—places such as Hewlett-Packard, Lincoln Electric, Southwest Airlines, ServiceMaster, Whole Foods Markets, AES, and so forth—tended for the most part either to promote from within or to seek diligently to do so. In various articles and reviews written since that book was published, this point has provoked a great deal of disagreement and discussion. The idea prevails that change, often required to implement high performance work practices, occurs more readily when outsiders are brought into the organization, and, further, that innovation and creativity are stimulated by bringing in "new blood." Both of these points have some merit.

But they are counterbalanced by the following. The only way to manage without knowing the specifics of the industry or, perhaps, even of the company that one is managing is to manage by the numbers, employing a financial orientation. In that sense, it is no surprise that business schools emphasize finance and accounting and other general analytical tools applicable in virtually any situation, for such schools believe they are training general managers and that to manage virtually any organization concepts are needed that can be applied in any context. But recall the evidence from the large scale study of internal innovation cited earlier in this chapter and the evidence from the survey of perceived barriers to implementing high performance work practices. Both of those studies, as well as others, lead inexorably to the conclusion that a financial orientation, with its emphasis on financial controls and, frequently, on the short-term, relates negatively to doing the things that need to be done to achieve profits through the effective management of people and of the employment relation that links them to the organization. Recall that strategic controls relied on deep, often intuitive understanding of the business and its relation to both competitors and the environment, and that much expert knowledge is tacit knowledge, something that cannot be represented in a set of financial statements that anyone with the training can interpret and improve. This implies that organizations need individuals who possess that tacit, intuitive knowledge, who are not just good general managers, but who actually know something about the industry and the business they are managing. For these reasons, it remains the case that organizations seeking to build an orientation in their management team associated with taking actions to achieve competitive advantage through people would be well-served to practice, to the extent feasible, promotion from within, choosing those individuals who have the requisite tacit understanding to eschew a strict reliance on financial controls and the consequent problems such a reliance often produces.

Promotion from within also helps to solve the other problem discussed, short-term time orientation. Discussions of a fluid managerial labor market may mirror current reality. The idea of "buying" rather than "making" executive talent may be appealing to organizations that are managing themselves—by not investing enough in training and by engaging in practices that encourage turnover—in ways that render management development a term without empirical content. But, managerial job-hopping inevitably leads to a short-term orientation and the associated problems that make taking actions with long-term payoff unlikely.

The problem of orientation and focus is also very much a problem of measurement. One of the positive aspects of the quality movement was a shift in measurement away from strictly financial indicators. Because quality was defined by the customers and their expectations and requirements, most quality programs gathered data on customer satisfaction as well as on the quality and cost of the firm's products and services. Because total quality management emphasized finding and fixing the root cause of problems, a corresponding development emphasized both understanding and measuring underlying processes. This was a useful counterpoint to the tendency of most financial reporting systems to measure only outcomes at an aggregate level, a set of measures not necessarily very useful in and of themselves for diagnosing the sources of a company's problems. One of the most useful aspects of the movement toward a balanced scorecard approach, in which financial measures are only part of a system that also measures customers, employees, and the organization's activities that permit it to compete effectively in the future (such as its success in developing and introducing new products and services), is, again, the supplementing of financial accounting measures with other indicators that can be used to manage the business but which have a broader focus. The problem with the actual implementation of the balanced scorecard is, as one manager from CPC International told me, that it is tough to maintain a real balance and not to let the financial indicators carry disproportionate weight and influence. Nonetheless, both total quality management practices and balanced scorecard measurement are useful in remediating the problems of both time horizon and focus that occur in traditional financial accounting and control systems.

If managers find it difficult to actually delegate—because of the social psychological forces that cause them to believe that work produced under more supervision, particularly if it is *their* supervision, is superior—then organizations must find ways to virtually force delegation. One of the simplest and most powerful is to increase the span of control—the number of people supervised—to the point that managers are forced to delegate because they cannot closely oversee the number of people they are managing. When Harry Handlin, at the time the chief operating officer of Lincoln Electric of North America, was asked why Lincoln was able to delegate so much responsibility to its front-line people, he responded in terms of the large spans of control characteristic of Lincoln, which also had the effect of reducing managerial overhead and associated costs. Prior to assuming his position at Lincoln, Handlin had been head of sales, and in that job he had had thirty-seven direct reports. As he noted, with thirty-seven direct reports, it becomes simply physically impossible to closely oversee what the people are doing and to manage them too closely.

In many organizations, managers complain that they are overworked and have too much to do, so they hire more assistants and institute more sophisticated management information and reporting systems to help them in their managerial tasks. When your organization's managers complain that they have too much to do and need more help doing it, you should take the complaint at face value—they probably do have too much to do. But before you add staff and fancy information systems to assist them in exercising control and overseeing work more effectively, you might ask a more basic question: Do they have too much to do because they are doing the wrong things, namely, supervising too much and not delegating enough? In most organizations I have seen, the answer to performance problems is not more managers but fewer, not more but less staff, and not more centralized information but distributed performance information that can be used by those who are actually doing the work to understand and self-manage their own work processes.

Self-managed teams also help substantially in forcing delegation and participation. This occurs because these teams mobilize collective social pressure for such delegation and participation. It is difficult for a single individual to complain to his or her manager about lack of delegation and supervision. The authority relation and the ability of the manager to exact retribution makes such behavior both unlikely and, probably, unwise. But, it is much more difficult for a manager to retaliate against an entire team. Numbers create strength as well as social support. Change to a more team-based structure usually, although not always, leads to more delegation and participation.

Overcoming the effects of social influence and a normative environment that says that what, in fact, is very poor management is actually good managerial practice, may be among the toughest to fix of the barriers to doing the right thing. After all, the stock market's reaction to the appointment of Albert Dunlap at Sunbeam is difficult to ignore. The key here would seem to be making sure that one has the right social influences, and this involves being in the right networks. One might be well-served to spend more time with the executives from Whole Foods, Southwest Airlines, ServiceMaster, Singapore Airlines, AES Corporation, and the myriad other organizations that manage people in ways that produce high performance work systems. One might also be well-served to spend more time outside of the United States. I find when I travel to either Europe or Asia and talk to managers, let alone politicians or labor leaders, about some of the typical U.S. practices that seem to me to make no sense and that actually destroy organizational competence and capability, they for the most part not only agree with me but are even more vehement and horrified than I am. What has come to be taken as "good management practice" in the United States is very, very culturally specific to the United States. Managing in a different way may require developing a broader world view and a much broader set of colleagues with which to develop and share ideas.

Each of these suggestions—promotion from within, using measures from total quality management and/or a balanced scorecard approach, restructuring to virtually force participation and delegation, and choosing the right reference group by which to be influenced—by themselves will probably not overcome the forces that impair the implementation of high performance work arrangements. Taken together, however, they can help organizations and leaders to move in the right direction. In the end, if not everyone or every firm can accomplish this, the result is simply greater returns for those who can.

CONCLUSION

It is not likely that what happened at British Land Rover, as related above, resulted from ignorance on the part of BMW executives about lean or flexible manufacturing practices and their effects on automobile plant productivity, quality, and employee motivation and satisfaction. The information on flexible or lean manufacturing is simply too well-diffused throughout the industry to make this scenario plausible. Rather, that particular case—and undoubtedly others hinging on factors and forces not considered here—reveals that smart people and organizations do dumb things because a profound gulf exists between knowing *what* to do and knowing *how* to do it and between *knowing* how and actually *doing* things more effectively. In many organizations and for many executives, this gap, often a quite significant one, exists between *knowing* and *doing.*

The gap is not surprising. Most business schools in the United States and abroad teach "what"—conceptual frameworks, decision-making processes, analysis—under the mistaken presumption that knowledge of what to do helps people make better decisions, design more effective organizations, and allocate resources and measure performance more effectively and that this will be sufficient to actually produce behavior that renders organizations and leaders more effective. Most research in business focuses on what to do—determining what practices are associated with successful reengineering efforts, for example, or identifying what organizations that are successful over long periods of time have in common, or isolating the practices required to build loyal customers and the consequent economic value. Do not get me wrong—knowing "what" to do is a necessary and useful precondition for knowing "how" and actually implementing that knowledge. But although necessary, it is clearly insufficient.

Executives and, for that matter, researchers on business and other organizations would be, it seems, well served to consider the links between knowing what, knowing how, and actually doing things differently. As the argument in this chapter indicates, important barriers stand in the way of actually implementing knowledge about effective organizational performance. It seems clear that in the future, success will come to those organizations and those leaders who not only know *what* to do but also *how* to do it and have the skill to actually accomplish change and implementation—thereby turning performance knowledge into organizational action and, as a consequence, superior organizational results.

6 ◆ The "New Employment Contract" and the Virtual Work Force

*I*ɴ ᴛʜᴇ ʀᴇᴄᴇɴᴛ ᴘᴀsᴛ, people went to work for an organization expecting, if things worked out, to stay with that employer indefinitely. The traditional, implicit "employment contract" offered people who worked hard and remained loyal to an organization careers and a long-term future in that organization, barring some economic catastrophe. John Kotter's study of fifteen highly successful general managers, published in the early 1980s, revealed that these individuals had, on average, spent about 80 percent of their careers with one company and approximately 90 percent of their careers in a single industry.[1] Things have changed. A subsequent study by Kotter of Harvard Business School graduates revealed a different pattern, with survey respondents reporting holding multiple jobs often with comparatively small companies.[2] Today, mobility across employers and even across industries is expected and is reflected in most individuals' career histories. A study using panel data reported that fewer men had strong attachments to their firms than in the past. "In the 1970s, 67 percent of men had strong tenure, changing employers no more than once in a decade; after 1980 the percentage of men with strong tenure declined to 52 percent. In the 1970s, 12 percent of men changed their employer four times or more, while in the 1980s, 23 percent did."[3] These trends have undoubtedly strengthened even more in the 1990s.

The change in employment stability reflects a change in employers' views of the employment relationship. In the relatively recent past, employers both valued and rewarded employee loyalty. Today, downsizing, outsourcing, and the externalization of employment, the use of contingent work arrangements, reign supreme. One article maintained that "about 25% of the work force is engaged in part-time or temporary employment; estimates suggest that 33% of the part-time and 66% of the temporary employees involuntarily hold these positions because no alternative employment opportunities are available. . . . [O]ne-fifth of this year's college graduates were hired for temporary or contractual positions."[4] Between 1991 and 1993, fully 20 percent of all new jobs created in the United States were temporary jobs.[5] Employment security is something from a bygone era. A survey covering the *Fortune* 1000, the five hundred largest service and manufacturing firms, revealed that between 1987 and 1993 the proportion of firms offering employment security to none of their employees increased from 47 to 63 percent, while the percentage offering employment security to all of their employees declined from 18 to 9 percent.[6]

The so-called "new employment contract" has redefined the relationship between organizations and their people. No longer do firms, particularly in the United States, offer the prospect of long-term employment in return for good performance and effort. No longer do firms think it wise to provide a "career" inside the company with all that implies, such as a sequence of positions and training and development opportunities. The word today is "employability"—organizations promise challenging jobs and interesting assignments that will help people build their skills but that offer no long-term promises of a career. Instead, the only promise is that the work and the skills acquired on the job will help to make the people more employable if and when they have to leave. Meanwhile, the implication emerges that since the organization won't look out for your interests anymore, you should look after them yourself, taking individual responsibility for your career.

At Sun Microsystems, following layoffs in 1991, the company decided that it wanted to foster "career self-reliance" and "career resilience."

Career Self-Reliance is . . . a lifelong commitment to the proactive management of one's career and a continual focus on increasing learning opportunities. . . . The rapidity of technological developments combined with the dynamism of the marketplace means that it is essential for employees to become "career resilient."[7]

Sun Microsystems has established a partnership with an outside vendor of career services, the Career Action Center, a nonprofit organization originally formed to provide career advice to women in the Silicon Valley. This organization provides career services (presumably to make Sun employees career resilient) on-site at various Sun facilities in the San Francisco Bay area. Employees of this outside vendor of career services meet confidentially with Sun employees to offer counseling and assessment to identify current skills, values, and interests; to provide guidance on training, including taking outside courses and eligibility for tuition reimbursement; and to help in meeting work-family balance issues.

What stuns me is that organizations are surprised by the consequences of all this. Although individual employees probably appreciate the career help and access to appropriate training opportunities, it is not at all clear that the firm, itself, has done something sensible. Having told people that they need to be "career self-reliant" and having provided them with the necessary resources, the companies are then surprised when they face the very turnover that their programs have helped foster. I recall some years ago talking to a person who worked at human resources at Apple Computer, one of the firms that pioneered the idea of "employability." When this person complained about the turnover in the organization (and, as is often the case, many of the people who left were among the best employees, those with highly marketable skills who could readily find other jobs), I replied that the organization had told employees that it would not offer them careers but rather the opportunity to "get ready for their next jobs." Apple had made its employees ready to move on, with consequences that were not necessarily what Apple, Sun, or other organizations with similar policies had either wanted or expected.

Unfortunately, managers tend to take the view that all is for the best in this best of all possible worlds of employment arrangements. They assume that what exists must be efficient and effective because otherwise it would not exist, that organizations adopting particular employment arrangements do so on the basis of sound reasoning and evidence. Therefore, they construct adaptive stories that explain these changes in the employment relationship as reasonable and sensible. Worse than that, however, organizations tend to be followers of fads and fashion. If it is in fashion to have a virtual work force with little attachment or connection to the firm—because everyone is doing it—organizations follow the lead and frequently blindly adopt practices that do not make much sense. Similarly, if many firms are downsizing and laying off employees, social pressures exerted on managers lead them to do so also, almost regardless of the rationale or the consequences of work force reduction.

The existing empirical evidence does not support the view that, for the most part, firms adopt new labor force management practices strategically. Rather, what the available data do portray is unplanned, haphazard management of the employment relationship. This ad hoc character of managing people must certainly negate much prospect of achieving profits through people. As one example, a comprehensive survey of more than nine hundred British establishments reported the following striking results.

> Just over a third of employers said their decisions on labour use were guided by a strategy or plan. . . . We found no evidence of formal statements of organizational policy on manpower utilization, and little evidence of analysis of alternative scenarios with costings. . . . [W]e uncovered little evidence of a strong linkage between labour use objectives and other areas of labour-related practice such as in recruitment, training, and remuneration. . . . The *ad hoc* character of decisions was underlined by the fact that in a significant number of our cases the initial decisions to seek flexibility were being questioned or had already been reversed.[8]

As another example, twenty-one companies that were members of the Work and Family Roundtable at Boston University's Center on Work and Family responded to a survey asking about their assessment practices regarding the use of contingent work arrangements. A highly nonrandom sample, these companies are among the most thoughtful and concerned about the impact of work arrangements on their organizations. Nonetheless, only 58 percent of them assessed the effectiveness of using direct-hire temporaries, 50 percent assessed agency temporary arrangements, and only 17 percent assessed their use of independent contractors and consultants. Perhaps even more striking, cost was the predominant criterion used, with only 14 percent of the firms assessing the work performance of independent contractors and 9 percent measuring supervisor satisfaction with these contingent workers.[9]

These data present a picture of little systematic evaluation of the consequences of contingent work arrangements even on the part of large firms concerned about labor force issues, and a very narrow, cost-based evaluation process for the most part when evaluation is done at all. A similar picture emerged when a colleague, teaching in a human resources executive program at Stanford on the subject of contingent work arrangements, asked the almost fifty executives attending whether and how they evaluated these practices. Many of them did not measure the effects at all, and those that did relied virtually exclusively on the impact on direct labor costs, with little or no consideration of the consequences for quality, productivity, customer relations, or other important outcomes. I have yet to encounter any evidence that most organizations implement contingent work arrangements in a thoughtful, strategic fashion.

But perhaps the most telling evidence for the absence of much planning or strategic thought in many organizations' downsizing and contingent work arrangements comes from surveys that document the extensive rehiring, as temporaries or contractors, of employees previously laid off. Because in many cases the employers had paid severance and other costs as part of the downsizing process, rehiring the same people soon thereafter as contractors or temporaries is expensive at best and foolish at worst. A Labor Department survey found that 17 percent of contingent workers had a previous and different relationship with the companies that now rented them. An American Management Association survey of 720 companies reported that 30 percent had brought back laid off employees either as outside contractors or as rehired employees. The president of one temporary help service that does a lot of business with Pacific Bell Telephone in California reported that "former employees make up 80 percent of the 900 to 1,000 people that his agency supplies to the phone company on an average day."[10] Even employers recognize and will occasionally admit their lack of planning and foresight: "Michael Rodriguez, Pacific Bell's vice president for human resources, conceded 'some of the work did not go away as quickly as we would have liked.'"[11]

What I argue in this chapter is that the "new employment contract" frequently does not make sense for many if not most organizations, and that the externalization of employment—taking workers out of their organizations through the use of outsourcing, temporary help, or contract employment—a process that thereby creates virtually "virtual" organizations, also is frequently misguided. Of course, sometimes managers inherit a difficult business situation in which it appears that downsizing is the only (or possibly the best) solution. This chapter therefore considers some ideas about how to avoid downsizing, even in difficult times, and, if downsizing proves necessary, how to reduce employment in such a way that the least organizational damage is done. I argue here that the idea of employment security, so out of favor in the 1990s, can, in fact, produce tremendous benefits if implemented sensibly. Moreover, efforts to avoid downsizing can be useful practice for organizations seeking to achieve the economic benefits that we saw in chapter 2 from managing their people effectively.

Before proceeding, however, we do need to dispose of the argument that I sometimes hear that the change in employment arrangements is not just imposed by companies but is sought by employees, who don't want long-term attachments to their organizations anymore. This argument presents two problems. First, people will learn to accommodate to their situations—if they don't foresee the prospects of long-term attachments to organizations, they will come to terms with this reality and appear to no longer desire more secure employment relationships.

Second, this argument is completely inconsistent with the existing evidence. A random sample of more than 2,000 people conducted in late 1994 asked a question about which of four statements "best describes how you think of your CURRENT job." Forty percent of the respondents picked the statement, "A LONG TERM job you will stay in," and another 20 percent picked the statement, "an opportunity for ADVANCEMENT in this SAME (company/organization)." Thus 60 percent of the respondents, even in late 1994, thought of their present job as being in an organization in which they would like to work over a protracted period. Only 15 percent described their current job as "Part of a CAREER or profession that will probably take you to DIFFERENT companies."[12] Moreover, even in a time of downsizing, outsourcing, and the breaking of bonds between people and organizations, 54 percent of those surveyed said they felt a lot of loyalty to the company or organization they worked for and 32 percent said they felt some loyalty. Only 14 percent reported that they felt either a little loyalty or no loyalty at all.[13] The idea that people don't want or expect stable employment relationships and are basically content to have a marketlike relationship with their employers is largely untrue—even if believing these myths comforts the managers who daily test the bounds of employee loyalty and commitment.

THE NEW EMPLOYMENT ARRANGEMENTS ARE ACTUALLY OLD

Undoubtedly, the connections between workers and the organizations producing goods and services with their labor has undergone and continues to undergo profound change. Not only do estimates indicate that about 25 to 30 percent of the U.S. labor force now works in contingent arrangements—including temporary help, part-time work, and outside contracting[14]—but further evidence shows that these arrangements are growing in importance. One analyst notes, for instance, that "employment in temporary help agencies rose 21 per cent from 1993 and 1994 alone."[15] Between 1982 and 1994, the temporary help service industry grew by 361 percent, with total job growth 26 percent for the same period.[16] Evidence from the Bureau of National Affairs indicates that 57 percent of firms used contractors for tasks that could be done by their employees, with 81 percent using part-time workers, 59 percent hiring their own temporary workers, and 84 percent using temporary help agencies.[17] The use of these practices had increased about 30 percent just over the preceding two years.

Nor are these changes confined solely to the United States. Results from a survey of 584 British firms found that subcontracting had become substantially more prevalent over the past ten years:

> The . . . survey . . . found that 77 per cent . . . of the firms surveyed used contractors for at least some activities and, of these 40 per cent showed an increase in use over the previous three years. . . . Secondly, subcontracting has not only been used more in traditional, ancillary services . . . but has also begun to replace the use of conventional employment contracts in a much broader range of occupational groups such as design engineering, marketing, and publicity. . . . Thirdly, the practice has been extensively adopted across all sectors of industry and types of establishments.[18]

Layoffs and downsizing have also become increasingly frequent, in part because such practices have become normatively valued.

> Xerox was considered a highly successful company in 1993 with a strong commitment to good union-management relations and to its employees. But when it announced its intentions to slash its work force by about 10 per cent, observers reacted not with concern about the potential costs of broken commitments, but with applause. An analyst with First Boston observed, "we are just starting to see these types of restructurings. These guys are ahead of the curve." By the end of the day, Xerox stock had risen by 7 per cent.[19]

This was the same company that, as part of its attempts to meet the competitive challenge that had seen its market share shrink from 82 to 41 percent between 1976 and 1982, had established a no-layoff guarantee in 1984, less than a decade previously.[20]

A Louis Harris and Associates Survey in 1991 reported that 50 percent of the firms had laid off substantial numbers of people within the previous five years. A survey by Wyatt Company published in 1993 found that 72 percent of the respondents had layoffs in the past three years, and a national probability survey of employees conducted in 1993 discovered that some 42 percent reported that their employer had conducted layoffs in the preceding year. Layoffs seem to be increasing in frequency and are no longer linked to the business cycle. The American Management Association reported that the proportion of firms planning to downsize actually increased between 1993 and 1994.[21] Between 1983 and 1993, the *Fortune* 500 firms reduced the total number of employees by 2.5 million, or by almost 18 percent.[22] The labor market is more and more like a spot market, with fewer and fewer of the internalized employment arrangements that employees had come to take for granted. Peter Cappelli has described this trend as removing employment arrangements that buffer jobs from market pressures and replacing them with arrangements that rely much more heavily on outside labor market forces to structure the employment relation.[23]

But this extensive reliance on the labor market, the use of contract employees and outsourcing, and high rates of dismissal and turnover are not some "new" employment innovation. These practices are, in fact, precisely how work was organized about a century ago. Despite the overheated rhetoric and the coining of new terms like *network organization*, these very old ways of organizing work predate regimes of regular employment and systematic administration of the labor force. Will today's organizations, in their efforts to outdo one another in reinstituting market mechanisms for governing the employment relation, wind up making the same mistakes made by employers more than one hundred years ago?

The evidence on how work was organized in the early days of the development of manufacturing in the United States is unambiguous.

> [T]he putting-out system was common: Merchants distributed raw materials and tools to household workers, who then wove the cloth or made the shoes and returned the finished product to the merchants for distribution and sale.[24]

In this system, the merchant-as-trader stood between those producing goods and the market purchasing them. The merchant had capital, in terms of inventory, at risk, but exercised no control over the methods or even the speed with which work was done. Even the early development of centralized factories changed the basic elements of this system very little, because "the factory was often no more than a congeries of artisanal workshops which had been mechanized and enlarged."[25] A system called inside contracting was prevalent in the organization of factory work.

> The contractor, who was a highly skilled foreman, arranged with the proprietor to deliver the product within a specified time at a specified cost. The proprietor provided the contractor with tools, materials, and money, and then left him in charge of production. The contractor hired and supervised a group of skilled workers, who in turn might employ their own unskilled helpers. This system was most common in . . . industries . . . where a high degree of skill was needed.[26]

In other instances, production decisions were left entirely to workers who organized themselves without a foreman or contractor. At the Columbus Iron Works in the 1870s, for example, the workers negotiated with the firm's owners on the rate to be paid for each rolling job, and then the workers decided collectively "how to pay themselves, how to allocate assignments, whom to hire, and how to train helpers."[27] The system sounds a lot like self-managed teams in today's parlance, except that, in this case, the workers were more like contractors than employees.

Employment instability was common, even for those production workers who had an employment relationship (as contrasted with a contracting relationship) with the firm. Dismissals were frequent. Supervision was often arbitrary and the workers recalcitrant, and the firing of workers was used to attempt to maintain a semblance of control in the establishments.

> One critic of this system told the story of an assistant superintendent making his rounds through the shop: "Bill," he said to the foreman, "has anyone been fired from this shop today?" "No," the foreman meekly replied. "Well, then, fire a couple of 'em!" barked the assistant superintendent, in a voice that carried. "It'll put the fear of God in their hearts."[28]

In addition to dismissals, layoffs were common, both as a consequence of the seasonality of some work—people would be hired for peak seasons and then laid off—and because of fluctuations in the economy, which were both frequent and severe in the late 1800s in the United States. It was uncommon to rehire those previously laid off for either the next season or when the economy improved, so employment stability was quite low. And, few employers tried to maintain employment stability through work-sharing arrangements or by guaranteed employment policies. "By 1920, only 15 companies had employment guarantee plans."[29]

"Because the employment relationship was one of weak attachment on both sides, the industrial labor market prior to 1915 was a market of movement, characterized by high rates of mobility."[30] At the Boston Manufacturing Company, only about 10 percent of the individuals who were working for the company at one point in time in the mid-1800s were still there just five years later.[31] The example of Ford Motor Company illustrates both the extent of turnover, its costs, and the company's response. "By December 1913, turnover had reached 380 percent at Highland Park—which meant that Ford had to hire 963 men to keep 100—and when the directors decided to issue a Christmas bonus that month to men who had worked with the company for three years or more, they found that only 640 qualified, out of some 15,000 employees."[32] Ford was operating an assembly line producing the Model T, and demand for the automobile was expanding rapidly. But an assembly line cannot have unstaffed positions—if the line is to keep moving, every part of the total assembly task had to have the necessary workers. With such a high rate of turnover and an unstable work force, the company was forced to spend a lot of money on recruiting and training new employees. It could reap no benefits from learning by doing or from experience. Because almost none of its people stayed long enough to develop ideas or firm-specific skills, little experience was available from which to learn. But, perhaps the greatest cost to the company was this: In order to ensure that the line could operate and fill the tremendous demand for the cars, which required that each assembly position be staffed, the company had to keep a reserve pool of people employed and potentially available to fill in for those who quit with little notice or who were absent from work.

Henry Ford had never been known for his generosity or for his love of the common working man. But, faced with the problem of actually running a factory that entailed a high level of interdependence among the people on the line, he decided to take a bold action that would ensure that he had sufficient employees to keep the factory operating: He instituted a substantial wage increase, the so-called $5 a day wage. In part this was because of the economics of the situation. The assembly line had reduced the time needed to assemble a car to 93 man-minutes from 728 just a year earlier, so in fact Ford could have easily paid $20 a day. The backlog of orders for cars was huge, and the cost of the $5 a day wage was $10 million compared to dividends of $11.2 million during the same period.[33] In part, however, the new wage policy arose because Henry Ford was influenced by Ralph Waldo Emerson's essay on compensation.

> "In labor as in life," wrote Emerson, "there can be no cheating. The thief steals from himself." . . . Trying to chisel down the price of labour is self-defeating. You get what you pay for. A wise employer should educate his workers, argued Emerson, and should generally seek to raise the level of their "good sense," vision, and quality of life.[34]

The reaction to Ford's wage increase was quite interesting. The wage, of course, had the desired effect of increasing the applicant pool and ensuring that those hired tended to stay in the job longer—few other earning opportunities at that time offered anything like that sum, and thus, the new wage policy did relieve Ford's labor supply problems.

> Henry Ford always liked to present the Five Dollar Day as a hardheaded matter of "efficiency engineering" with "no charity in any way involved,"

and he took pleasure in subsequently reporting it to be "one of the finest cost-cutting moves we ever made."[35]

But others, particularly in the business establishment, did not react favorably to the wage increase and some of its moral—as contrasted with strictly economic—underpinnings. The *Wall Street Journal* was particularly upset.

> [T]he *Wall Street Journal* accused Henry Ford of "economic blunders if not crimes," which would soon "return to plague him and the industry he represents, as well as organized society." In a naive wish for social improvement, declared the newspaper, Ford had injected "spiritual principles into a field where they do not belong"—a heinous crime—and captains of industry lined up to condemn "the most foolish thing ever attempted in the industrial world."[36]

Ford's action, of course, turned out to make brilliant business sense. This tale holds important lessons, not the least of which is that the comments and advice of business journalists can be taken with a grain of salt and that the blandishments of fellow managers can be disregarded if you are reasonably sure that you understand the economics of your business better than they do.

The employment relationship and its various trappings, including rules and procedures to provide some assurance of due process, career ladders to motivate both effort and loyalty to the company, and benefits, including retirement, that also would tend to bind people to their employing organizations, arose to solve real business problems. With no long-term connection to the employing organization, it was relatively easy to get employees to strike, to sabotage production, and to basically engage in work place conflict with often despotic foremen operating what had come to be called the "drive" system of management.

How can firms create a learning organization, to use the current parlance, if people aren't there long enough to learn or to use their learning in enhancing operations? How can one build competence in work organizations facing turnover approaching 400 percent annually? But perhaps, most importantly, how can firms achieve any sort of competitive leverage through their work force and their culture with such a minimal level of attachment in the employment relationship?

Growing evidence exists that using contract employees can have adverse, even physically dangerous, consequences. In the petrochemical industry, "between 1986 and 1990, an increasing proportion of explosions and fires . . . have involved contract employees. . . . Of the eleven work place accidents known to involve explosions, fires, and spills in the U.S. petrochemical industry from January to June 1991, nine were reported to involve contract employees."[37] Another study covering a slightly longer time period found that "13 out of 23 major accidents in the petrochemical industry involved contract workers."[38] These safety problems arose because contract employees received less training and less managerial oversight and frequently had substantially less tenure on the job and therefore less wisdom and experience. A similar picture emerges from a study of mining. Between 1987 and 1990, independent contractors accounted for 17 percent of all fatalities in mining but they constituted only 10 percent of the employees. In surface mining, since 1989 independent contractors accounted "for 16% of surface mining employee hours but 46% of the fatalities."[39]

The issues of skill acquisition and adequacy of training and managerial oversight highlighted in this research should be of concern to all employers, even if few face as severe life and safety consequences. Furthermore, evidence shows that the use of contingent employees adversely affects regular employees. In a study of three divisions of a large aerospace company that designed and manufactured sophisticated equipment for air and space craft, Jone Pearce found that "employees with contractor co-workers reported less trust in their organization than did those in employee-only work units."[40] How can firms achieve economic success employing a work force that lacks trust in management?

It is essential to remember that, although purchasing goods and services, including labor, on a market-like basis can provide some benefits, sustainable competitive advantage is most certainly not one of them. What one organization can purchase, another can as well. Any organization can use a temporary help agency, outside contractors, or a flexible labor force only temporarily associated with the firm. The differentiation, if it is to emerge from the firm's human assets, must come from assets unique to the organization that are not continually thrown onto the market to work for the competition. This does not mean that firms should internalize all transactions and never rely on the market to purchase anything. It does mean, however, that a diminished attachment between organizations and their labor force must, of necessity, mean that its labor force cannot provide the firm with any sort of competitive leverage vis-à-vis other firms. As such, pursuing a contingent work force strategy belies the often made claim that "people are our most important asset," and to the extent that noble sentiment is based on business fact, use of a contingent work force can create the same difficulties for contemporary organizations that firms of more than a century ago faced.

THE CONSEQUENCES OF DOWNSIZING

Few systematic studies have been made of the effects of a contingent work force on organizations, so the arguments about the potential problems must necessarily rely on logic, case examples, and the limited available data. The evidence on organizational downsizing, however, is much more comprehensive. The evidence indicates that downsizing is guaranteed to accomplish only one thing—it makes organizations smaller. But, downsizing is not a sure way of increasing the stock price over a medium- to long-term horizon, nor does it necessarily provide higher profits or create organizational efficiency or productivity.

An article examining the stock prices of downsizing firms showed that, two years after an initial increase, the stock prices of two-thirds of the companies lagged behind those of comparable firms by 5 to 45 percent; in more than half of the cases, stock prices lagged the general market by amounts ranging from 17 to 48 percent.[41] This result is not surprising in the context of other studies showing that downsizing does not necessarily increase productivity or profits. One methodologically sophisticated study examined the approximately 140,000 manufacturing plants that were in operation in both 1977 and 1987 using data from the Census of Manufacturers. Thirty-two percent of these plants had increased both productivity and employment over the decade; 26 percent had increased productivity while reducing employment (downsizing); 14 percent had experienced both declining productivity and employment; and 29 percent had increased employment while productivity had declined.[42] More than one-third of the plants that had cut employment experienced a *decrease* in productivity, while 52 percent of the plants that grew employment over the period *increased* productivity.

Survey results generally reveal a similar pattern: Sometimes downsizing is successful, sometimes not, in about equal proportions. The American Management Association has been conducting regular surveys of downsizing to assess its extensiveness, its causes, and its effects. The 1994 survey results reported that "slightly more than half of the firms that have downsized since January 1989 report an increase in operating profits following the cuts, and just over one-third said that worker productivity improved," while 86 percent of the downsizing firms reported that employee morale declined.[43] If, in fact, downsizing does not solve basic issues of profitability and productivity, it follows that firms embarking on downsizing will be led to do it repeatedly. In fact, the 1994 AMA survey reported that "downsizing tends to be repetitive: on average, two-thirds of the firms that cut jobs in a given calendar year do so again the following year."[44] Other surveys reveal similar results. A 1991 survey by Wyatt of over 1,000 firms "suggested that most restructuring efforts fall far short of the objective originally established for them."[45]

In some sense, the limited economic benefits to downsizing are not that surprising. Merely cutting staff, after all, will not necessarily fix problems with the organization's products or customer service, its process technology, the time needed to get products or services to market (cycle time), or even, as it turns out, its cost structure. Second, cutting staff is an activity that is readily copied, so as a source of competitive advantage over a long period of time, its efficacy is necessarily limited. And third, downsizing has a number of often unmeasured or unanticipated costs associated with it that also limit its economic benefits. A Louis Harris Survey of more than three hundred large companies in the United States reported that in 40 percent of the companies, downsizing resulted in undesirable consequences for the organization.[46] As shown in Table 6-1, many of these undesirable consequences are both quite prevalent in downsizing firms and reasonably predictable—things such as lower morale and unanticipated severance costs. What the data also show is that companies often carry out downsizing in ways that lose the wrong people or wind up simply substituting temporary or contract employees for permanent employees that have been laid off.

Moreover, when firms lay people off, they frequently lose an important reservoir of skill and wisdom.

John Challenger, executive vice-president of Challenger, Gray & Christmas . . . thinks that shrinking companies are at risk of "corporate Alzheimer's."

He argued that the success of a firm depends not only on its skills and knowledge but also on its collective business experiences, successes and failures, culture, and vision, and numerous other intangible qualities.[47]

Because downsizing has such limited positive effects, current rhetoric praises growth. But in this as in many other areas, the gap between what firms say and what they actually do is quite wide. Even as they talk about people as key strategic assets, firms jettison these assets with abandon.

THE CONNECTION BETWEEN EMPLOYEE TENURE AND ORGANIZATIONAL PERFORMANCE

The new employment arrangements, including contingent work arrangements and emphasis on the "new employment contract," because they diminish the connection or attachment between employees and employers, lead to more turnover at a minimum and often to a less motivated and committed work force. Accumulating evidence shows that tenure offers important organizational returns in the form of enhanced customer service and satisfaction as well as productivity. Given

Table 6-1 CONSEQUENCES OF DOWNSIZING

Consequence	Percent of Firms Reporting
Lower morale among remaining work force	61
More need for retraining remaining employees	41
More use of temporary workers or contractors	36
More use of overtime	35
Increased retiree health care costs	30
Entire functions contracted out	26
Wrong people lost	20
Severance costs greater than anticipated	16
Too many people lost	6

Source: Mitchell Lee Marks, "Restructuring and Downsizing" in *Building the Competitive Workforce,* ed. Philip H. Mirvis (New York: John Wiley, 1993), 75. Copyright © 1993 John Wiley & Sons, Inc. Reprinted by permission of John Wiley & Sons, Inc.

this evidence, then, adopting strategies that encourage reduced tenure on the part of the work force would appear to be shortsighted.

One study of 1,277 employees and more than 4,000 customers from a personal lines insurance company revealed that both employee job satisfaction and satisfaction with their ability to provide service increased linearly with firm tenure. While 79 percent of the employees with more than five years of tenure with the firm reported being very satisfied or satisfied with their jobs and 86 percent reported being satisfied with their service capability, only 65 percent of employees who had been in the firm less than one year were as satisfied with their jobs and 74 percent with their capability of providing service.[48] The results from examining customer satisfaction revealed that "as service employees gain more experience, they become more aligned with their customers."[49]

A study of 771 Sears stores correlated employee tenure with results of a "60-second survey" conducted semiannually with a sample of the stores' best customers, measured by their charge purchases. A clear inverse relationship appeared between turnover and service—the lower the employee turnover in a particular store, the higher the store's score on the customer service measure. Higher customer service operations had, on average, turnover rates of 54 percent while lower customer service stores had turnover rates of 83 percent on average.[50] The research on Sears also examined the relationship between tenure and full-time employment status and customer service as assessed by the survey of customers. This analysis revealed that "stores with more regular employees also score much higher on customer satisfaction measures."[51] The study provided support for the relationship between customer service and the nature of the employment relationship.

> As employees become more attached to Sears—measured by reduced turnover and a higher percentage of full-time workers—regular customers who visit those stores experience better service. Employee attachment leads to customer attachment. . . . [S]tores with employees who exhibit greater commitment as measured by reduced turnover and ratio of full- to part-time employees also experience greater perceived customer service.[52]

A study of Ryder Truck Rental's turnover rate and workers' compensation claims, covering some eighty-seven districts and about 10,000 employees, provides further evidence on the economic benefits of employee attachment. Districts that averaged less than 9.5 percent turn-over in 1988 and 1989 experienced a workers' compensation claim rate of 16.1 percent. Districts that experienced a 20 percent or higher vol-untary turnover rate had a worker's compensation claim rate that was some 50 percent larger, or 24.0 percent.[53] The Ryder study also exam-ined the relationship between tenure—the opposite of turnover—and financial performance. Districts that had average employee tenure of greater than 8.33 years earned 120 percent of the firm's average return on net controllable assets, while districts with average tenure of less than 5.75 years earned only 82 percent of the average return on net controllable assets.[54] A time-series analysis at Ryder indicated that "im-proved management of the HR [human resources] work environment will lead to improved financial performance and a reduction in control-lable costs."[55]

Arguments in favor of the high turnover caused by using contingent work arrangements and frequent layoffs emphasize that turnover brings in new blood and helps introduce new ideas. The argument continues by claiming that "efficiencies may result from replacing full-time em-ployees who leave the organization with part-time personnel or with entry-level personnel, thereby reducing . . . costs."[56] A study of a na-tional sample of 333 hospitals, however, showed that turnover among registered nurses was linearly related to nonpersonnel operating and personnel costs per patient day and found no evidence that a modest level of turnover positively affected performance. The study concluded that "organizational or human resource factors such as turnover among key personnel have a significant marginal effect on productivity even after supply and demand characteristics are controlled. Indeed, human resources management may be integrally linked to objectives of cost efficiency and productivity."[57]

Examining the substantial economic returns from having loyal cus-tomers, Frederick Reichheld noted that "employees who are not loyal are unlikely to build an inventory of customers who are."[58] A study of automobile repair garages in one national chain revealed that the top third in terms of employee retention were also in the top-third in productivity, with sales per employee that were 22 percent higher than those in the bottom third.[59] Even in the high turnover fast food indus-try, a study of one national chain showed substantial variation in turnover ranging from 100 to 300 percent, with stores with comparatively low employee turnover enjoying profit margins more than 50 percent higher than stores with high employee turnover.[60]

Tenure not only affects customer satisfaction and economic performance, it also affects the ability to accomplish the work place transformation that can help customer service and work place productivity. Recall that the study of change in the use of flexible manufacturing in automobile assembly plants found that those plants that had managers with longer tenure tended to make more change. A similar finding comes from a study of transformational change in the Ford Motor Company, where the most profound changes were made by managers who had apparently plateaued in their careers and, therefore, had longer tenures in their jobs. That study also reported that "given the findings regarding positive affect [attitude] and transformational change, senior management must be increasingly sensitive to attitude and morale issues."[61] Thus, we see again the potential for a vicious cycle of organizational decline. Organizations that downsize and thereby reduce both tenure and morale as they get into trouble set in motion forces that significantly reduce their ability to change and adopt those very practices that can alter the poor productivity and customer service and the resulting diminished economic performance.

Nor is it the case that turnover or its converse, employee tenure, is some exogenous factor, like an act of God, outside of management's control. Starbucks, the operator of retail coffee stores, for instance, provides all employees, even part-timers, with health insurance, stock options, and training and career counseling. Its turnover is about 60 percent annually, well below the 300 percent average for the restaurant industry.[62] Chevy's, a restaurant chain serving "Fresh Mex" cuisine, has held turnover to 31 percent in management and 91 percent among hourly employees using an unusually generous combination of benefits, quarterly meetings that give employees a chance to discuss work-related issues, tangible financial rewards for length of service, a sense of ownership and involvement in the organization, and a policy of listening to and respecting employees. The organization has thus recognized and responded to the direct costs of turnover—recruiting and training replacements—as well as the indirect costs from reduced customer service and productivity.

"Our underlying philosophy is, the guest comes second, the employee comes first," said Fred Parkin, vice president of human resources for the San Francisco-based chain. "If you take care of the employees, they'll take care of the guests, and the business will take care of itself."[63]

Clear evidence exists showing that use of part-time, fixed-term contract, and temporary help increases turnover. Many people believe in the market, including the labor market, and the idea behind such arrangements is to encourage a market-like orientation. But a company that sends the message that it will lay off its employees at the first sign of trouble and that its people should always be apprised of the labor market encourages its people to be continually job shopping and at risk, therefore, of job-hopping. Such an orientation diminishes attachment and increases turnover. And, as the old adage maintains, "when the ship threatens to sink, the best swimmers are the first to jump." Thus, firms that indicate that they will downsize at the first sign of trouble will be continually at risk of losing their best people first, thereby exacerbating the performance problems that initiated the downsizing.

COMMITMENT IS RECIPROCAL

If you want to see the sheer foolishness of the "new employment contract," try one of the following thought experiments. Think about meeting someone and falling in love. You tell the person, "I care about you and want you to be with me. Come be with me, take care of me, be loyal to me and devoted to my interests—and by the way, when I find you no longer interesting or useful, you're out." Let me suggest that this is not likely to be a very effective personal pick-up line. Nor is it a very effective corporate pick-up line, even if it is what many organizations implicitly (or explicitly) say to their work force.

Or try going home to your spouse and children with the following redefinition of the "new family contract": "Because of increasing instability in the economy, I can no longer make credible long-term commitments for your support and education. I face career instability, and, therefore, how can I promise that I will provide ongoing financial support? In this era of rapid change, we need more family unit flexibility to deploy our personnel resources as the situation dictates. In fact, what I will help you do is to become family-circumstance resilient, so that you are better able to cope with changing family circumstances." I suspect your family members will think you are nuts, and, moreover, if you attempted to act on the basis of such beliefs, I doubt if your family would stick around very long.

Both of these thought experiments strike most people as implausible because each violates a universally-held social norm—the norm of reciprocity. Reciprocity has been uncovered in every human civilization ever studied and has even been observed among baboons—it is truly a ubiquitous rule of behavior. The norm of reciprocity means that favors get returned and social obligations are repaid. Commitment is reciprocal. It is difficult to think of situations, at least in healthy, adult relationships, in which one side is committed and the other is not. For me to be committed to you requires that you, in turn, be committed to me—otherwise the situation will be unbalanced and inherently unstable.

Jack Stack, the successful chief executive of Springfield ReManufacturing Corporation and one of the proponents of "open-book" management described in chapter 3, had this to say about mutual commitments and employment security:

> I had always figured out how to maintain full employment, because I totally believe that when you bring people into your workforce, they're taking on debt, they're building families. They're trying to go forward in terms of their lives. To pull that out from under them is probably one of the biggest disgraces I could ever imagine![64]

The company lives by these values. When in 1986 General Motors canceled an order that represented about 40 percent of Springfield's business for the coming year, the firm averted a layoff by providing its people with information on what had happened and letting them figure out how to grow the company and achieve the productivity improvements that would obviate the need for layoffs.

Consider a firm that decided to make the mutuality of commitments and obligations between the enterprise and its people visible and explicit. Berlin Packaging is a growing, successful, privately-owned company with recent sales of over $120 million that provides packaging solutions to customers in numerous industries. The company has its own manufacturing plants and also subcontracts and purchases from

others. Andrew Berlin, the president, has developed a culture that recognizes the value of people and of aligning management processes with
the business strategy. As part of a change program to more closely align
people with the business, he developed a statement of the *mutual* obligations between the company and its people. I present this T-account,
or people balance sheet, in Exhibit 6-1, to illustrate how a firm that
recognizes the reciprocal nature of commitment has made the mutual
obligations explicit to all.

Much as they might like to, corporations cannot repeal the norm of
reciprocity or the mutuality of obligations. To tell employees that the
organization has no long-term commitment or obligation to them is
fine, as long as the firm is willing to bear the consequence of a mutual
lack of long-term attachment and commitment on the part of its employees. As we have already seen in this chapter, turnover is expensive
and downsizing has few if any benefits, particularly if one takes a
longer-term view. The "new employment contract" purchases presumed
flexibility at what is frequently a very stiff price.

AVOIDING DOWNSIZING

Some readers will say at this point that trying to offer a secure working
environment and building long-term relationships with employees is
fine for companies that are doing well and are growing consistently. But
what happens in times of economic stress due to the economic fluctuations that affect even the best-managed companies? What should
companies do about people who, because of changes in technology or
market conditions, are simply no longer needed and too expensive to
maintain in the firm? In response to these points, I would say first, that

Exhibit 6-1 MUTUAL OBLIGATIONS AT BERLIN PACKAGING

Berlin Owes the Employee	The Employee Owes Berlin
Rewards	Productivity
Chance to Grow	Profitability
Job Security	Loyalty
Collegiality	Teamwork
Leadership/Coach	Work Ethic
Training	Innovation

downsizing and layoffs are not inevitable and that organizations do have other choices. The automobile industry, for instance, is cyclical, and most firms lay off employees during economic downturns. Employment security, however, is one of the pillars of Japanese employment systems. Consequently, even in a social environment in which employment security is much less common, Japanese automobile manufacturers operating in the United States have adhered to their employment security practices, despite their cyclical industry and their use of fewer temporary workers than in Japan, which makes work force adjustment during downturns in demand more difficult. "None of the transplants have had any layoffs of core employees to date."[65]

Firms have a number of options for avoiding layoffs, even in the face of economic pressures. Firms that view their people as assets and manage in such a way as to achieve profits through people tend to use these options. The following are the most straightforward steps for avoiding downsizing or for mitigating its impact.

- ◆ Proportionally reducing work hours that spreads the pain of reduced employment costs across the entire work force.

- ◆ Reducing wages for all employees (possibly weighted so that the highest paid take larger pay cuts) to reduce the wage bill.

- ◆ Taking work previously outsourced (such as maintenance or subcontracting) back into the organization.

- ◆ Building inventory while demand is slack.

- ◆ Freezing hiring to avoid making overstaffing worse.

- ◆ Having people do other things, such as deferred maintenance and repair, taking training courses, and similar activities for which they were too busy when business was better.

- ◆ Refraining from hiring to meet peak demand, which makes reductions in employment almost inevitable when demand decreases.

- ◆ Encouraging people to develop new products, services, or markets so that their skills can still be used by the firm.

- ◆ Putting production or staff people into sales to build demand.

Although none of these actions is particularly novel or even difficult, nevertheless, according to the American Management Association's 1994 Survey on Downsizing, little evidence shows that firms use these methods to try to avoid layoffs or to mitigate their consequences. Rather, "voluntary separation plans show a continuous upward trend. Policies intended to 'share the pain' are generally in decline."[66] This evidence speaks to how organizations actually view downsizing and their employees. Research evidence indicates that companies that implement at least some of these suggestions can minimize downsizing. One study of 152 organizations, for instance, found that when groups of employees were covered by variable compensation, so that pay adjusted according to organizational fortunes, employment levels were less variable.[67]

Organizations can do even more creative things if they are serious about either avoiding or minimizing layoffs. Have you ever seen larger organizations laying off people in one division or unit even as they were hiring in another? This has been common in some of the regional telephone operating companies and in many other organizations. It is disheartening to employees and costly to the organization, which faces recruiting expenses in one unit even as it confronts severance costs in another. In the early 1980s when Minnesota Mining and Manufacturing faced the prospect of layoffs, it implemented a policy called the Unassigned List. Under this policy, people whose positions are eliminated have six months to find another job within the company. During that period, workers receive their salaries and benefits and even any salary increases due them. During the first four months, employees are offered a generous severance package of one and one-half week's pay for each year of service, and older workers are eligible for a preretirement leave package that maintains benefits and accrues service credit toward retirement. The program has been quite successful in retaining talent in the organization and in ensuring that those who leave do so with a good feeling about the organization and its willingness to honor its commitments and value its employees.

> [O]f the approximately 200 people who went through the unassigned process during the first three quarters of 1994, only one or two of them made it to day 180 without finding work. On average, those who do find other positions within 3M, which is approximately 50% of the people who go through the process, do so within three and a half months.[68]

A similar approach is used by Hewlett-Packard, another firm that tries to provide some measure of employment security. When, for instance, the company exited the fabrication business at its Loveland, Colorado, division, leaving four hundred surplus workers, it facilitated their move to other HP facilities; provided help to employees relocating to distant facilities, giving them priority in job assignments at other H-P locations; loaned employees to divisions with short-term hiring needs; and permitted employees to be reclassified to lower pay levels and other jobs. More than 50 percent of the employees were retained in the company.[69]

Companies facing only temporary slowdowns due to seasonal fluctuations in demand or a downturn in the economy have the option of "loaning" surplus workers to nearby firms, a tactic used by Brooks Beverage Management Inc., a soft drink bottler.[70] A company might also develop projects internally that absorb surplus labor. At Harman International, with 8,000 employees worldwide in the business of manufacturing high-quality audio and video products, productivity improvements permitted employees to produce nearly three times the dollar value that they had only three years previously. The company's chairman, Sidney Harman, stated that "We have no greater responsibility to our employees and our shareholders than to free employees from the threat of job loss, simply because they respond to our urging for greater productivity."[71] The company developed a program, called Off-Line Enterprises, that involved creating "a job bank of projects that assembly workers, or employees supporting assembly operations, could be temporarily redeployed to work on until demand for their labor picked up again."[72] Among the things the company did was to train employees to become salespeople, build products customarily purchased from outside suppliers, provide service personnel usually obtained through outside suppliers, such as security guards, and convert waste byproducts into salable products.[73]

If companies are serious about seeing their people as assets and as the key to profits and, as a consequence, about avoiding layoffs, almost anything is possible. Consider the case of Pinnacle Brands Inc., one of the top five trading-card manufacturers—and the only one that survived the baseball strike that began in 1994 and extended into the following season. With no baseball being played, not many baseball cards were sold, and the company faced a loss of $40 million in trading card revenue. What the company did was to issue a challenge to its people—if they could find a way to replace the lost revenue, they could keep their jobs.[74] People, working in teams that often crossed departmental boundaries, figured out ways to cut costs and came up with new product ideas that replaced lost revenue. Instead of laying off 190 people, the company wound up getting through the crisis without layoffs. Thus, the fundamental question confronting organizations facing economic stress is are they serious about treating their work force as assets rather than costs?

DOWNSIZING SENSIBLY

Even for firms that need to reduce the number of employees, downsizing can be accomplished while still treating people as important assets and maintaining morale and trust. By contrast, other ways of downsizing reduce morale, diminish trust, and signal that, whatever the rhetoric, management neither respects nor values its work force.

> At Tenneco, where 1,200 employees were laid off over a six-week period, many learned of their fates when confronted by armed guards carrying boxes for them to use in clearing out their desks. At Allied Bank of Texas, department heads called meetings and then read the names of those to be laid off in front of their coworkers.[75]

Contrast those incidents, or the description of layoffs at Apple Computer from chapter 1, with the following events at New Zealand Post. When the Post became a state-owned enterprise on April 1, 1987, as part of the reform of the New Zealand economy, it was expected to operate as an efficient commercial enterprise. On that date, it got a new name, a new insignia, new employment contracts, new rules, and a new CEO. At that time, the organization had about 11,500 employees and was overstaffed. It had too many small facilities and did not contract out either enough or the right activities. Like many public organizations, it had been, to some extent, used as an employer of last resort as a way of coping with unemployment. Within a few years, its employment had fallen to about 8,500, a decrease of almost 30 percent, but the reductions were accomplished without leaving the organization weakened by a distrustful and unmotivated work force.

One of the things the organization did right was to do a large number, although not all, of the eventual layoffs almost immediately. As soon as he took over the organization, Harvey Parker, the managing director at the time, announced a 20 percent across the board budget cut and let the individual managers figure out how to make the cuts. This step got a lot of the pain out of the way as well as communicating that change was necessary. In contrast, New Zealand Telecom, created at the same time, waited some eighteen months before taking any initiatives to change the organization. The Post also shared a lot of budgetary and financial information with its people and established clear targets and goals, including an emphasis on customer service and productivity, that served to motivate the work force and to clarify what was needed and why.

Unfortunately, many organizations, such as IBM, Digital Equipment, and others engage in round after round of employee layoffs. Case study evidence shows that repeated waves of downsizing make the implementation of high commitment work practices almost impossible, although a one-time downsizing does not. Continuing rounds of layoffs create uncertainty that undermines the willingness of people to change because they view "it as increasing company profits as their plant went out of business."[76] One company that experienced technological change and that made inevitable reductions in the work force suffered as, "with repeated underestimates of the required work-force reductions, workers no longer believed the projections that were made or the promise that early retirements and annual turnover would be used instead of layoffs."[77] Without credibility or trust in management, implementing high involvement work practices becomes substantially more difficult.

The New Zealand Post endeavored to treat its people, including those being laid off, well. The organization worked hard during the restructuring to place employees elsewhere in the organization. When people could not be placed elsewhere, they received handsome redundancy packages, averaging $20,000. Because about 65 percent of the employees were female, in many instances earning a second income for the family, and many of the employees of both sexes were quite senior—as most employees had worked only for the Post for their entire working careers—the organization's demography made the redundancy packages reasonably attractive. The management told the truth about what they were doing and why, and the resulting credibility helped tremendously. But the key was that the "people went with dignity."[78] The company let staff know as far in advance as possible about departures. Unlike at those companies that announce who is laid off and then escort them out the door with guards, the Post held parties for those leaving. The organization offered assistance to individuals looking for other jobs and preparing resumes. The Post allowed the work force to identify those who might be more willing to leave—in some instances, people who weren't targeted to be laid off offered to go in place of some who had. Finally, a number of the Post managers told me that because New Zealand had a safety net—a program of income maintenance—individuals did not fear the future as much as they might otherwise have.

Another example of an organization that handled the need for layoffs sensibly is Carlton & United Breweries, a large Australian brewer. When the company confronted the fact that some of its breweries were inefficient and possibly overstaffed, it considered simply announcing a reduction in the size of the work force. But the firm had embarked on a program of work redesign that was intended to implement high performance work practices. Its managers decided that an announcement of layoffs was inconsistent with the new culture of participation and empowerment they were trying to build and would probably have adverse effects on both motivation and trust. Yet, the business necessity for doing something was real and compelling. What the company did was to go to the union that represented most of the workers in the brewery and to lay out the financial situation, providing access to any books or records that the union leaders might want to see. The company and the employee organizations then reached joint decisions about how large a reduction in staff was necessary and other ways to address the business issues. In the end, fewer layoffs were required than the company had anticipated but, more importantly, the decisions on staffing levels were made in a way that was consistent with the high commitment culture that Carlton & United was attempting to build and reinforce.

Virtually all of the things I have described that either avoid layoffs or make them less traumatic cost resources, both of time and money. Generous severance is obviously more expensive than less generous payments and giving people assistance in finding other jobs and time to do so and to say good-bye also incurs costs. Carlton & United Breweries' consultation with its work force clearly delayed the speed of adjustment in the size of its work force. I asked Elmar Toime, the current chief executive of the New Zealand Post who had come to the firm in 1987 with Harvey Parker, why the organization was willing to incur these costs. He replied that they weren't really costs at all but instead an investment in building a relationship with the remaining work force that would permit the organization to prosper in what is, after all, a people-dependent, service business. His answer reflects a time horizon and perspective that is, unfortunately, all too rare. But it reflects an approach to management that is likely to be more successful.

> Memories of how victims of reductions are treated stick in the mind of surviving employees for a long time to come. If they observe that affected employees are treated poorly—given short notice, a piddling severance, and nothing in the way of personal or career counseling—then surviving employees are bound to fear that they are next in line for arbitrary and insensitive treatment.[79]

The following list summarizes the lessons from organizations that have shed people in ways that did not destroy their culture or the commitment and motivation of those who remained.

- ◆ Reduce staff levels promptly once the decision is made to do so.
- ◆ Reduce employment levels, to the extent possible, all at once rather than in repeated waves.
- ◆ Share economic and performance data on the reasons for the downsizing.
- ◆ Provide notice of the decision.
- ◆ Involve people in the decisions on how many staff to cut and who should leave.
- ◆ Provide people with fair severance and benefits.
- ◆ Let people leave with dignity, having ceremonies or social functions to let them say goodbye.
- ◆ Provide career transition assistance, such as outplacement, career and vocational interest assessments, and so forth.

THE VOLKSWAGEN EXPERIENCE

Volkswagen presents a useful example of how to handle work force reductions. In late 1993, the company was faced with stagnating sales, extremely low profit margins, and the need to dramatically increase productivity, quality, and customer responsiveness in order to be competitive. From a level of 103,000 employees in 1993, it projected a decrease to just 71,900 by the end of 1995, a reduction of some 31,000 people or 30 percent of its work force.[80] In fact, it took actions so that it decreased employment to 91,000 people by 1996. The company, moreover, remains committed to maintaining 58 percent of its jobs within Germany, a comparatively high-wage country. Volkswagen's efforts were part of a larger cultural change at the company that involved removing layers of management, instituting teamwork, and increasing the skill level of its work force. What I want to highlight here, however, is how the company handled the downsizing issue.

It is important to note that Volkswagen began this effort with some distinct advantages.

> In introducing variable forms of employment, Volkswagen was able to build on certain stable values: a level of wages virtually unrivaled in the region, a high level of social benefits, and finally a strong sense of security—as the jobs concerned had hitherto always carried life-long guarantees. . . . All these values have made Volkswagen such an attractive employer that applicants have often tended to put greater stress on working for the company than on the type of job concerned.[81]

Volkswagen proposed reducing the average working week from 36 to 28.8 hours, with a simultaneous reduction in earnings for the entire work force. But, monthly income was not reduced as much because redistribution of other income elements brought salaries back up to near their pre-reduction levels, although annual income fell, on average, about 12 percent. The annual income of Volkswagen employees was comprised of several elements: "monthly salary; a special one-off annual payment amounting to 96% of a twelfth of the gross annual salary earned during the previous year; holiday pay over and above the monthly salary . . . paid on two fixed dates; a Christmas bonus calculated according to the number of years' service in the company."[82] The company took some of the once-a-year payments and distributed them equally over the twelve months, brought some negotiated raises forward, and contributed an additional 2 percent of monthly income to achieve its goal of providing workers with the same monthly income they had previously received, thus allowing them to meet their ongoing financial obligations.

The company instituted two other programs to help manage the necessary reduction in work hours. One was a "block time" program, targeted at workers between 18 and 30 years of age. The program entails a period of limited duration unemployment, during which the employee undergoes training and skills acquisition. "This model converts the 'normal' double load of work and training into a combination which allows the employee scope to work and earn money as well as to upgrade his skills over the course of the year."[83]

The company also recognized that not everyone wants to work the same number of hours throughout their working life. So, it instituted a flexible working program that entails a phased increase or decrease in working time. This program "fits with the idea of Volkswagen being a 'family.' Older employees are able to gradually withdraw from work. . . . [T]he system allows for a working week which progressively increases for freshly qualified employees and . . . is gradually reduced for older employees."[84]

Volkswagen's experiment with the four-day, shortened work week made headlines when it was announced and was not greeted by universal approval from commentators in the business press or by other executives. The change did cut personnel costs by some 15 percent. More importantly, almost half of a sample of Volkswagen employees said they were "satisfied" or "very satisfied" with the new working arrangements, while only 16.6 percent were "dissatisfied" or "very dissatisfied." And, a survey of over 1,000 people in the country at large found that the Volkswagen model was evaluated positively by 51 percent of the respondents and negatively by only 29 percent.[85]

Volkswagen is an unusual company. It is headquartered in a country with a strong union movement and with mandated codetermination. It is a large employer in that country, and its actions, such as laying off people, have important consequences for governmental expenditures on unemployment benefits. Perhaps because of these factors, or because of the character of its leadership, Volkswagen has taken a different approach to the problem of excess employees.

> Throughout the world, mass unemployment has become one of the most pressing problems of modern times. The automotive industry has been hit by a crisis of restructuring and excess capacity. It would have been easy enough for Volkswagen to follow the example of many other companies and simply shed jobs. But, as "Every Job has a Face," the company therefore decided . . . to break out of the vicious circle of mass unemployment. *It is*

all very well for market trends, technological progress, or productivity to define personnel requirements—but these factors alone should not be allowed to dictate the nature of the solution to the problem.[86]

Meanwhile, Volkswagen's economic recovery has continued, and its profits have increased. Its program of cultural change might not have been possible or nearly as successful without its heroic efforts to maintain its commitment to its work force. But in any event, the company followed a course of action consistent with its values and its beliefs, and it did so thoughtfully and creatively.

CONCLUSION

The two decisions considered in this chapter—where to draw the organization's boundaries or how much temporary help and contract employment to use and what implicit or explicit agreement about employment continuity to offer employees—are two of the most basic, important, and fundamental choices organizations make. Much of what else managers do with respect to managing people will be dictated by these two choices. Given that fact, the evidence we have seen about the absence of planning, thought, and evaluation given these decisions is truly startling. Firms should draw at least this lesson from the material presented here: the economic and social importance of adopting a strategic, thoughtful, and comprehensive approach to evaluating these two basic questions of outsourcing and employment security.

Making smart decisions about these issues requires in the first place that managers take a longer term view of the consequences of staffing decisions. Downsizing may cut labor costs in the short run, but it can erode both employee and eventually customer loyalty in the long run. And, most basically, these decisions need to be evaluated! Outsourcing affects more than direct labor costs and should be assessed accordingly. Managers should ask not just what people cost but what they do and what value they create for the organization. Asking about productivity and other measures of effectiveness, assessing the reactions of managers and coworkers, and evaluating the impact on customer service, broadly defined, are crucial steps for ensuring that decisions about the use of contingent workers are truly thoughtful and sound.

As you can tell, my overall judgment is that organizations, particularly in the United States where they are free of virtually any regulations or constraints on their behavior, have moved too far in undermining employment security and using contingent labor. How can I talk about employment security in the current economic environment, given the prevalence of downsizing? First, it is an empirical fact that high commitment work systems frequently include some form of employment security, as we saw in chapter 2. Second, employment security relates logically to other elements of high performance work arrangements. Employees "are more willing to contribute to improvements in the work process when they need not fear losing their own or their co-worker's jobs. Employment security contributes to training as both employer and employee have greater incentives to invest in training when they expect their relationship will endure."[87] Third, the norm of reciprocity means that employees will not commit to a firm and its success unless the firm demonstrates a reciprocal commitment to its people.

Numerous examples besides those mentioned here might be used to show the connection between people and profits and the positive effects for firms that did not turn to downsizing at the first sign of economic distress and that handled work force redundancy with care and respect. Charles Schwab, for instance, the extremely successful discount stock brokerage firm, attempts to maintain employment during the periodic downturns in the securities industry. It does so because it does not want to lose its investment in training and loyalty in a work force that it believes provides the service edge that gives it an advantage over the competition.

It is not necessary, as some of my colleagues believe, to confront the competitive environment with a new social contract and a flexible work force. "Calling a layoff at the first sign of financial stress is a little like getting a paper cut and calling the paramedics."[88] The New Zealand Post is today one of the most efficient postal systems in the world, and it is probably the only one that has actually cut the price of a stamp. It is very profitable and earns an excellent return on its invested capital. Are these results a consequence of an approach to people that states "the Post's job is to equip people with the skills to be mobile but to give them a job that makes them want to stay"?[89] In a people-dependent, service business, such an approach to employment must certainly help. As Peter Hartz, the senior personnel executive at Volkswagen, reminds us, the competitive environment defines the requirements, but each company can define the solutions. In fact, the job of leadership is precisely the crafting of creative responses to competitive conditions that build competence, capability, and commitment in people and avoid destroying organizational memory, wisdom, and loyalty.

As we have seen in this chapter, little evidence exists to support the view that downsizing solves organizational profitability or productivity problems or that a contingent work force provides much competitive leverage. On the contrary, quite a bit of good empirical data opposes both these trends. Managers must decide whether they will be swept up in the fads and rhetoric of the moment or will recognize some basic principles of management and the data consistent with them. The great irony in all of this is that at a time when most employers offered reasonably stable and secure employment, any particular firm drew little advantage from doing so—it was just one of the many. But in today's world of downsizing, outsourcing, and separating human assets from the organization, firms can gain a tremendous advantage by being different: They will attract and retain a better work force and capitalize on the skills and knowledge developed by that work force.

7 ◆ *How Common Approaches to Pay Cause Problems*

*I*F YOU WERE to ask me what could you do to inflict the most damage on an organization, I would answer: tamper with its pay system, and do so following the current "conventional wisdom" about pay. That wisdom is based on the following three elements:

1. Cutting labor costs is important for cutting overall costs, and cost-cutting is important in an increasingly competitive world. Competitive position—for both firms and nations—is significantly determined by their relative rates of pay or at least by their labor costs.

2. Effective compensation practices reward individual efforts and individual achievement. Merit pay is a great idea, and the only issue is in how to implement it effectively. Compensation based on piecework—paying for individual work accomplished—is even better for those situations where individual work output can be measured. People want to be differentially recognized for their performance and more collective pay schemes—such as profit sharing or gain sharing, or even stock ownership—simply encourage free riding and shirking.

3. Pay systems and the associated measurement practices (such as performance reviews) required to implement them are critically important for organizational effectiveness. If the incentives (both monetary and nonmonetary, but particularly monetary) are not

right, organizations will have problems. "Fixing" compensation practices, therefore, should be a high priority for any organization that wants to enhance its performance. Call a compensation consulting firm immediately!

It is my observation that pay practices, and particularly changes premised on the three assumptions above, frequently get in the way of efforts to build productivity and profits. This occurs even when, and sometimes because of, the use of compensation consultants who, for the most part, merely do what the organization requests. Thus, if a compensation consulting firm is called in to install a merit pay plan, it will install one, even if by doing so it causes the myriad problems discussed later in this chapter. If a consulting firm is requested to make pay more differentiated on an individual basis, it will do so, even if it thereby sets up destructive internal competition and destroys efforts to build teamwork. In pay, as in many other management practices, the first principle ought to be "first, do no harm." Thinking about pay ought to be based on logic and evidence, not on belief or ideology. Unfortunately, it often isn't, and great harm may be the consequence.

Every organization compensates the people who work for it. Consequently, every organization has to decide what to do about pay, regardless of any other rewards it offers its people. It *must* make these basic decisions about pay: first, how much emphasis to place on pay as part of the management system; second, how much to pay, what level of compensation should be implemented; and third, whether to administer pay on an individual, group, or larger collectivity basis. Making those decisions using the best available evidence and reasoning is important for preventing the problems caused by poorly designed pay systems.

What I am going to argue may shock you. But I hope to convince you of three things:

1. Pay rates are much less important than most managers think, and even lower labor costs may not be the basis for competitive success.

2. Individual merit pay and even piecework, although growing in popularity, have numerous problems, and the research evidence suggests that they are frequently ineffective.

3. Believing that pay and the associated measurement systems used to implement pay will solve all productivity problems is almost certainly a prescription for ruin.

At the end of the chapter, I will talk about how to make decisions about pay consistent with achieving profits through people—but if I can prevent you and your organization from doing harm, we will be well on our way to building more effective management practices and more productive organizations.

LABOR COSTS, LABOR RATES, AND ECONOMIC PERFORMANCE

Many firms' management strategies focus on cost reduction. In the short run, labor costs are usually the most controllable. Rates of pay and staffing levels can be more quickly adjusted than can capital equipment and other physical infrastructure. Many firms, therefore, particularly those facing intense and increasing competition, become obsessed with reducing labor *costs,* often by reducing labor *rates.* Many of the efforts to reduce labor costs begin (and often end) by focusing on labor *rates,* or the pay per unit of time. Thus, for instance, in the early 1990s, Ford Motor Company decided not to award merit raises to its white-collar employees, "reflecting a new cost-cutting program."[1] Given Ford's emphasis on building commitment in its work force, the decision was unexpected and inconsistent with its implicit management policies.

> The decision to defer raises at a company that has long credited the hard work of its employees for its financial and sales success was "certainly difficult," the spokeswoman said. But she said Ford "is pretty lean already" and that it has been difficult to find ways to reduce expenses further. Merit raises were viewed as a "controllable cost," she said.[2]

But, labor *costs* are not the same thing as labor *rates*—the rate of pay people receive. Labor costs reflect both the rate of pay but also what people produce. Higher paid people who produce proportionately more can actually reduce labor costs. New United Motor Manufacturing has paid the highest wage in the automobile industry, a premium of about 10 percent. But the plant was almost 50 percent more productive than similar plants. With 50 percent more productivity one can afford to pay a ten percent higher labor *rate* and still have lower labor *costs*. In the steel minimill industry study described in chapter 2, the number of hours required to make a ton of steel was 34 percent less under commitment systems; consequently, the labor costs to make steel will be less under commitment compared to control systems even though the wage rates were, on average, about 19 percent higher.

Not only are labor costs not the same as labor rates, but labor costs are not necessarily the most important source of competitive advantage. In fact, in some cases, labor costs are virtually irrelevant to organizational success.

One day I arrived at a large and prominent discount department store with a shopping list. As you may know, in the United States we have developed these very large stores, on the order of 100,000 square feet or so, that permit one to go shopping and get exercise at the same time, the exercise coming from wandering vast spaces looking for specific items. On this particular day, however, I thought my luck had changed, because soon after arriving at the store, I encountered a sales associate. I approached the person and inquired whether he could tell me where to find the first item on my list. He immediately replied, "no." Giving the same response on items two and three, and seeing that I had a long list, the nice young man told me that the particular store (and chain) had a lot of employee turnover and, in fact, he had only been in the store two hours. At the rate I was going finding the items on the list, I would soon be in the store two hours myself.

The question this incident raises is: What is that person's value to the organization? Not only can't he sell any of the merchandise, he can't even locate it! No matter how little he is being paid, the organization has paid too much, for the issue is not what labor costs, but what it can do, what it can produce, what value it provides to the organization. If you really want to cut labor costs, I can tell you how to do it very effectively—close down. For on the day you close, the organization's labor costs will be zero. In fact, organizations are really not interested in minimizing labor costs. They are presumably interested in maximizing profits, productivity, or performance, and that is often something very different.

Aaron Feuerstein, the owner of Malden Mills of Lawrence, Massachusetts, received a lot of well-deserved publicity when, after a fire destroyed his mill, he kept his nearly 1,000 employees on the payroll while the factory was being rebuilt, at a cost of some $15 million in wages. Talking about why he hasn't followed the lead of some of his competitors and moved his (unionized) plant to the South, where wages are lower and the likelihood of unionization less, or even offshore, he noted:

A great many of those companies failed anyway, despite the lower wages they spent so much money to find, and Feuerstein is sure he knows why: They gave too much attention to costs and not enough to quality. . . . "Why would I go to Thailand to bring the cost lower when I might run the risk of losing the advantage I've got, which is superior quality?" . . . [L]ower wages are a temporary advantage. Quality lasts. . . . Any idiot with a strong enough stomach can make quick money . . . by slashing costs and milking customers, employees, or a company's reputation. But clearly that's not the way to make a lot of money for a long time. The way to do that is to create so much value that your customers wouldn't dream of looking for another supplier.[3]

At Levi Strauss, Peter Thigpen, at one time the worldwide vice president of manufacturing, told me about his experience prior to implementing modular production and gain sharing. He was, as are most people in manufacturing, obsessed with costs and, given the difference in the wage rates between the plants in the United States and those in low-wage, developing countries, he was spending a lot of time trying to figure out what to do so the company could keep at least some of its U.S. plants open. Then he did a study and learned several things. First, the direct labor cost component in a typical pair of jeans was about 15 percent of total costs. Second, approximately 95 percent of the time that material was in the plant, nothing was being done to it; it was simply sitting in work in process inventory. Third, the basis of competition in the apparel industry was changing from strictly cost to delivery so that retailers could control their own inventory levels and quality. So, Thigpen concluded, he was spending close to 100 percent of his time trying to get about a 20 percent improvement for something that only accounted for 15 percent of the cost in any event, and cost was not even the sole, or perhaps the most important, basis of success.

Nor is the Levi's example unusual. At USX, the large U.S. manufacturer of steel, 1992 labor costs were only 20 percent of total costs. At machine-tool manufacturer Giddings and Lewis, direct labor is only 10 percent of total costs.[4] Even at Solectron, a contract manufacturer of electronic components, direct labor now accounts for well under 30 percent of total costs, with much of the remaining direct costs coming from materials. And this is a company that, as a contract manufacturer, does not do a lot of product development or consumer marketing, large cost components in many firms. At Solectron, better materials handling and quality processes are much more important to being a cost effective manufacturer than are direct labor rates. It is increasingly the case that the critical competitive factor in many firms is not direct labor costs, which, in business after business, are a small fraction of total costs. Even more important to success are quality, service, and the technical characteristics of products.

Consequently, even holding aside the question of whether minimizing or cutting costs is the road to success, it seems clear that worrying about labor rates is seldom useful even if the organization is concerned about costs. About the time this book was written, the Canadian Automobile Workers went on strike against General Motors over the issue of outsourcing. General Motors wanted to outsource more of its parts and components manufacturing, frequently to non-union firms, because these firms are able to pay lower wage rates and therefore presumably

Table 7-1 HOURS REQUIRED TO ASSEMBLE A CAR OR TRUCK FOR VARIOUS NORTH AMERICAN AUTOMAKERS

Company	Labor Hours Required
Nissan	27.36
Toyota	29.44
Honda	30.96
Ford	37.92
Chrysler	43.04
General Motors	46.00

Source: Oscar Suris, "Chrysler Leads Big Three in Efficiency of Car Factories, But All Trail Japanese," *Wall Street Journal,* 30 May 1996, A2. Reprinted by permission of the *Wall Street Journal,* © 1996 Dow Jones & Company, Inc. All Rights Reserved Worldwide.

have lower costs. But compelling evidence suggests that inefficiency and costs at General Motors have comparatively little to do with wage rates. In early 1996, the Harbour Report provided data on average assembly times, measured in labor-hours, for assembling automobiles. These numbers are reproduced in Table 7-1. The numbers are somewhat higher than those found in the worldwide automobile assembly study conducted by M.I.T. because the Harbour figures include manufacturing time for sheet metal stampings, engines, and transmissions.

The data in Table 7-1 show that General Motors, on average, takes more than 68 percent more labor hours to make a car than does Nissan and more than 20 percent more hours than Ford. This difference in productivity is a major source of the company's cost problems—and it has nothing to do with what it pays its people. It is virtually impossible for General Motors to "solve" its cost problems solely by adjusting wage rates, given the magnitude of the difference in the hours required to assemble an automobile. Nor is it sensible to try to do so.

The example of machinery manufacturer Cincinnati Milacron, a company that had virtually surrendered the market for low-end machine tools to Asian competitors, is instructive.

[I]n the last two years, Milacron overhauled its assembly process, abolishing its stockroom and reducing job categories to one from seven. Without any additional capital investment, it cut labor hours by 50% and now exceeds Taiwan's productivity by a third. As a result, Milacron's new . . . line . . . has pulled even with its foreign competitors.[5]

What is true for companies is also true for countries: Little evidence supports a high correlation between labor *rates* and labor *costs,* and, moreover, policies to push down compensation rates, most notably in Britain, have for the most part been abject failures. In Great Britain, the 1980s saw government try to improve the unemployment rate and the competitive position of British industry by attempting to lower the relative rate of pay in the country.

In July, 1980, Margaret Thatcher claimed that, "one of the main reasons for today's distressing unemployment figures . . . is that we have paid ourselves far more than other countries for doing the same job. . . . We have to reduce unit labour costs in this country if we are to reduce unemployment." A decade later . . . Mrs. Thatcher was again focussing attention on unit labour costs as a prime cause of the UK's economic problems.[6]

But the evidence on hourly labor costs, labor output (productivity), and consequently, the labor costs for each unit of production, comparing Great Britain, France, Japan, the United States, and West Germany, from 1979 to 1989, shows a high correlation between hourly labor rates and labor productivity. "This is what might be expected, given that high productivity businesses can afford high pay levels, that firms in low labour cost economies have less incentive to improve productivity by introducing advanced technologies, and that countries which specialise in high value-added products need a more skilled, and higher paid, workforce to produce them."[7]

The data from the decade of the 1980s shows that "in Britain's case . . . it seems clear that any competitive advantages from low labour costs are outweighed by the disadvantages of even lower levels of labour productivity, with the result that unit labour cost levels are the highest of any of the . . . economies."[8] Another analysis of the performance of the British economy, and the effect of labor costs, reached a similar conclusion: "The narrow obsession with labour, and the negative control of labour costs through sacking, is an indicator of the British management problem."[9]

What is salient in managers' attention becomes focal, guiding decisions and strategies. Everyone can focus on only a limited range of things. The problem with the frequently observed obsession with reducing labor rates and even labor costs is that the issue comes to exclude other, possibly more important considerations, such as productivity achieved through the implementation of high involvement work arrangements as part of a redesign of the system of production. We saw an example of this in the apparel industry, where the possibility of competing on quality and delivery was overlooked by firms that focused almost exclusively on labor rates and the costs of doing individual tasks. It is important for managers to recognize the real bases of competitive success, which are frequently quality and service as well as costs; to recognize that labor costs are often a small component of total costs; and in general to take a broader, more sophisticated view of both costs and competition.

PROBLEMS WITH INDIVIDUAL MERIT
OR PERFORMANCE-BASED PAY

In addition to obsessing over labor rates or the rate of pay, many companies today also try to reduce or manage their labor costs by implementing variable pay schemes based on individual performance, in the belief that paying for individual productivity is the best and surest way to increase organizational performance. Although variable pay systems that attempt to differentially reward individuals are clearly currently on the increase, such systems are frequently fraught with problems. Incentive systems that reward groups of employees or even the entire organization, as through profit or gain sharing or stock ownership, typically have fewer of these problems and, as I will argue later in this chapter, are therefore customarily preferable.

At the outset, it is important to distinguish between merit pay systems and piecework, as the problems of the two are not identical. Merit systems typically provide differential raises or bonuses based on performance evaluations and are often administered in the context of a program of wage and salary administration that has prescribed wage ranges assigned to positions and a fixed raise pool determined centrally based on budgeting considerations. By contrast, in a piecework system, individuals are paid on the basis of their productivity, objectively assessed, with typically (and preferably) no upper limit on what they can earn. Changing the rates or capping compensation because "people earn too much" is a certain way to ensure that no one trusts management and to eliminate incentives for enhanced productivity. A sales commission system is a common piecework-like system, in which the sales person earns a fixed percentage of all sales (or, in some cases, of revenue collected). Among the most common and notorious problems that plague either or both of these pay systems are the following.

1. Subjectivity and capriciousness that reward political skills or ingratiating personalities rather than performance.
2. An emphasis on the success of the individual sometimes at the expense of the success of his or her peers, consequently undermining teamwork.
3. An absence of concern for organizational performance.

4. Encouragement of a short-term focus and discouragement of long-term planning.
5. The tendency of such systems to produce fear in the work place.[10]

But perhaps the greatest problem is the symbolic message such systems send. "By making pay contingent upon performance (as judged by management), management is signaling that it is they—not the individual—who are in control,"[11] and as a consequence, "performance-related pay may lower the individual's feelings of competence and self-determination, and run counter to an intrinsic reward policy."[12]

Let's consider the problems of so-called merit pay systems first. Many, if not most, merit pay plans are administered in the following fashion. A manager is given a budget for raises that is specified as a proportion of the total salaries paid to his or her direct reports. The manager must then allocate that raise budget across the subordinates, presumably basing the raises on their individual performance and achievements. Already two serious problems are apparent. First, the percentage of total salaries to be allocated as raises is itself arbitrarily determined. It is frequently based on the rate of inflation, the company's position in the overall labor market in terms of salary and where it desires to be in that market, whether or not the firm had a good or bad year, what comparable firms are doing, and so forth. But these factors are combined in a judgmental fashion, meaning that the size of the pot of money available for merit pay is seldom determined in a very objective or transparent process. Moreover, since merit pay is often pegged to the rate of inflation and inflation has been running at about three percent annually, "companies have found it hard to motivate workers with such tiny pay raises."[13] Second, the competition for raises is zero sum. Since there is a fixed raise budget, every dollar you get, I can't. As a consequence, what I want to happen is for those competing with me for raises to have very bad years so I will look better by comparison. As most executives will tell you, individual merit pay does virtually nothing to encourage teamwork and cooperation and, to the contrary, provides disincentives for helping coworkers.

The foregoing issues are virtually universal, but some organizations make matters even worse by providing salary ranges for jobs. A person who has had a job for a while in which he or she excels, therefore receiving comparatively large raises, will find one day that his or her raises are limited by approaching the salary ceiling for that job. At that point, any pretense toward pay based on performance disappears, since the salary becomes determined by the prescribed range for the job and no longer by performance.

Consider the following tale told to me by a division manager at AES Corporation to explain why that organization does not have human resource people and why it administers its salaries the way it does. Prior to coming to AES, this individual worked in the chemicals division at Diamond Shamrock. On one occasion he came into a job in a division in which the traffic manager, Rudy—the person who arranged for the shipment of the company's products—was clearly doing an exceptional job. Rudy negotiated great freight rates, obtained good delivery and service, expedited shipments when needed, and was exceptionally knowledgeable about freight and transportation issues. He was saving the company literally millions of dollars. Moreover, everyone who had contact with him was in general agreement about Rudy's outstanding performance. He was a star. Since Diamond Shamrock had a merit-based raise system, the executive requested a large raise for Rudy. He was told that such a large raise was impossible. In fact, because Rudy had worked both at the company and in his present position for a long time, he was up against the top of the prescribed salary range for his job. So, he could receive only the increase in the range, which was basically the cost of living.

Needless to say, his boss was nonplused. Here was someone doing a terrific job on every dimension. How could he be rewarded? He was told that Rudy could be financially rewarded only if his job could be reclassified, and the easiest way to do that would be to give him a couple of subordinates. Then he could be upgraded because of his "managerial" responsibilities and could be compensated more adequately for the outstanding job he was doing. But in this process, the organization would have to waste money paying for two positions that it didn't need and that nobody wanted. The point of this tale, which is quite common, is that in a system with salary ranges attached to positions, unless those ranges are quite wide, people will soon run up against the top of the range, and whatever pretense the system made to being performance or merit based disappears.

And if that isn't bad enough, the process that determines the "worth" of various jobs frequently also contains perverse incentives. One of the factors frequently used to determine the value of a particular job is the number of people supervised, as in the preceding example. This leads to what a consulting colleague has referred to as the "body count" mentality, in which managers seek to have as many levels and people reporting to them as possible, because these factors influence their pay. Needless to say, eliminating levels of hierarchy in such a system becomes virtually impossible, because eliminating layers, unless the compensation system is also changed, reduces or eliminates the possibility of obtaining a raise. The system I have just described was exemplified in the famous Hay compensation system, in which pay was determined by the number of Hay points a job warranted. Some people will tell you that this is changing, that broadbanding (having wider salary ranges for jobs) is becoming more common, and that rewarding people simply for the number of subordinates and their level in the hierarchy is diminishing. I am sure all of these changes are occurring, although they have yet to spread very much to Europe. But even in the United States, these new pay arrangements remain the exception and are often implemented with great difficulty. Most organizations are still saddled with pay systems that don't make much sense.

Another problem with merit pay is that, in many instances, it is not based very much on "merit," at least as that term is commonly defined. Performance is frequently judged against objectives that "bear little relationship to work practice" and are possibly even "engineered purely for the purposes of having an individual PRP [performance-related pay] scheme."[14] Certainly for some jobs, such as being a professional athlete, an individual's performance can be fairly objectively and unambiguously assessed. Such jobs have the following characteristics: well-defined, specific, and well-known dimensions of performance, actions, and behaviors; consensus on the relative importance of the various performance dimensions; and clear visibility of the individual's contribution to performance, either because the individual works independently of others or because measurement and assessment is sufficient that each person's contribution can be seen. Garen Staglin, a vocal advocate of piecework and the chief executive of Safelite, a windshield manufacturing and repair company that uses a piecework system, nevertheless noted that "business must . . . have a capacity to track individual performance, that typically comes only with highly computerized operations."[15] Moreover, for individual incentive plans to work, management must be willing to share some of the rewards from increased productivity with the workers rather than passing all the benefits on to shareholders or owners, and the company must "have a realistic hope of expanding sales, so that higher productivity does not lead to morale-destroying layoffs."[16]

Most jobs and most business organizations frequently have few of these characteristics. Job goals are often quite general—developing subordinates into more capable leaders and managers, reducing cycle times for implementing new products or services, exercising leadership, helping to instill customer focus and enhance customer service, and so forth. One can tell if the goals are being more or less achieved, but measurement is often imprecise. Furthermore, performance is frequently multidimensional and the trade-offs among the various dimensions change over time and are not often agreed upon even at a point in time. Most importantly, organizations are characterized by pervasive interdependence among positions—and this interdependence is even greater in places that take the idea of "teams" seriously. Organizational work is done with and through other people, which makes assessing a single individual's contributions perilous and frequently impossible. Herbert Simon, winner of the Nobel prize in economics, wisely recognized this problem:

> In general, the greater the interdependence among various members of the organization, the more difficult it is to measure their separate contributions. . . . But, of course, intense interdependence is precisely what makes it advantageous to organize people instead of depending wholly on market transactions.[17]

In other words, in those organizational situations in which piecework or merit pay is most likely to be readily implemented, because individual contributions can be unambiguously measured, organizing the work inside an organization as contrasted with leaving it in a marketlike relationship probably makes less sense.

When merit pay is actually implemented in a setting characterized by interdependence and multidimensional assessments of performance, invariably a large subjective component occurs in the evaluation process. One way of helping to overcome this subjectivity is to use peer and subordinate evaluation, or "360-degree feedback." Such systems help for the same reason that when ten people estimate anything, the estimate derived from averaging their answers is likely to be more accurate: More information from multiple sources helps to reduce measurement error. But not too many organizations have implemented 360-degree feedback systems yet, and, in any event, these systems don't overcome one of the most important biases affecting the evaluation of work: the rater's personal commitment to and involvement in the assessment.

Whenever the same individual makes a series of decisions at multiple points in time, inevitably later decisions are affected by earlier ones. In the performance assessment context, if a supervisor has made a decision to hire or promote a given person, subsequent appraisals of that person will be affected by that earlier choice and the resulting commitment created by it. How can I say you aren't a great employee if I was influential in hiring you in the first place? I could, I suppose, admit I made a mistake. But in an uncertain and ambiguous setting, it is more likely I will evaluate your work more positively as a way of ratifying my original good sense in selecting you in the first place.

This is exactly what was found in two studies relevant to the performance appraisal task. The first was an experiment in which subjects played the role of vice president of a retail company with multiple stores, with the decision being a choice among three candidates to fill a vacancy as manager at one of the stores.[18] Subjects were provided detailed performance and biographical data on each candidate. Subsequent performance data presented to the subjects indicated that the promoted manager was not doing well. In one situation, the subjects actually chose the manager. In another, subjects were told the manager was chosen by their predecessor. In each instance, they received the same performance information and had to make recommendations about pay increases and bonuses and the manager's promotion potential and to project future sales and profitability for the store. The results showed that "subjects who were responsible for the promotion decision gave higher pay increases and bonuses, evaluated the manager's potential more favorably, and projected higher sales and earnings than did the subjects who were not responsible for the promotion decision."[19]

Of course, this was just an experiment. But when the study was repeated in a field setting, the results held: Raters who had input into and agreed with a promotion or hiring decision rated the individual more favorably than did raters who did not have any involvement with the decision; conversely, when raters had input into the decision but disagreed with it, they rated the person more negatively than did those who had not been involved. Moreover, the study found that the "escalation biases accounted for more variance in performance appraisals than did the measure of clerical ability used to select employees into these jobs,"[20] a test that was a statistically valid predictor of performance.

In some sense, these results are not surprising. But they do call into question how "objective" performance appraisals are and, therefore, the likelihood of merit-based pay having much to do with meritorious performance on the job. The results also suggest that, for merit pay plans to be reasonably fair and objective, individuals not involved in and committed to the decisions that put people into their present positions need to do the ratings.

The problems with individual merit or pay for performance systems are both pervasive and well-known, even though such pay systems proliferate. A Hewitt Associates survey found that of the 61 percent of the companies in their sample that had adopted variable compensation systems with budgets of $5 million or more, 48 percent of the plans failed to achieve their goals in 1995.[21] A study by William Mercer found that 73 percent of the companies responding had made major changes to their performance management plans in the preceding two years, but 47 percent of the companies reported that the systems provided little value to employees, and 51 percent of the employees said that the performance management system provided little value to the organization.[22] Based on these and many other surveys showing similar results, some observers have concluded that "most plans share two attributes: They absorb vast amounts of management time and resources, and they make everybody unhappy."[23] But these plans persist nonetheless because of the tendency of organizations to overemphasize pay as a solution to all of their performance or management problems (more on this below) and because of a set of beliefs, held with almost religious fervor, that individually-based merit pay is right and therefore, with enough diligent effort, the firm will finally find a system that works.

Piecework systems presumably overcome some but not all of the problems just discussed. Plans based on objective performance, such as the number of windshields installed, as at Safelite, allow less room for subjective judgment and bias. But piecework does not overcome the short-term focus or the emphasis on individual rather than team or organizational performance. "In the real world, pay for performance can also release passions that turn workers into rival gangs, so greedy for extra dollars they will make another gangs' members look bad to make their own look good."[24] This is precisely what happened at Lantech, a manufacturer of packaging machinery with 325 employees. Pat Lancaster, the chairman of the company, stated that "Incentive pay is toxic. . . . By the early Nineties I was spending 95% of my time on conflict resolution instead of on how to serve our customers."[25]

Sales commissions, although widely used in retailing—between 1981 and 1990, the proportion of sales representatives paid just on salary declined from 21 percent to 7 percent[26]—frequently suffer from many of the same problems as other forms of piecework. Sears abandoned a commission system at its automobile repair stores when California officials found widespread evidence of consumer fraud, with employees recommending unneeded repairs to unsuspecting customers, for example. Faced with resistance and resentment from the sales force, Dayton Hudson cut back broad commission schemes after just two years in operation. Other stores have acted similarly, in response to fundamental quality and service issues.

> Highland Superstores Inc., an electronics-store and appliance-store chain based in Plymouth, Mich., has just eliminated commissions, placing clerks on full salaries, and has begun an ad campaign to alert customers to the change. Highland Superstores' compensation plan, which was based almost entirely on commissions, caused salesmen to become so aggressive that they alienated consumers; the plan also created a high turnover rate among clerks at the stores.[27]

The distrust of salespeople paid on commission and the incentive of such individuals to act in ways that are not necessarily in the best interests of either the customers or the organization has led General Motors' Saturn car division to pay its salespeople salaries rather than commissions, to "engender good customer service and teamwork among the sales force."[28] In addition, the various discount stock brokers, such as Charles Schwab and Fidelity, pay their representatives salaries rather than commissions on individual trades, a payment scheme that has not inhibited the growth of either of these highly successful organizations. Nor has it adversely affected customer service and customer retention. In fact, people from Schwab will tell you that it has been one of their secrets to success.

It is also the case that piecework has a terrible history in the United States because of employers' tendency to reset the incentive rate if employees do too well. And, "individual output-based incentive schemes, and particularly piecework, are . . . very much identified . . . with the past emphasis on a Taylorist control strategy and the ills associated with it."[29] Because of the problems with piecework, even firms known for paying for productivity on a piecework basis now have substantially more sophisticated pay systems. Lincoln Electric, for example, is famous for its piecework system as well as for its outstanding performance in making arc welding equipment and supplies and electric motors. "While Lincoln is famous for piecework, almost half of a worker's pay typically comes from the year-end bonus,"[30] which is determined by the firm's profitability as well as the worker's rating on the attributes of quality, productivity, dependability, and cooperation. Thus, an important component of the financial incentive is based on the success of the total firm, and individual employees are graded on factors that include how well they cooperate with their peers to produce Lincoln's excellent results.

If piecework has so many problems, sound evidence should show that moving to a more group-based system enhances performance, and, in fact, a rigorously done field study demonstrates precisely this. The study was conducted at a manufacturer of fabricated tubular exhaust components for the automotive industry with gross sales of $35 million and 405 hourly and fifty-nine salaried employees in 1985. "For 35 years, all of the company's hourly personnel had operated under an individually-oriented standard hour plan which paid a base hourly wage plus incentive wages for parts produced in less than standard time. . . . Groups of employees were given a raise in hourly wages equal to the average incentive wages earned by that group during the preceding five years."[31] In 1985, the company implemented a gain sharing plan that paid plant-wide bonuses for performance improvements. Because when it shifted to gain sharing the organization implemented a new labor-hour accounting system that calculated labor efficiency differently, it was not possible to investigate the direct effects of the change on productivity. Other outcomes could, however, be assessed.

Survey responses obtained two months before the transition and again 15
months later revealed improvements in perceptions of teamwork and concern for performance . . . time series analysis of over four years of objective
data showed a significant decrease in grievances and a significant increase in
product quality occurring at the time of the intervention. . . . [D]efective
products per 1000 shipped decreased from 20.93 under piecework to 2.31
under gain sharing.[32]

Furthermore, if individual merit pay has the numerous problems
described, then evidence should show that instituting such a system
does not positively affect performance. Again, a carefully-designed
study of twenty offices of the Social Security Administration that implemented merit pay as part of the Civil Service Reform Act of 1978
provides data relevant to this question. Using careful time-series analysis techniques, the study reported the following: "Our analysis of the
effects of the implementation of a performance-contingent pay program for managers indicated that its implementation had no statistically significant, gradual, permanent effect on the general trend of
organizational performance in 11 out of 12 tests."[33]

The evaluation of any change in incentive arrangements must be
carefully done to rule out alternative explanations for the results. Implementation of piecework incentives, for instance, frequently accom-
panies openness about performance data, and, on occasion, a new
policy of letting individuals know how well they are doing compared
to their fellow workers. On occasion, piecework may be implemented
in a way that specifies a goal or norm for behavior. Each of these
changes—providing individuals with information on how they are doing, providing information on how well they are doing compared to
others, giving them a specific goal or objective, and providing a financial incentive—can be the cause of increased performance. In one classic
case used to demonstrate the effectiveness of contingent (in this instance, nonmonetary) rewards, Emery Air Freight experienced much
better performance in its call centers and freight loading operations.
The improvements, in fact, occurred virtually overnight. A careful reading of the implementation of positive reinforcement, however, reveals
evidence that prior to the implementation of the program, employees
had little or no knowledge of how well they were doing along critical
performance dimensions nor much understanding of the critical aspects
of performance. One could argue that it was this knowledge of results

as well as the establishment of clear goals, rather than any incentive effects, that accounted for the improvements observed.

Because of the various problems with individualized merit pay and piecework, a growing trend is to move away from individualized pay.[34] Nevertheless, many companies continue to implement individual incentive programs as they seek to make pay both more variable and more dependent on performance. Even though "these conventional incentives focus on individual performance, not on business success, and can interfere with teamwork and problemsolving . . . nearly all firms (90%) still use such incentives to some degree."[35] These individually-based incentives fit well with the American ideology of individualism and also fit with the ideological belief that some form of financial incentive is crucial to organizational success and to solving organizational performance problems. This last myth, about the importance of financial rewards, is considered next.

HOW IMPORTANT ARE FINANCIAL INCENTIVES?

As Alfie Kohn has noted, "It is difficult to overstate the extent to which most managers and the people who advise them believe in the redemptive power of rewards."[36] The key word in that sentence is "believe," because little evidence demonstrates the efficacy of rewards, although much evidence indicates that rewards and their design loom large in management attention. That is undoubtedly because changing incentives is relatively quick and easy to do—certainly much easier than changing the culture, altering the nature of the work, increasing trust, or fundamentally redoing the relationship between people and the organizations that employ them. Also, particularly in the United States, we believe in the power of incentives; therefore, ignoring the possibility that new incentive schemes might solve organizational problems seems somehow risky or foolish.

Consider the following striking example illustrating the magnitude of our collective belief in the usefulness of incentives. On Wednesday, October 23, 1996, Air Products and Chemicals, a $4 billion manufacturer of industrial gases and chemicals, reported fourth-quarter and full-year results showing little revenue or profit growth over the preceding year. Annual sales increased less than four percent and earnings after one-time items and earnings per share rose just over four percent. The company's stock, selling at about seventeen times earnings, declined in price during the following week from the low 60s to the high 50s. And then, on October 31, the company announced a set of new management compensation and stock ownership initiatives. One of the initiatives required "company officers to attain an investment position in Air Products' stock at least equal to . . . sums ranging from two to five times their base salary." Another initiative introduced premium-priced options to encourage earnings momentum. The objective of all of the initiatives was to "strengthen the alignment of financial interests between our management team and our shareholders by significantly increasing the portion of total executive compensation determined by Air Products' short and intermediate term financial performance."[37]

The stock market apparently thought this move was *the* answer to the company's problems. In the absence of any other news about the company, on the day of the announcement of the new compensation arrangements Air Products stock closed at 60, up 1 and 1/4. The next day, November 1, the stock rose an additional 4 and 3/4 points, closing more than two points higher than its previous high for the year. In two days, the stock price had risen more than 10 percent on the strength of an announcement of a change in management incentives. The *Value Line Investment Survey*'s report on the company dated November 29, 1996, noted, "Investors seem pleased with the recently announced changes in executive compensation. . . . Since this announcement was made, AP's stock has advanced nearly 15%."[38] The implicit theory must be that prior to this announcement and the change in compensation arrangements, Air Products' executives were not sufficiently motivated or committed to doing a good job and making good decisions. Thus, this change in the financial reward system would now create more intelligent, dedicated, and hard-working executives. I had previously met many of this company's most senior executives, and they had impressed me as being very intelligent, dedicated, and quite hard working and motivated. It is difficult to believe that these changes in compensation were going to produce dramatic changes in either behavior or competence. Rather, the changes in pay practices simply provided reassurance to the financial markets, which seem to believe that incentives are all-important.

Little evidence supports this view. Literally hundreds of studies and scores of systematic reviews of incentive studies consistently document the ineffectiveness of external rewards, as admirably demonstrated in summaries by Alfie Kohn.[39] That extensive review concluded that *"rewards usually improve performance only at extremely simple—indeed, mindless—tasks, and even then they improve only quantitative performance."*[40] Relevant to the Air Products stock price reaction, a study of the effect of having incentive plans for top executives on shareholder returns found no effect,[41] a result replicated cross-culturally as well in the United States by Graef Crystal's examination of CEO compensation.[42] Again, economics Nobel prize-winner Herbert Simon provides some important insight:

> Although economic rewards play an important part in securing adherence to organizational goals and management authority, they are limited in their effectiveness. Organizations would be far less effective systems than they actually are if such rewards were the only means, or even the principal means, of motivation available.[43]

One of the reasons that financial incentives are relatively ineffective is that "in studies dating back to the 1940s, employees always have ranked other items, such as being shown appreciation for work done, feeling 'in' on things and having interesting work as being more important to them than their salaries."[44] Some of the most successful companies, such as Southwest Airlines and AES, have as one of their core values having fun. When a colleague and I interviewed people at Southwest Airlines, we were told numerous times about executives who turned down offers, often with substantial salary increases, to stay at Southwest. When we asked why, we were invariably told that the alternative work places were unpleasant. Time is priceless—no amount of money can purchase yesterday. Many people want to enjoy what they do, and a place that makes work fun and meaningful will attract and retain exceptional people. I heard similar stories at AES. Many of the employees at the Thames, Connecticut, power plant had alterative offers for more money, but came to work at AES, or stayed there, because of the discretion they were given, the learning that came as part of being given a lot of responsibility, and the good working climate that made the job enjoyable.

Hal Bennett, an entrepreneur involved in turning around a software company, has said that people will work hard if the atmosphere is fun, and it is possible to make most jobs fun if management sets out to accomplish this and basically gets out of the way and facilitates the work process. Bennett's comments, and the record of AES, Southwest, and other organizations speak to the power of nonfinancial incentives to maintain interest and enthusiasm at work. At Apple Computer in its early days, employees didn't work eighty or ninety hours a week to maximize the expected value of some discounted stream of future earnings or to maximize shareholder wealth; they did it because the work was fun and challenging and because they were changing how the world viewed personal computers.

Not only are financial incentives not the most important thing to most people, but a substantial body of research has demonstrated, both in experimental and field settings, that large external rewards can actually undermine intrinsic motivation. This process involves self-perception and retrospective sensemaking: If someone works for a large reward, when called upon to account for his or her behavior, the reward is a salient explanation—I did it for the money. When working hard for less money or for money that is less salient a rationale, people will come to see intrinsic interest in the work or the organization itself as their motivation.

An emphasis on financial incentives is controlling, and this control can set up psychological reactance in which people rebel against attempts to control their behavior. "By making that bonus contingent on certain behaviors, managers manipulate their subordinates, and that experience of being controlled is likely to assume a punitive quality over time."[45]

Deming and others in the quality movement have argued that firms emphasize financial incentives too much. Incentives, over time, come to be taken for granted and seen as rights—and, consequently, no longer produce extra effort. Incentives, particularly individual financial incentives, strain if not rupture interpersonal relationships, which is why so many of the organizations that stress teamwork and the quality of the interpersonal environment as an important component of job satisfaction don't use individual incentives. For instance, not only does Southwest Airlines reward on the basis of seniority rather than merit for its unionized employees, it basically has forgone individual incentives even at the executive ranks in favor of profit sharing and stock ownership, thus emphasizing collective rewards that build a common identification with the total organization's success. At AES, rewards are based partly on individual performance but largely on the performance of the total organization and the person's department or facility, thus building a sense of concern for the collective. Contrast this with what typically happens under individual incentive systems with the accompanying measurements of individual performance:

> Peter R. Scholtes, senior management consultant at Joiner Associates Inc., put it starkly, "Everyone is pressuring the system for individual gain. No one is improving the system for collective gain. The system will inevitably crash." Without teamwork . . . there can be no quality.[46]

All this is not to say that pay is unimportant to people. If individuals are not treated fairly, pay becomes a symbol of the unfairness and a source of discontent. If the job, or the organization, or both, are basically unpleasant, boring, or unchallenging, then pay may be the only source of satisfaction or motivation in the work environment. But, creating a fun, challenging, and empowered work environment in which individuals are able to use their abilities to do meaningful jobs for which they are shown appreciation is likely to be a more certain way to enhance motivation and performance—even though creating such an environment may be more difficult and take more time than merely turning the reward lever. This truth is recognized in the actions and decisions of many firms that are generally known as having more progressive employment policies and that are trying to build high performance work systems. As Bill Strusz, Director of Compensation at Xerox's U.S. Customers' Operations division, is fond of saying, if you focus solely on compensation and change compensation only, you will get two results: nothing will happen, and you will spend a lot of money getting there.

USING COMPENSATION TO PRODUCE PROFITS THROUGH PEOPLE

How can we understand the role of pay and its use in developing high commitment work arrangements? This task is important because innovations in pay practices arise continually, such as pay for skill or knowledge or for the number of certified competencies an employee acquires or using so-called broadbanding, that is, fewer but wider pay grades for broader job classifications. It is impossible to predict what new approaches to pay might develop in the future. After all, a large compensation consulting industry is in operation, with an interest in devising new ones all the time. Managers need a way of sifting through these various innovations, and fortunately, parsing them out is fairly easy.

We should begin by recognizing that pay has both substantive and symbolic components, and in many instances, the symbolic aspects of pay are as or even more important than the substantive ones. Two such symbolic messages come immediately to mind. If the organization enjoys increased profitability and performance as the result of the efforts of its people, then considerations of equity virtually demand that the entire work force, not just some senior managers, share in the returns through higher pay. Otherwise, organizational participants will feel cheated and will probably withhold effort and initiative. Not to share rewards equitably with organizational members sends the message that shareholder and senior management interests dominate, and this can be alienating. Stuart Hampson, chairman of the John Lewis Partnership, a retailing organization in the United Kingdom and the largest employee-owned firm in the world, stated this effect clearly.

> It cannot be right that in most businesses, incentives and rewards are focused on senior management and high flyers who . . . reap a disproportionate share of the company's success. . . . If it's worth a company's while to produce a generous package to make a chief executive feel valued and motivated, it must be worth the company's while to do the same at other levels of the business.[47]

Second, pay can send a signal about the value the organization places on its people. Although pay is not the only, or perhaps even the most important signal, in the absence of other behaviors, individuals will look to how well they are paid as a signal of whether or not the organization really values its people.

Substantively, more consistent evidence supports the effectiveness of incentive compensation at a more aggregated level, such as the division or the total organization, than at the level of the individual. In other words, profit sharing, stock ownership, gain sharing, and group bonuses seem more consistently to produce positive results than do individually-based incentive schemes. A study of thirty companies in the United Kingdom that have more than 10 percent of their issued shares held by or for employees, for example, reported that these companies "outperformed the FTSE All-Share index by 89 percent since . . . January 1992."[48] Not only do these collective reward practices produce better returns, they are also part and parcel of the use of high performance work arrangements.

One concern often heard about collective bases for rewards is the so-called free-riding problem, the idea that individuals who receive rewards based on the results attained by the group and the efforts of others may be tempted to shirk and will thus benefit disproportionately from the efforts of their colleagues. Although concern about free-riding is prominent in many economic theories of behavior, the empirical evidence for its substantive importance is surprisingly meager. People frequently do what they feel is right or fair and will often expend substantial effort not to let their colleagues down.

> The logic of the problem of collective action is . . . compelling. . . . The problem with this logic, however, is that the empirical evidence for its ability to predict actual behavior is either scant or nonexistent. . . . Under the conditions described by the theory as leading to free riding, people often cooperate instead.[49]

So, don't be reluctant to implement collective bases of rewards because of the fear of free-riding. The evidence for the effectiveness of various group incentives is compelling, while the empirical evidence for free-riding is sparse.

Perhaps the most useful way to look at pay is to note that incentive systems are an important component and determinant of an organization's culture. As such, incentive and pay schemes can be used to shape how individuals think about and approach the organization and their work. Put simply, most economic and many social psychological theories of incentives take individual motivations as given, emphasize pay, and treat as informal rewards things such as prestige among peers and group norms. In contrast, "large Japanese firms take a much more active role in shaping employee motivation than organizations are usually given credit for. They do this in part by turning small work groups and company ideology into official reward mechanisms with powerful consequences for individual motivation."[50] This possibility of shaping how employees relate to the work place rather than taking employee preferences and motivations as givens is characteristic of many successful U.S. firms, as well.

Terry Besser's study of compensation practices at Toyota Motor Manufacturing, the plant in the United States that produces almost all the Camry cars sold in America, illustrates this process. Toyota has three forms of monetary compensation: regular pay, bonus pay, and special monetary awards. Production, skilled maintenance, and clerical workers are paid by the hour and receive overtime pay. Except for clerical workers, all are called team members and belong to work teams. After attaining eighteen months seniority, all production workers receive the same pay. Bonus pay is a percentage of wages. Consequently, team members receive the same bonus after eighteen months on the job. Team leaders receive only a 5 percent differential. Consequently, "81 percent of TMM's employees receive roughly the same pay with distinctions based on job category, not individual performance."[51] Special award money goes to groups that have made suggestions that result in safety, cost, or quality improvements. Awards go equally to all group members. Instead of giving the awards in cash, they are provided in the form of merchandise certificates redeemable at local general merchandise stores. "Gift certificates require the purchase of a tangible item which continually reminds the team member and his/her family of the rewards for *kaizens* [small, incremental improvements in the work process] in a way that money spent on a few beers, or put in the bank, would not."[52]

Equal pay promotes feelings of equality and helps strengthen the bonds among team members and, in fact, among all people in the plant. The bonus system and rewards for suggestions promote the belief that individuals will benefit to the extent that the organization is effective. The company uses recognition ceremonies and awards such as plaques to highlight quality, safety, and attendance achievements. Through the provision of job security, the use of job rotation and enrichment, and rewards that build a sense of shared community, Toyota has been able to make tolerable what is essentially boring or dull work—by placing it in a social context in which peer support and group membership become valuable rewards derived from work.

The community of fate and the work team alleviate some of the worst effects of monotonous work. . . . [T]hey do not, however, transform the jobs themselves into interesting work. . . . [T]he actual work people perform is the same at TMM as at non-team, large-batch assembly operations. The difference between a job in a team organization, like Toyota, and that same job in a non-team organization is primarily in the context of the job, i.e., in the social milieu of the work team and in the feeling of community of fate.[53]

Although most traditional approaches to understanding pay emphasize individual incentive effects, increasing evidence shows that such a view is much too narrow. Pay not only sets the social context and shapes the environment, as at Toyota, but pay systems can either inhibit or promote organizational learning. Consider the positive effects of gain sharing, for instance. To view gain sharing simply as an incentive system is incorrect, for this perspective fails "to capture the potential for organizational transformation of these plans."[54] In an innovative longitudinal study at a manufacturing plant that had introduced a suggestion system along with a gain sharing plan, Jeffrey Arthur and Lynda Aiman-Smith examined 436 suggestions made during the first four years of the plan. They noticed a distinct time trend. The proportion of suggestions dealing with material savings and with doing previously contracted work more cheaply in-house decreased over time, while suggestions for changes in the work process and product improvements increased over time. They argued that gain sharing, by changing the fundamental social system in the plant through participative management, labor-management cooperation, and increased communication and information, facilitated second-order, deeper learning. This study and others that have demonstrated the effects of gain sharing and similar interventions suggest that the impressive results may occur as much through learning and fundamental organizational change as through simple incentive mechanisms.

It is also important to remember that appropriate compensation policies are only one element in a set of practices that constitute high performance work arrangements, and that while compensation practices can affect the organization's culture and its social system, these practices do not, by themselves, determine that culture or the nature of the employment relation. The example of United Airlines illustrates all of this quite well. In July, 1994, United became the largest employee-owned company in the United States when, in return for substantial wage concessions, managers and unionized pilots and mechanics received stock and representation on the board of directors in return for wage concessions. By January, 1997, the pilots, who had led the employee buy-out, voted down a new contract offer by a four-to-one margin and poor labor relations at the airline made the news. Some observers took this as a signal that employee stock ownership was ineffective, in spite of the massive systematic empirical evidence to the contrary.

In fact, the United case illustrates several things. First, simply changing one organizational practice—compensation—will not necessarily overcome a history of adversarial labor relations and implement high performance work arrangements. Second, compensation arrangements by themselves can affect but cannot fully change an organization's culture. In the United case, flight attendants did not participate in the wage concessions or the stock ownership, making the labor situation worse. However, the basic problem was with the persistence of outmoded views of the labor-management relation on the part of both the United management and its unions, public relations language to the contrary:

> From the outset, it lacked farsightedness: both workers and managers seemed to see it as a one-off cost-cutting exercise. . . . [S]enior managers now express the view that the ESOP should be seen as no more than a temporary restructuring tool.[55]

When it was time for a new round of bargaining with the pilots, United's management decided to hold a practice run-through of the arbitration process mandated by the contract, something that deepened employee mistrust.[56] The pilots and other employees were unhappy that large bonuses were given in 1996 to six hundred top managers even as employee salaries were contractually restrained. This decision and the reaction it provoked illustrates a third important point: Both economic sacrifice and economic gain should be shared. Finally, the United example demonstrates the critical role of point of view and perspective in affecting reactions to compensation arrangements and the resulting motivation and satisfaction. Within the company, management attributed much of United's improved economic performance since 1994 to macroeconomic factors, while its employees saw the rebound as a result of their hard work. As Joseph R. Blasi, a professor of labor relations at Rutgers noted, "Management and labor never really changed their fundamental points of view."[57] Thus, the new compensation arrangements, never part of a totally changed work system, had only limited impact.

Employee stock ownership and what it symbolically represented certainly helped, but by itself it was simply insufficient to change the management-employee culture at United Airlines.

CONCLUSION

It is patently incorrect to view individual motivation as either fixed or determined exclusively by forces outside of the organization, although clearly the larger social context matters. Rather, individual motivation and the relationship of people to one another and to their organization are shaped by what the organization does—including what it does in its compensation system. Unfortunately, many organizations use compensation practices that do harm on multiple levels—and then try to fix that damage by further tinkering with the incentive system that created the problems in the first place.

Organizational incentive systems send important messages about how and what the organization thinks of its members. A system that is reasonably complicated and comprehensive, rewarding myriad micro behaviors, sends the message that management believes people won't do what is necessary unless they are rewarded for every little thing. A system of micro-level behavioral or outcome incentives also tends to convey an absence of trust, implying that people must be measured and rewarded for everything or they won't do what is expected of them. A system that focuses on reducing labor rates sends a message that the organization does not value or respect the contributions of its people. Rather, the objective is to pay as little as possible and, perhaps, get by with as low quality a work force as possible.

Individual incentive schemes erode teamwork and trust and set people against one another in a competition for rewards. Such systems do not promote sharing knowledge. Why should I teach you if we are competing for a fixed pool of salary raises? Such systems also don't do much to promote concern about organizational well-being. Climbing the corporate rank or salary ladder becomes a more important objective than ensuring the organization's overall success, particularly if job security is limited and the real goal is to get ready for a move to the next job, building a track record through a salary history and not by actual accomplishments.

By emphasizing financial rewards above all else, organizations signal that money is basically all they provide to those who work in them—not fun or meaningful work, only pay. Intrinsic motivation diminishes. Most perniciously, in their emphasis on financial incentives, managers and their organizations neglect and ignore other, nonfinancial aspects of the motivational environment.

Clearly, the problems discussed in this chapter do not afflict all organizations. Many have learned the lessons of cooperation and teamwork and the importance of fun as a basic principle of organization. But, too few firms are in this category, and the learning is coming too slowly. Perhaps this is because the compensation consulting industry sells services that tinker with incentive systems, touting this as a panacea and continuing to fix and adjust the incentives when the first plan fails. Perhaps it is because, at least in the United States, many people believe in a simple economic ideology that emphasizes incentives. Perhaps it is because adjusting rewards is easier than remedying basic problems of too much stultifying control and too little meaning or enjoyment in the job. But for whatever reasons, managers should ignore the many blandishments and the temptation to try to solve most of their organizational problems through pay. Rather, they should keep the myths and issues discussed in this chapter firmly in mind when thinking about their pay systems and about how they want to build their organizations.

8 ◆ *Can You Manage with Unions?*

WHY SHOULD ORGANIZATIONS CARE whether they can succeed in working with unions? Aren't labor organizations relics of a bygone age, out of place and in rapid decline in a world of global competition? Maybe and maybe not. Managers need to be able to develop cooperative and positive working relationships with labor unions for several reasons.

1. Most industrialized countries other than the United States have much higher rates of unionization. If a company is going to be a truly global player, it had better not only get used to working with labor, but actually develop some skill and maybe even some comparative advantage in doing so.

2. Even in the U.S. labor environment, simply extrapolating declining union density (the proportion of the labor force covered by collective bargaining) may not be wise. Unionization has never been simply about money; it has also been about job security and control over the work environment. A climate of economic insecurity potentially favors unionization. As autonomy, even of professionals, erodes in organizations that do not implement high commitment work practices, the attraction of unionization increases. In fact, managed health care, with its regimentation and loss of autonomy by doctors, has stimulated even physicians in both public and private hospitals and clinics to join labor organi-

zations.[1] If union density begins to recover, firms that work constructively with labor will enjoy an advantage over those whose labor relations are stuck in the dark ages.

3. Some, although certainly not all, of contemporary labor organizations actively advocate and negotiate for the implementation of many elements of high performance management practices. Therefore, these organizations can be important allies in making the change to high commitment management.

4. Finally, and most basically, firms cannot be serious about "putting people first" if they are unwilling or unable to work constructively with employees' representative organizations.

But many managers and organizations have a long way to go to begin working constructively with labor organizations and profiting from doing so. A mind set or perspective obstructs their progress. Mention the words "labor union" to a group of executives, particularly U.S. executives, but many others as well, and their blood pressure goes up. Management ideology in the United States "has never accepted the legitimacy of union representation. . . . While firms that were unionized during the period 1935–1955 eventually learned to live with their unions . . . firms that were not unionized during that period often determined to stay that way."[2]

This negative reaction stems from the perception that labor unions are, for the most part, impediments to management control in the work place and hindrances to achieving competitive levels of costs, quality, and productivity. The conventional wisdom maintains that even if the labor movement had at one time been necessary to achieve socially useful gains in areas such as occupational safety, child welfare and protection at work, and obtaining higher wages and better benefits, those days are past. Today, many managers would argue, governments in the major industrialized countries enforce laws about wages and hours, work place safety, and child labor, and market forces should control wages in industries that increasingly compete on a worldwide basis. Unions are seen as industrial fossils, remnants of some bygone era. And, union effects on productivity are presumed to be deleterious. The assumption is that "unencumbered by the interests, goals, and countervailing power of unions, non-union employers are free . . . to set the terms and conditions of employment that they believe will maximize performance and profitability."[3] These unencumbered choices will presumably be more efficiency-producing than those made under union influence.

Because of these beliefs, management, again led by U.S. executives, has decided to fight unions. Union organizing campaigns are resisted vigorously and decertification elections to remove unions as bargaining agents for a firm's employees are also increasing in frequency.[4] The proportion of the U.S. labor force covered by collective bargaining has decreased dramatically to less than 15 percent, a figure that masks the real extent of union decline. Unions remain strong in the public sector, where some 43.5 percent of workers are covered by collective bargaining.[5] Teachers, police and firefighters, municipal workers, and health care employees, for example, are all frequently unionized largely because elected officials are reluctant to take the aggressive posture of many of their private sector counterparts. Much of the decline of unionization, therefore, has occurred in the private sector, where the proportion of organized workers approaches 10 percent.

Although labor movements in other industrialized countries tend to be stronger than in the United States, the decline in unionization, while far from universal, is becoming widespread, particularly over the last decade or so. Because the decline in unionization in the United States has proceeded more rapidly than in other countries, however, the difference in union density (the proportion of the work force unionized) between the United States and other countries more than doubled from 1970 to the late 1980s. "In 1986–1987, U.S. density was 36 points below the average, compared with 17 points below the average in 1970."[6] U.S.-based firms tend not to have to work with labor unions, which has at times presented problems when the companies open operations overseas requiring that they manage with unions and works councils. In many instances, they are neither temperamentally nor managerially prepared to do so.

It is important to recognize that the decline in unionization does not simply reflect the result of unencumbered employee choices or the operation of market forces. It has been assisted by actions of the state. When U.S. President Ronald Reagan fired air traffic controllers who went on strike in 1981, he helped set the tone for labor relations generally and legitimized the hiring of replacement workers. Laws in countries other than the United States have also been changed and government policies instituted to weaken the role of trade unions in the labor market. Great Britain, under former Prime Minister Margaret Thatcher, introduced tough labor legislation and followed policies designed to weaken the labor movement generally and the coal and transport unions specifically.[7] The Employment Contracts Act in New Zealand has made operating a non-union work place easier. Ironically, this law was passed under a labor party government. Labor law reform in Germany, undertaken to enhance labor market flexibility, has also begun to slightly weaken the power of unions. In each instance, these state interventions were made under the presumption that national economic well-being and international competitiveness would be enhanced by weakening unions.

Managements' and governments' beliefs about harmful effects from unions and the concomitant effort to weaken them, a growing trend in many industrialized countries, is unfortunately not based on much actual evidence that unions are inevitably or invariably harmful to organizations, their productivity, or their profits. In fact, the data are remarkably clear in the other direction: Absolutely no evidence exists that unions adversely affect productivity, the rate of technical innovation,[8] the competitiveness of companies or industries on a worldwide basis,[9] or, except under conditions of high economic concentration, firm profitability.[10] Research from the construction industry shows that, under some circumstances, unions actually increase productivity, for instance in the building of commercial office space[11] and private hospitals.[12] The general conclusion now is that "it is the *state of labor relations rather than unionism and collective bargaining per se that determines productivity.*"[13]

A study of 115 relatively small manufacturing companies distributed over a number of industries in the United Kingdom, each with between 80 and 200 employees, investigated the determinants of organizational innovation. Innovation was believed to be important because "firms which are skillful at innovation—the successful exploitation of new ideas—will secure competitive advantage in rapidly changing world markets; those which are not will be overtaken."[14] The study examined innovation along a number of dimensions including new products, production technology, production processes, and work organization and administrative practices. The research concluded that "unionised companies are more innovative than non-unionised companies."[15]

Another claim, frequently made but also not supported by the data, is that unionization hinders the adoption of high-involvement work practices and work place innovations, such as the use of teams. It is certainly the case that examples can be found of unions that have resisted work place change. For example, "a union local at a large manufacturing plant that recently won a quality award refused to participate in the company's quality efforts when invited to do so."[16] But large sample quantitative studies generally find unionization has either no effect or a positive effect on work place change. Robert Drago's study of the survival rates of quality circles in a sample of establishments in metropolitan Milwaukee, found that unionization was *positively* related to the survival of quality circles. In fact, unionization was more predictive of quality circle survival than any other factor examined in the study, including a measure of the extent of participative management.[17] A study of 325 manufacturing plants that examined union effects on quality and employee participation efforts showed that "workplaces with employee participation achieve greater improvements in quality than more traditional workplaces. . . . [E]stablishments with jointly administered programs achieve quality improvements substantially greater than those achieved through either management-controlled programs or traditional collective bargaining relationships that exclude direct participation activities."[18] When the plant had a participation program jointly administered by the union, the likelihood of achieving much higher quality was almost 40 percent and the odds of achieving no improvement was only 14 percent. "When participation programs were controlled by management . . . these likelihoods are reversed."[19]

A study of over two thousand workplaces in Australia concluded that "those workplaces with active unions and bargaining relationships reported *twice* the level of work restructuring of other workplaces."[20] Examining the proportion of an establishment's core employees who received formal off-the-job training and using a nationally representative survey of U.S. establishments as the source of the data, Paul Osterman found that "unionism is . . . significantly related to training effort by establishments."[21] Because the analysis controlled for numerous other possible explanations of training effort, the union effect is net of factors such as establishment size, gender composition, and the educational attainment of employees and the skill requirements of the job. Thus, the existing evidence is consistent with the view that union involvement is likely to increase the training effort and enhance the success of quality improvement efforts as well as positively affect the continuation of work place reforms, compared to situations that are management-controlled and nonunion.

The problems experienced by management and their organizations from organized labor are frequently due to the failure to achieve a mutually beneficial relationship and accommodative working arrangement. In this struggle, neither side is wholly blameless. American management has been unusually vigorous, compared to management in other industrialized countries, in resisting unionization. Labor leaders, for their part, have occasionally eschewed opportunities for building cooperative working relationships. In the steel industry, for instance, a pattern of joint labor-management cooperation and consultation was established with the impetus of the federal government during World War II, the government's interest being to maximize wartime production and to avoid labor disputes that might cripple the war effort. When the war ended, the steel union leadership, under Phil Murray, did not try to extend the pattern of interaction that had been established and, instead, reverted to the typical arm's-length bargaining over a narrow range of economic issues.

Many U.S. labor leaders, as contrasted with their counterparts in other countries, traditionally have forgone trying to have a say in work place governance and have been content simply to bargain over wages, benefits, and working conditions. This strategy has left these union officials largely ignorant of how well the companies were actually doing and uninformed about their business or technology strategies. Both they and their company counterparts have often preferred to have union members uninvolved in any form of joint decision making that might benefit both unionized workers and the firms that employ them. More recently, some labor leaders, particularly in the automobile and the steel industries, have pushed for greater involvement in joint efforts to improve organizational competitiveness and to increase productivity by using the talents and knowledge of all people. It is now the case that "joint labor-management programs have been established at approximately half of all unionized establishments."[22] And, the debate on union involvement has largely shifted from whether to participate to how and under what conditions to participate. Nonetheless, efforts at joint union-management cooperation and decision making have been resisted on occasion by labor leaders and union members who have feared being coopted and becoming too friendly with the "enemy."

The existing data support the idea that "the labor-management climate is a key determinant of whether positive collective voice effects or negative restrictive union effects are dominant."[23] This chapter first reviews the benefits of moving from an adversarial to a more cooperative labor relations climate and then provides evidence that such benefits are substantial. I also describe the case of Magma Copper, which illustrates how to move from suffering the price of war with employees to enjoying the benefits of labor peace. The chapter then considers why some firms have forgone opportunities to eliminate unions when they have had the opportunity to do so and why some firms have even invited union representation.

Throughout this discussion, it will be clear that unions have the potential (obviously not always realized) to enhance organizational performance. This is because unions often, although not invariably, take a longer term view of organizational success and performance and thus can help management resist short-term pressures to curtail training, cut wages, and lay people off, actions that produce immediate economic gain at the cost of the long-term strength and viability of the organization. Certainly little evidence shows unions to be invariably harmful to organizational well-being, and some progressive labor organizations and leaders have pushed for arrangements that closely resemble the various practices associated with high performance work arrangements. All of this suggests that, instead of a generalized negative approach, managers would be well-served to be more nuanced in their thinking about unions and to manage their union relationships in ways that create economic value rather than destroy it.

ECONOMIC GAINS FROM COOPERATIVE UNION-MANAGEMENT RELATIONS

A number of studies have documented a significant correlation between labor-management relations in unionized plants and measures of organizational performance. A study of twenty-five automobile manufacturing plants, for instance, found a strong positive relationship between participation in suggestion programs, involvement in quality of work-life programs, and workers' attitudes and both direct labor efficiency and product quality. The same study also found strong negative relationships between the grievance rate and the disciplinary actions rate and both labor efficiency and product quality.[24] Although this study was cross-sectional, and therefore open to the interpretation that positive performance made good industrial relations possible rather than the other way around, a number of longitudinal studies demonstrate the causal effect of industrial relations climate on organizational effectiveness. As one example, a study of nine unionized paper mills over the 1976 to 1982 period reported that the more grievances filed, the lower was the plant's productivity.[25] A study of eighteen General Motors plants over a nine-year period also found an effect of industrial relations performance on economic performance.[26]

One of the more interesting quantitative demonstrations of both the dimensions of labor-management relations and their effects on a number of aspects of manufacturing performance comes from a study of the primary manufacturing facility for Xerox located in Rochester, New York. The plant was organized by the Amalgamated Clothing and Textile Workers Union and the study covered the period from January 1984 through January of 1987. The basic premise of the study was that economic performance was affected by two things: first, how conflicts were resolved in the work place, and second, how (and whether) common concerns were pursued through cooperative activity.[27] One interesting finding of the study was that "even within this single manufacturing complex, widely recognized as a leading example of new developments in industrial relations, there is wide variation in the patterns of labor management relations."[28] Some areas were characterized by close supervision and little cooperation on common problems, reflecting an adversarial climate, while other areas featured autonomous work groups and a high level of problem solving.

Ten indicators or measures were used to distinguish traditional from transformational labor relations within the Xerox manufacturing plant.[29]

1. The frequency of conflict;

2. The speed of conflict resolution;

3. The number of grievances that went to the third and fourth steps in the process;

4. The extent to which there was minor problem solving;

5. The degree of major problem solving activities;

6. The amount of informal worker autonomy;

7. The amount of formal worker autonomy (the number of autonomous work groups in operation);

8. The frequency of feedback on cost, quality, and schedule;

9. Frequency of worker-initiated changes in work design; and

10. The extent to which problems were settled informally prior to initiating grievance procedures.

Table 8-1 presents the differences in performance on measures of cost, quality, adherence to production schedule, and productivity between the traditional and the transformed labor relations units. The data clearly indicate that "traditional labor-management patterns were associated with higher cost levels, more worker hours lost to scrap, a higher level of monthly defects per worker, greater delivery variance, greater productivity variance, and a lower net return from hours worked."[30]

Some vivid case examples, many in the steel and automobile industries, further demonstrate the benefits to be gained from moving from an adversarial to a more cooperative labor relations climate. At New United Motors, in order to forge a different relationship with the United Auto Workers' Union, the joint venture agreed to a much higher level of union involvement in decision making. Applications for the hourly jobs of Team Members and Team Leaders were jointly evaluated by managers and union officials.[31] The union also played a role in selecting the management personnel that did not come from General Motors. Furthermore, management at NUMMI was committed "to joint union/management investigation of work problems; advance consultation on layoffs, schedule changes, and major investments; and joint union/management review of unusual or mitigating circumstances in advance of discharges or suspensions."[32] General Motors learned an

Table 8-1 ECONOMIC PERFORMANCE DIFFERENCES BETWEEN
            TRADITIONAL AND TRANSFORMED LABOR RELATIONS
            IN A XEROX MANUFACTURING PLANT

Measure	Traditional	Transformational
Production-related spending	5.0	2.3
Worker hours lost to scrap	.0008	.0002
Defects per worker	1.2	0.7
Delivery variance (deliveries ahead or behind schedule; negative values indicate deliveries are ahead of schedule)	.006	−.003
Productivity variance (variance from internal standard productivity performance)	−.35	−.24
Net return to direct hours worked	5.1	6.1

Source: Joel Cutcher-Gershenfeld, "The Impact on Economic Performance of a
   Transformation in Workplace Relations," *Industrial and Labor Relations Review* 44
   (1991): 254.

important lesson about union-management cooperation from the
NUMMI experience as well as from its past unsuccessful history of
adversarial labor relations. When it established the Saturn Corporation,
it set up an organization in which "all management positions are co-
occupied by representatives of the company and the union," a degree
of codetermination that is unusual even by German standards.[33]

   In the steel industry, the LTV Corporation has achieved excellent
results in a new plant that makes zinc-galvanized steel for automobile
manufacturers and employs about one hundred people, seventy-one of
whom are union members. In the plant, union members constitute the
hiring committee for new workers. Job classifications are not used, and
pay is based on the number of skills people acquire. Employees get a
pay raise after a six-month trial period, and, beyond that, "pay increases
are based on learning how to do different jobs."[34] People in the plant
"make sales calls, visit customers to solve any quality problems, and
help select suppliers."[35] Senior workers train newer employees and both
desirable and less desirable jobs are shared among the work force.

Management and labor wear the same uniforms, all parking is unreserved, and workers and management share the same cafeteria. Most importantly, when the plant was established, the company agreed that it would not try to avoid the union if the union would, in turn, explore working with management cooperatively, with a goal of boosting productivity.

This new way of working cooperatively was developed in an industry, steel, that has been noted for its adversarial labor relations.

> "When I came into this industry in the 1950's, the attitude was the less you did the better—people looked for hideaways so they could sleep," Mr. Vernon, the plant manager said. "Later, when I went into management, my job was to find the guys sleeping and give them a talk."[36]

Although the LTV arrangement developed in a new plant without a history of on-site conflict, and NUMMI and Saturn both represented start-ups to some degree, the case of Magma Copper, described below, offers a dramatic illustration of both the transformation of an adversarial culture in an existing work place and documentation of the substantial economic gains that accrue to the organizations that have leaders who are able to effect such changes.

THE CASE OF MAGMA COPPER

The fourth largest copper mining company in the United States, Magma Copper was created as a spin-off from Newmont Mining in 1987. It had 4,300 employees, 75 percent of whom were represented by one of nine unions;[37] its sales were about $700 million. In 1988, Magma's shareholder equity (the number of shares times the price per share) was worth about $200 million, and the company was saddled with a huge debt burden of $400 million. Because it was the industry's highest cost producer,[38] Magma's very survival was in doubt. In 1989 it faced the task of negotiating new contracts with its unions, the largest of which was the Steelworkers' Union. The company's relationship with its unions had been hostile, to say the least, a relationship typical of other mines in the state. Arizona copper mining had been characterized by a years' long war with labor, with the companies backed by the state, which supplied police and National Guard to ensure strikebreakers access to the mines.[39] Phelps Dodge, another company with copper mines in Arizona, had invited a series of bitter strikes in the early 1980s to break the union and was well on its way to becoming a completely non-union operator. Magma management were very much caught up in the Arizona copper mining environment and mind-set. "The unions viewed management as an autocratic group that cared little for the employees. Management viewed the unions as inflexible and short-sighted."[40]

In 1988, Burgess Winter, an Irishman, left Kennecott Copper to become president and CEO of Magma. He set out to establish a different labor relations strategy, designed to produce outstanding economic returns. In 1996, Magma was purchased by BHP, the Australian steel and minerals corporation, for $2 billion. In just eight years, the shareholders enjoyed a ten-fold return on their investment, not in a high technology or other glamorous industry, but in copper mining. They achieved this return not because management continued to wage war with the work force, finally managing to break the union, but because the new leadership of Magma had the wisdom and courage to pursue a collaborative partnership with the union and the workers it represented.

The July 1989 contract negotiations represented a turning point for Magma. They had been conducted under the usual, adversarial conditions, with both sides bracing for a strike.

> The company brought in sleeping trailers and soup kitchens and made plans to hire replacement workers. Sporadic violence erupted; bombs were placed in the company's underground mine, shots even fired at Mr. Winter's home.[41]

Although the contract was finally signed without a strike, the working environment was poor. The accident rate in the mine was increasing, little progress was being made cutting operating costs, and an expansion and modernization program was providing little benefit. Magma had spent several hundred million dollars installing new, state-of-the-art equipment, but the equipment would not be worth much if the employees would not use it effectively and were tempted to sabotage the production process. The new labor agreement contained within it a provision calling for the parties to work toward joint cooperation, a provision that few probably took seriously when it was inserted. But that fall, Burgess Winter decided to try a different approach.

Mr. Winter told Marsh Campbell, Magma's vice president of human resources, that he wanted to end the company's us-versus-them adversarial relationship and to find a way to tap employees' knowledge—and their help—in turning the company around.[42]

Campbell had twenty-five years of experience in labor negotiations.

Campbell saw old hostilities and resentments preventing both sides from discussing future possibilities without a dramatic breakthrough. He believed ... management and the unions first had to deal with the deep-rooted animosities that clouded every discussion and then to jointly create a plan for the future. Campbell recommended Magma take a fresh course—one based on honest, candid discussion of mutual objectives and a joint willingness to do things differently.[43]

The company and the union began the reconciliation process by jointly hiring an outside consultant, Bob Mueller, to help them work through the residue left by years of hostility and bitterness. "Through this single participative act of selecting the consultant, a foundation of trust was laid and a working relationship forged."[44] On October 17 and 18, a two-day off-site meeting with seventeen high ranking union and management personnel was held. After spending the first day venting their pent-up emotions, the participants on the second day established a Joint Union-Management Cooperation Committee (JUMCC), "a high-level policy committee responsible for overseeing, developing, and implementing cooperative labor relations at Magma Copper."[45] On October 20, 1989, workers arriving at Magma were treated to an unusual sight: At the plant gate, Burgess Winter and "United Council chairman/boilermaker journeyman Harry Clark greet[ed] Magma employees with copies of the commitment to cooperation."[46] Marsh Campbell has said that, fortunately, the company was too poor to afford fancy offices in a city. Its headquarters were at the mine. That made it somewhat easier and more natural for the CEO to be at the work site, but by making the difficult effort personally to deliver copies of the new cooperation agreement to arriving workers, Winter and Clark sent an important symbolic message to the work force: Things were going to be different.

A statement of principles and philosophy had come out of the union-management meeting, a portion of which is reproduced as Exhibit 8-1.

Note that the agreement specifically mentions job security and also explicitly recognizes the role of the union. The statement of principles was followed shortly by an extensive set of training activities for the company's nearly four hundred supervisors. Between 1989 and 1993, the company spent more than $5 million on "employee-management training and other employee-involvement efforts."[47] Winter, the CEO, spoke at each of these training sessions at both the opening and closing, again providing visible evidence of senior management's commitment to the process. The company also sponsored a "series of two-day meetings comprising local union leaders, shop stewards, and mid-level managers and supervisors. These meetings were designed to be educational, team building workshops. . . . Over ten months, about 700 employees from the San Manuel and Pinto Valley operations attended those meetings where past concerns were addressed, major issues tackled, and plans for the future forged."[48]

Exhibit 8-1 SOME OF THE PRINCIPLES AND PHILOSOPHY
EXPRESSED IN THE 1989 UNION-MANAGEMENT
COOPERATION COMMITTEE JOINT STATEMENT

Our vision is to create an economically viable, profitable company that provides job security.

To accomplish this economic viability, the Company and Union mutually recognize the link between productivity and job security.

In creating a company with a high degree of economic viability and job security, everyone must be committed to the principles of fairness, honesty, and integrity.

The Company and the Union recognize the role of collective bargaining but are committed to moving more concerns into the area of joint problem solving.

The above must be accomplished with regard and recognition as to the dignity and existence of the Union and the Company.

Source: George W. Bohlander and Marshall H. Campbell, "Problem-Solving Bargaining and
Work Redesign: Magma Copper's Labor-Management Partnership," *National Productivity
Review* 12 (Autumn 1993): 522. Copyright © 1993 (John Wiley & Sons). Reprinted by
permission of John Wiley & Sons, Inc.

The company and the union also launched a series of work improvement projects on a substantial scale.

> Each of the company's five divisions was asked to make a quantum productivity gain or cost savings through adoption of a significant "breakthrough project." . . . [T]ackled projects needed to have definable outcomes in time and measurement for initial and ongoing results *and* they had to champion the cooperative labor-management partnership. Projects were started and completed through the use of . . . teams composed of equal numbers of employees, supervisors, and/or managers.[49]

The new working relationship and the success of the productivity and work improvement projects inspired the company and the union to reconsider the contract they had signed in 1989. Both parties voluntarily agreed to sign a new contract eight months prior to the old one's expiration in the summer of 1992. This 1991 contract was unusual in several respects. First, it was fifteen years in duration. The three-year negotiating cycle traditional in the copper industry hampered productivity because little was done in the last year of the contract. Second, the new contract guaranteed no work stoppages for eight years. "That's enough time, says Mr. Winter, for the sweeping management changes and worker-participation programs . . . to show results."[50] Third, the contract created "joint labor-management 'work redesign' teams to develop ways of increasing productivity, including how jobs are structured and managed."[51] The contract also created joint problem-solving teams to resolve contract disputes and provided for binding arbitration over economic issues. Reflecting the new management-employee relationship, the contract was developed in a different way.

> [C]ontract proposals were developed by five joint labor-management teams (overall there were 40 representatives from each side) and then refined by a 28-member core team, also equally balanced between union and management representatives.[52]

The company and the union approached designing and negotiating a contract the same way they approached all other work place issues—jointly, collaboratively, and cooperatively. Marsh Campbell, the human resources executive intimately involved in this effort, drew this lesson about the building of trust in a situation that had once been hostile.

[A] compelling issue for labor and management has been the building of a trusting relationship. Since 1989, both sides have taken specific steps to demonstrate their commitment to cooperation. . . . [N]early all these actions have been jointly driven, for example: the joint hiring of consultants; the jointly written statement of the principles and philosophies of the cooperative relationship; joint creation and membership in the JUMCC; the joint participation of senior company officials and union officers in organizational development workshops and training sessions; joint membership in division strategic planning committees, department steering committees, and design teams.[53]

Another important step in building a different union-management relationship entailed implementation of a new gain sharing program.

The concept of gainsharing is simple: any employee-generated economic benefits from increases in productivity and cost reductions are shared between the company and the workers. In reality, the concept is far more complicated and must consider the complexity of integrated copper production, variations in ore grade, the impact of capital projects . . . and the need for accurate measures. . . . [T]hrough the commitment of labor-management teams, Magma was able to solve tough plan design issues. . . . The plans were implemented in July 1991 and are considered to be a major ingredient in the goal to further boost productivity.[54]

By 1992, just three years after the company and the union began working in a different way, Magma Copper was well on its way to economic recovery. In July 1992, *Business Week* ranked the company first in percentage stock price appreciation on the New York Stock Exchange during the first half of that year. Between 1988 and 1991, operating costs per pound of copper decreased 24 percent, production from the company's mines grew 30 percent, and "employee-management cooperation has proven to be the basis for Magma's astonishing 50 percent increase in productivity."[55]

One of the most noteworthy results of the Magma turnaround was the development of the Kalamazoo ore body at the company's main mine in San Manuel, Arizona. The ore in that mine was scheduled to run out in 1997, at which time the mine would close and 1,300 jobs would be lost. The Kalamazoo (or "K") ore body at the same site, it was believed, could not be mined economically because of its inaccessibility. "The company had spent more than $150 million trying to come up with new technology to develop the K but had abandoned the project."[56] One of the breakthrough project teams tackled the task of developing this ore body. They recommended implementing high-performance work teams and giving employees a say in work scheduling, team composition, and work methods. They also recommended a change in the role of the supervisor to that of facilitator and supporter.[57] The results of the team's efforts were so successful that the Kalamazoo ore was mined economically.

> When the pilot program began in October 1990, the mining rate was 1,000 tons of ore a day. By December 1990, the high-performance team of 150 employees increased extraction tonnage to 6,000 tons a day while reducing production costs from $7 to $5.25 per ton of ore. . . . [B]y the end of the second study in 1991, the mining rate of ore reached 11,000 tons a day, nearly double the design rate, and extraction costs fell to $3.80 per ton of ore mined. . . . According to study goals, when mining cost at the San Manuel mine fell below $4 per ton of ore, then nearly $100 million would be committed to the complete development of the K-orebody. Extraction costs at San Manuel dropped below $4 per ton of ore in September 1992.[58]

The company's successful efforts to change the way it worked with its unions and the economic results it garnered brought it extensive publicity and favorable comment. The organization itself "believes it enjoys a substantial competitive advantage in the mining industry as the foremost innovator of high-involvement human resource programs and processes—processes that are beyond 'change.'"[59] But, although extensively discussed in the mining industry as well as in general industry publications, surprisingly, the lessons from the Magma experience have not been widely imitated by other firms either in mining or in other industries with a unionized work force. Many of the changes made at Magma entailed a sharing of power with employees and their organizations that leaders are often not willing to undertake, regardless of the economic benefits from doing so.

WHY KEEP A UNION?

It is one thing to decide to work collaboratively with a labor union, recognizing the costs of conflict and the benefits from mutual collaboration, but it is something else again to decide not to attempt to weaken or get rid of a union that has weakened to the point that efforts to eliminate it would be likely to succeed. Instances in which opportunities to weaken or eliminate a union were forgone seem to defy the conventional wisdom of the benefits of union avoidance, but many good reasons support going against the crowd.

In the late 1980s, the American Telephone and Telegraph plant in Mesquite, Texas, near Dallas, faced severe operating problems.[60] A manufacturer of power supplies and energy equipment, including rectifiers, controllers, and distribution equipment, the factory was far from world class standards in cost, cycle time, access to customers, and quality. Its material handling and quality problems were so severe that the plant was closed on average one day a week, and scrap costs were in the millions of dollars per year. The plant had experienced a series of layoffs with employment falling from 3,500 in 1985 to 2,000 by 1988, and rumors were circulating that the plant might shut down completely, with the production moving to Mexico. Trust in the work place was almost nonexistent. The workers did not trust the management who, they felt, "expected them to check their brains at the door."[61] Management believed the employees basically were seeking to avoid expending any more effort than necessary and did not care about the wellbeing of the company. The employees did not trust the union and its leadership either. In fact, just before the turnaround in the plant started, the local union went into receivership.

When Ken Weatherford was brought in to turn the plant around, in addition to reorganizing the manufacturing process and making a number of cultural changes, he had to decide what to do about the plant's union. With the threat of closure hanging over the work force, many factors contributed to making decertification of the union a very real possibility: the factory's jobs paid well compared to other jobs in the local labor market; the rank and file employees highly distrusted the union leadership; the union was in receivership; and the plant was located in a conservative, right-to-work state. But instead of trying to weaken the union, Weatherford worked with it. Along with other managers, Weatherford developed a series of initiatives that included the following: "Consult with union leaders and involve them in the process of making changes and of formulating new employee policies, such as an absenteeism policy, a 'poor performers' program, more flexible work rules, and others."[62] Moreover, when the decision was made to establish a team to act as agents of change, the local union president helped choose the members.

This seemingly strange course of action is actually quite sensible. First of all, in a plant already confronting substantial performance problems, it made little sense to create even more problems and issues by taking on the union. Enough had to be done to implement focused factories and just-in-time manufacturing without diverting time and attention to an attempt to rid the plant of the union. Second, in a plant facing considerable change and, consequently, having a pressing need to communicate both the need for change and the content of new work processes, the union afforded yet another channel of communication and was another possible agent of change, as long as it was on Weatherford's side. Finally, in a plant in which trust and cooperation among the entire labor force would be useful, if not essential, to accomplish the necessary changes, beginning the process with a fight with the union would send the wrong message. It would indicate that the new management was not interested in working with employee representatives and, to some degree, would create an even more adversarial relationship with the work force.

A similar situation confronted the New Zealand Post in its post-1987 incarnation as a state owned enterprise expected to earn a profit and operate like a commercial business. In the past, compulsory unionization had covered employees up to the most senior levels, but, with labor law reform, this was eliminated. The postal union that had organized the Post went bankrupt and was put into receivership before being taken over and merged into a new union. Confronting a very weakened union with almost no financial resources, what did the management of the Post do?

First, they made things as easy as possible for the new union. The company continued the payroll deduction of dues and forwarded the funds to the new union—even before it was asked to do so. The company has consistently pursued a policy of cooperation with the union, which includes sharing financial and operating information as well as business plans with union leaders. This contrasts sharply with the policies pursued by New Zealand Telecom, which has fought the union and, in 1994, suffered a very tough strike that eroded both employee and public support for the company.

The chief executive of the New Zealand Post, Elmar Toime, noted that cooperating with the union has helped to build trust in the organization. The union permitted consultative groups to discuss the provisions of the contract then under negotiation, an arrangement similar to that at Magma Copper. Toime believes that labor has a valid voice in representing workers. Although it is only one of the organization's constituencies, it is an important one. He noted that the Post had to undergo some very fundamental cultural change—from thinking and behaving like a government monopoly to operating like a profit-making business facing increasing competition and deregulation in many of its markets. Toime believes that the union helped substantially with this cultural change process and that the change would have been much more difficult without the union's support. Moreover, he has argued that many administrative advantages derive from dealing with one relatively strong union that can help with internal communication and the mobilization of employee support.[63]

Is the New Zealand Post's relationship with its union unusual? Absolutely. I have met senior managers in many companies and have frequently attended catered lunches in the executive dining room. But it was only at the New Zealand Post that the luncheon attendees included the leader of the New Zealand Post's union, Hamish Fraser, whose interaction with the senior managers was easy, familiar, and collegial. This is not to say that disagreements do not arise between the Post and its union. But the relationship, built in part by management's past behavior, has made working with the union and deriving benefit from that relationship easier.

The answer as to why keep a union, then, is that a union can actually be an important ally in difficult organizational transformation efforts. A friend who formerly worked at one of the major strategy consulting firms' European offices related the following illustration of this.

> I worked on a case of a department store that needed to change its strategy and its customer service approach. In this store, the most effective part of the management team were the union leaders, because they understood the importance of change and subsequently got the whole staff lined up in support of our change effort. The management, in contrast, was totally clueless about what to do and how to support the change effort.

Even in instances in which management may be more competent, the general point still holds: Unions can be, and frequently are, important advocates of change and can be helpful in communicating the need for change and in mobilizing support from the firm's people. Moreover, maintaining a relationship with an organization representing the employees helps to build trust and confidence in the work force. Finally, the alternative—taking on the union—is frequently unattractive because it merely adds another problem, and an unnecessary one at that, to management's tasks.

WHY ENCOURAGE UNIONIZATION?

It is one thing to work cooperatively with an existing union or to forgo the opportunity to eliminate a union when prospects exist for doing so, but it is something else again to actually *encourage* unionization in non-unionized establishments. But, believe it or not, examples, albeit not many, of this behavior exist. Most readers will have heard of United Parcel Service (UPS), a more than $18 billion package and overnight mail delivery company operating throughout the world. Many readers probably know that UPS is organized in the United States by the Teamsters union. What few probably realize is that unionization was actually encouraged by management early in the company's history. The company was founded in 1907 by Jim Casey and his brother George with the original name of the American Messenger Company.

> In 1919 Jim Casey, realizing that labor unions were unavoidable in the near future, invited the International Brotherhood of Teamsters to represent UPS drivers and part-time hourly employees. He explained to his co-workers, "I think it's possible to be a good UPS member and union member at the same time." Because of this early relationship, UPS was able to forge a flexible union-management partnership with such noteworthy features as variable start time, working as directed with minimum work rules, working across job classifications, combinations of inside and outside labor, part-time employment for half the work force, and mandatory overtime as needed.[64]

UPS clearly has benefited from the more positive relationship with the union that accrued from its initial invitation extended to the Teamsters. This does not mean that its labor relations have always been frictionless or that it has never had a strike. But, the tone of its relationship with the work force and their representatives was determined by this early move.

Nor is the idea of encouraging union organization simply an idea from the distant past. Recently, Levi Strauss and Company, the apparel manufacturer, which was already partially unionized, decided not to stand in the way of unionization at the remainder of its U.S. plants.

> Levi will allow the Amalgamated Clothing and Textile Workers Union, which represents one-third of its 18,000 workers at 30 American plants, to sign up thousands more as long as the union helps the company revamp its production system. . . . Levi has waived elections in favor of collecting signatures on membership cards—to avoid the adversarial atmosphere that inevitably comes with elections.[65]

Levi was prompted in this move by its adoption of the modular production process, described in chapter 2, requiring apparel employees to work in teams. By involving the union in the work place, Levi avoids violating current U.S. labor laws prohibiting company-dominated worker committees. Moving to modular production is not an easy change. People's pay, no longer based on individual piecework, depends on plant-wide gain sharing and other team-based incentives, and company surveys indicated that employees find working in teams more stressful. By actively involving the union, the company believed that the change in work arrangements would proceed more smoothly.

> "The more workers in the union, the greater their voice, and that drives the process forward," said Ronald Martz, manager of Levi's plant in Harlingen, Tex., which is serving as a laboratory to develop the new system.[66]

Another contemporary example of employers encouraging union organization comes from the U.S. automobile industry. In this industry, the major manufacturers have been trying to move production to more efficient suppliers and to become less vertically integrated. This change has been fiercely resisted by the United Autoworkers Union, which sees outsourcing as both a loss in membership and a loss in its ability to influence wages and working conditions for the benefit of its members. The outside suppliers have, for the most part, resisted unionization, forcing unions to mount expensive organizing campaigns with uncertain results.

> But now, in an unusual twist, Ford recently encouraged its main seat supplier, Johnson Controls Inc., to allow the UAW to organize two of its plants. . . . Ford said that by letting the union into those facilities, Johnson Controls

would help the automaker justify its increasing use of outside suppliers and ease tensions with the UAW over the outsourcing issue. . . . "Ford doesn't want the headache" of having to grapple with the union over outsourcing, says Sean McAlinden, a researcher with the University of Michigan's Office for the Study of Automotive Transportation. He notes that even with Johnson Controls paying UAW wages, Ford will be paying less for its Johnson-made seats than if it made its own seats in-house.[67]

Ford has gone even further. When unionized workers at seat-making factories at Johnson Controls went on strike, the company offered to continue supplying seats by using replacement workers and management. Ford refused. Ford considers its warm relations with the union an important strategic, competitive advantage and did not want to jeopardize the trust that had accrued from years of working cooperatively.

"It is not in the best interests of our employees or of Ford Motor Co. to accept seats made by replacement workers," John Devine, Ford's chief financial officer, told reporters. "Our relationship with the union and the respect we have with our team inside Ford are too important to us."[68]

In each of these instances, the company in question decided that it did not want to spend time and effort avoiding unionization or worrying about the possibility of becoming unionized. Each example also illustrates a bargain: The company will work with the union, even to the point of encouraging union membership, but in return, the union is expected to work with the company to accomplish economic objectives for the benefit of both the organization and its employees. By the same token, companies that spend time and effort fighting unions should not be surprised when the union leadership does not work cooperatively with the firm. The implicit theme in each of the above examples is that, particularly for organizations facing change and competition, unions can actually help the process of work place change and transformation—if they are induced to serve as partners in the business.

These three examples are, however, atypical in one very important respect. UPS has a particularly strong culture that has served it well over the years. It is a firm that consistently practices most of the elements of high commitment work practices described in chapter 3. Levi's and Ford are both known as being progressive employers. "Ford's relations with the UAW are the most amicable among the Big Three."[69] Clearly these firms, although they are more likely to embrace unions and to work with them cooperatively, actually need unions less than do other employers.

Need unions? Absolutely. Recall that earlier in this chapter we reviewed systematic empirical evidence indicating that unions were *positively* associated with training expenditures, with the persistence and success of employee involvement, with the success of quality improvement programs, and with organizational innovation. These data come from studies of large samples of firms and establishments. Case study evidence, too, is consistent with these results. "Many of the best-known examples of high-performance production systems are occurring in unionized plants—such as Corning, Saturn, Xerox, Levi Strauss, NUMMI, and AT&T."[70] The specific case of the evolution of bargaining in the steel industry provides some evidence as to why these positive effects can occur.

As noted previously, the American steel industry had very adversarial labor relations, in part a result of adverse product market conditions. The industry had lost market share to imported steel so that by 1985 imports constituted almost a quarter of the market.[71] As a consequence of increased foreign competition, competition from other metals such as aluminum, and growing productivity in the face of declining demand, steel employment fell precipitously, from 604,000 people in 1973 to 237,500 in 1985, just twelve years later. Steel production began to recover after the mid-1980s, and the steelworkers' union, under the leadership of Lynn Williams, began to adopt a different approach and bargaining strategy. As it prepared for negotiations in 1993 and 1994, "The USWA made it clear to industry that it wished to continue to move away from the traditional adversarial approach to collective bargaining in steel, and toward a cooperative approach that was more concerned with the long-run survival of both the union and the industry it represented."[72] Consequently, in 1993, the United Steelworkers of America adopted a "New Directions Bargaining Program" for future negotiations. Over the next three years, virtually all of the provisions of the program were successfully negotiated with the major U.S. steel manufacturers, including National Steel, Inland Steel, USX Corporation, Bethlehem Steel, Wheeling/Pittsburgh Steel, Allegheny Ludlum, LTV, Lukens, and Northwestern Steel and Wire. Table 8-2 lists both the objectives or

Table 8-2 UNITED STEELWORKERS "NEW DIRECTIONS
BARGAINING PROGRAM" AND ELEMENTS OF HIGH
PERFORMANCE WORK ARRANGEMENTS

New Directions Objectives	High Performance Work Practices
Employment security	Employment security
Union and employee involvement at all levels, from the shop floor to the board room	Self-managed teams and participation
	Selective Hiring
Restructuring work to reduce costs and to make the work place less authoritarian, safer, more fair, and more involving	Emphasis on training
	High and contingent pay
"Upside" protection, should the company prosper during the agreement	Information sharing
	Reduction of status differences
Health-care cost reductions through managed care; funding of retiree health care costs	
Revitalized apprenticeship and training program	
Investment commitments	
Company neutrality in union-organizing campaigns	
Elimination of remaining contracting-out problems	
Development of a joint public policy and legislative agenda, including labor law reform, health care, trade, and a steel tripartite commission	

Source: Adapted from Carl B. Frankel, New Directions Bargaining in the Basic Steel
Industry (Pittsburgh, PA: United Steelworkers of America, undated), 4–5.

provisions of the steelworkers' contract and the elements of high performance work arrangements described in chapter 3.

The degree of overlap between the two is striking. Obviously, the steel bargaining objectives included elements (for instance, coping with the problem of health-care costs for retirees) that are not part of high performance work arrangements. But, the steel agreement did cover employment security, incentive pay (in the form of bonuses or profit sharing if the firms did well), training (apprenticeship programs), information sharing (including sharing information at the board of directors level), and delegation of authority and decentralization, potentially in teams, so that productivity would be enhanced and the quality of work improved. Although implemented only recently, the available evidence is that the new model not only is working well from a bargaining point of view, but it has had real benefits for the industry and those who work in it. This steel industry example illustrates that union bargaining results and moving to high performance work systems are not necessarily antithetical to each other and, in some cases, are extremely complementary.

The steel industry example illustrates another potential positive consequence of unionization: stimulating the sharing of best practices across firms and stimulating interfirm cooperation. Cooperation and learning from other firms is difficult for many U.S. companies to do. A few years ago, I attended a meeting of the human resource managers from the companies involved in Sematech. Sematech was a consortium of semiconductor manufacturers jointly sponsored by the voluntarily participating organizations and the U.S. government to facilitate the development of processes and equipment to solve problems of U.S. competitiveness. The organization, in short, was designed to foster learning and cooperation for the mutual benefit of all industry participants. At this meeting, human resource materials—yes, human resource materials—were marked "confidential," and it was clear that, in spite of several years of history, cooperation and sharing of insights and wisdom came with difficulty to this group. Unlike the case in some other countries such as Japan and Sweden, few interfirm organizations in the United States exist to help diffuse high performance management systems.

Learning across organizational boundaries requires both information transmission and collaborative partnership structures to help diffuse the tacit knowledge so important to the management process. The implementation of cross-organizational learning requires either competitive pressure or other stimuli to overcome the internal organizational obstacles to work-place reform. In the steel industry case of "New Directions Bargaining," and in other instances, the union has really taken the lead in fostering interfirm learning about new work arrangements and in stimulating, through contract negotiations, work-place innovation and change. As always, such positive effects are not guaranteed and require union leadership that understands the elements and the importance of high performance work arrangements for both the companies and the union members. But, enough instances show that unions have helped to diffuse work place change and foster intercompany learning that this potential benefit should not be ignored.

Ironically, well-managed, progressive firms may not need unions to encourage training, to help maintain employee involvement and quality-improvement initiatives, and to implement provisions that closely resemble high performance employment practices—because they are already doing these things. So, the very organizations that are the most likely to fight unionization and to see unions as problems are those that can actually benefit the most from what unions have the potential to contribute to the effective management of people.

9 ◆ Market Failures and the Role of Public Policy in Producing Profits Through People

I HAVE DEMONSTRATED in previous chapters the economically significant connections between how people are managed and firm performance and the high performance management practices that, for the most part, produce these economic gains when systematically and systemically adopted. Most people, particularly economists, assume that since firms seek to maximize profits, they will seek to implement these optimal arrangements in their employment relationship. Consequently, many economists, business journalists, and business leaders believe that "the role of government intervention should be largely limited to ensuring the existence of competitive market conditions."[1]

I have also demonstrated, however, the comparatively slow diffusion of high performance work arrangements and presented some of the reasons why smart firms don't always do the wise thing. These data call into question the idea that competitive market conditions will be sufficient in and of themselves to lead firms to the practices that generate profits through people. Moreover, the position that government policy should be strictly limited to ensuring the existence of competitive markets is both unrealistic and naive. Even in the United States, let alone in other industrialized countries, governments intervene a great deal in labor market arrangements, and public regulation has existed for some time. Virtually all countries have minimum wage laws, policies setting the rules for collective bargaining, occupational safety and health regulations, rules that mandate permissible work hours and control eligibility for overtime pay, and rules governing child labor, among other such intrusions into the labor market. A pure free-market economist could argue that in each instance, public policy has interfered with the abilities of the parties involved to reach some mutually acceptable agreement, if such an agreement falls outside of the scope permitted by existing law or regulation. That is true, but it is implausible that this system of regulations will be repealed. Thus, no government is completely neutral with respect to the structure and governance of the employment relationship, and it is a myth to think that it ever will be. So, the question becomes not whether government intervention has an effect—the answer to which is invariably yes—but whether, on balance, the effects of government policies and actions help or harm the effective implementation and diffusion of high performance management practices.

Unfortunately, discussions of the role of government policy in producing profits through people are too often characterized by assertion and stereotyping rather than by actual examination of the data and logical analysis. Commenting on just one aspect of government intervention in the labor market—litigation concerning employment discrimination—John Donohue and Peter Siegelman noted, "much of the debate over the future of civil rights in employment has been characterized by high ratios of rhetoric to fact."[2] To get beyond ideology and belief, this chapter reviews some quantitative and case data to demonstrate the following points:

1. Capital markets show considerable myopia with respect to high performance work practices.

2. The performance of the U.S. economy, often assessed by the amount of job creation, may not be as positive as frequently asserted.

3. Government intervention in labor markets does *not* appear to have much impact on organizational adjustments to changes in product market demand; or, in other words, the supposedly harmful effects of legislated employment security policies such as those found in

Europe on the ability of employers to adjust levels of staffing are empirically negligible.

4. Existing government policy, particularly in the United States but increasingly in other countries as well, is not neutral but is actually harmful to the adoption of high involvement management arrangements.

5. Government policy, at all levels, can do many things to strengthen the competitiveness of firms by encouraging the implementation of more effective ways of managing people.

Why should we care about public policy concerning labor market issues in a book for managers about the link between people and profits? First, executives actively participate in the formulation of public policy on employment issues. In the United States, the National Labor Policy Association, an organization representing primarily large companies, has persistently lobbied for reforms in laws governing unions and other matters. Companies, along with trial lawyers, have vigorously resisted proposals to change at-will employment laws in an effort to curtail wrongful discharge suits, primarily because the firms are unwilling to agree to due process firing provisions included in most of these no-fault reforms. The National Association of Manufacturers and the Business Roundtable, industry trade associations, and other such organizations actively lobby to influence public policy on work place issues. Corporate involvement is even greater in other countries that pursue more activist labor policies. It is important that this business involvement be thoughtfully based on the true long-term interests of these organizations and not on opinion or ideology ungrounded in information and analysis.

Second, public policy frequently directly affects a number of the most important aspects of the employment relationship. Recall our discussion of the new employment contract and the contingent work force in chapter 6. Practices such as dismissal and the use of part-time and temporary help are profoundly affected in the United States and other countries by both direct regulation and indirect government policies. Similarly, the relationship between unions and employers responds not only to the applicable rules and regulations but also to government actions that make conflict or cooperation more likely. The level of training, an important component of high performance work systems, is influenced by government policies such as those in force in Singapore, Australia, France, and other countries where a company either spends some proportion of its payroll costs on training or pays a tax to the government.

Third, state action has important symbolic and indirect effects on the employment relation. The state has substantial legitimacy in most industrialized countries and thus serves as a role model on many issues, including managing the work force. If the government supports union-busting and the use of contingent workers, uses low commitment management practices, and pursues adversarial relations with its own work force, these policies send a message to private sector employers about prevailing normative values and sanctioned behaviors. If, on the other hand, the government leads in instituting high performance work practices and in working collaboratively with employee organizations, this behavior, too, sends an influential message. Thus, state action has both direct regulatory and legal effects as well as consequential symbolic, normative influences on the governance of the employment relation. For these reasons, at a minimum, public policy issues loom large in any attempt to understand the diffusion, or lack thereof, of high performance work practices in a given context.

A full discussion of governmental policy regarding the employment relation would require a book or many books. This chapter first presents data that help to make the case that simple market effects neither fully explain what exists nor, particularly in the short term, lead to optimal individual firm decisions. I then illustrate how government actions can and do actually harm the management of the employment relation. Finally, I present a number of examples of government actions that have enhanced the management of the employment relation and, as a consequence, organizational performance and competitiveness, although these examples, needless to say, don't often come from the United States.

GETTING THE FACTS STRAIGHT

Before embarking on our brief exploration of the actual effects and potential contribution of public policy and state action to organizational performance as achieved through the implementation of high commitment management, we first need to clear up some inferential and factual problems that plague many popular discussions of this topic. Perhaps the most pernicious is the fallacy of presuming that labor market arrangements are solely responsible for a set of observed macro-economic outcomes and the resulting error of using aggregated measures of national economic performance to make inferences about the optimality of various employment relation structures. Many examples of this logical fallacy exist, but here I highlight just one representative instance.

In an article in 1996, *The Economist* contrasted the effects of two economic models, which it called stakeholder capitalism and shareholder capitalism. Stakeholder capitalism is characterized by, among other features, employment security, particularly for "core" employees, laws that make dismissals and layoffs more difficult and requirements for joint consultations (with unions, for instance) in the case of significant layoffs, employee participation in company management, and a long-term perspective on the development of the business, including employees and their capabilities.[3] These factors are important, since many of them—security of employment, training and skill development, and employee participation—are central elements of high performance management practices. The article presented a long discussion of data on economic growth, the proportion of GDP invested in capital, productivity and productivity growth, the fraction of GDP invested in research and development, and unemployment rates. Based on these data, the article concluded as follows:

> The overall impression . . . is that the stakeholder economies, most notably Japan, outperformed the shareholder ones in the first few decades after the war; but that gap has narrowed significantly in the past 20 years or so. . . . This prompts several questions. Is the stakeholder magic wearing off? . . . Did the superior performance of these economies actually stem from factors that had nothing to do with stakeholding? . . . [T]he stakeholder mode . . . is under serious attack at home.[4]

Think about it. Surely outcomes such as the unemployment rate and the rate of economic growth are affected by monetary and fiscal policy—things such as interest rates and the size of the budget deficit or surplus, not just labor market arrangements. Certainly investment is affected by policy variables such as tax rates, as well as by the rate of economic growth in the country in question. It seems almost ludicrous to attribute the macroeconomic performance of national economies to their legal, normative, and employment relations policies without considering monetary or fiscal policy at all. In fact, the unemployment rate—the economic outcome most often considered in these analyses—varied between about 12 percent in Germany and 23 percent in Spain in 1997, *even though there is very little variation in the policies and regulations governing labor market arrangements in Western Europe.* It is empirically impossible for something that doesn't vary—labor market policies (constrained, by other things, by the rules of the European Union as well as by custom and politics)—to explain something that varies substantially.

The empirical problem stems from having too few observations and too many potential explanations. Evaluating a stakeholder or shareholder model, or the effects of various employment relations practices, at the level of the national economy thus becomes empirically difficult if not impossible. A much better way to approach this issue is to do what the numerous studies cited in chapter 2 have done: draw a large enough sample of companies so that the effects of management practices can be assessed after statistically controlling for other variables that would logically be expected to affect outcomes of interest. The idea that high rates of German unemployment are the result of Germany's codetermination laws and other labor regulations, ignoring, among other things, the relative strength of the German currency and the central bank's inflation fighting vigor, is simply nonsensical. If one is going to use comparisons of employment relations policies at the national level, then at a minimum these comparisons should be used to explore outcomes more proximately related to labor market policy, things such as the level of strike activity, skill development, and similar labor market outcomes.

A second confusion that plagues the discussion of the role of the state and labor market public policy is the relationship between job creation and other measures of economic performance. Not only does much popular writing misattribute macroeconomic performance to human resource regimes, ignoring small factors like monetary policy and interest rates as well as government surpluses and deficits, much of that writing praises the performance of the U.S. economy, and by inference, its labor market policies, by highlighting the comparatively large number of jobs created in the United States. Hold aside for the moment whether the jobs being created are "good" (high paying) jobs. One popular joke, for instance, has one person saying to another, "the economy is really doing well—look at all the jobs that are being created." The second person replies, "I know. I have three of them." Much more fundamental questions are whether job creation correlates positively with other accepted measures of economic performance and whether it is under the influence of governmental economic policy at all. Let's look at the data.

Many people would use as indicators of an economy's performance the rate of inflation (the lower the better), the rate of unemployment (again, the lower the better), and the rate of economic growth or growth in GDP (gross domestic product; the higher the better). Growth, in particular, has become a hot topic in a debate over the highest rate of noninflationary growth possible in the U.S. economy and what policies might promote such growth. In a study looking at economic statistics for comparatively wealthy democracies in the period following World War II to 1987, Harold Wilensky found that "except for 1980–1984, job creation rates are statistically unrelated to unemployment rates."[5] In fact, the relationship between job creation and unemployment is often *positive*.

> The great job creation machines are often great unemployment machines. For example, three of the top four job creators rank quite high in average unemployment rates since 1950.[6]

Not only is job creation unrelated to the unemployment rate, it is also empirically uncorrelated with either economic growth or the rate of inflation.

> In fact, if we combine low inflation, high growth, and low unemployment in an index of economic performance, weighting the three components equally . . . we see that in the entire postwar period from 1950 on, two of the six consistently poor job creators—West Germany and Austria—were excellent economic performers; that the Netherlands and France had sustained periods of good economic performance; that Belgium performed well before the first oil shock and was average to above average after; and that only Great Britain had both consistently poor job creation and poor economic performance. Conversely, two of the top four consistent job creators—Canada and Australia—had consistently mediocre to poor economic performance.[7]

How can this be? Wilensky's empirical analysis of the correlates of job creation revealed the following:

> The major causes of job creation are beyond the reach of economic policy, although they can be affected by family and retirement policy. The major causes are *demographic* (the age structure of the population and migration rates) and *social structural* (the rate of family breakup as it relates to poverty and the history of female labor force participation).[8]

Before the business press gets all excited about the great record of job creation in the United States, they would be well served to examine the empirical evidence that shows first, that "job creation is significantly and positively related to average migration rates,"[9] second, that "data on divorce rates for five-year intervals from 1970 to 1985 show positive correlations in all periods" with the rate of job creation,[10] and third, that "most of the sources of job creation . . . are beyond the reach of economic policy, except those policies that would directly discourage low-wage work."[11]

Finally, we need to consider the validity of a common criticism of government intervention in the governance of the employment relationship: that it inhibits labor market "flexibility." Thus, "institutional wage-setting systems, social security provisions, rigid working-time regimes, and legal layoff and dismissal restraints imposed in many European countries came to be widely regarded as essential in causing labor cost 'stickiness' and employment inertia."[12] This labor-cost stickiness and inertia in firms' ability to adjust employment levels to changes in product market demand are generally believed to account for the recent low rates of job creation in Western Europe. For the moment, forget about whether such flexibility—often defined as the ability to lay off employees or to engage them without constraint under contingent work arrangements—is actually beneficial. Let's ask a more basic question: Does government intervention in the labor market actually affect flexibility?

Fortunately, a great deal of empirical evidence is now available to illuminate this issue. One type of study examines whether differences exist across countries (or in a given country over time as its labor market regulations change) in the relationship between changes in the national economy, that is, changes in industrial output, and changes in employment. Other studies have examined differences in job stability, turnover, and the relationship to dismissal practices. Still other studies have examined more micro-level institutional policies and employer behavior. This welter of evidence leads to one conclusion: "The genuine impact of employment security policies has been frequently overstated in the current debate on labor market flexibility."[13] How can government policies have so little effect? Because the decisions of firms themselves and other, non-governmental policy factors affect and constrain the ease and speed with which employment and, for that matter, wages adjust to changes in aggregate demand.

> Even in the absence of exogenously imposed statutory or union constraints, modern labor markets have been found to generate a high degree of de facto job stability. Where legislators have imposed legal rules and procedures for employment terminations, these were frequently *congruent rather than in opposition to firms' own work force adjustment preferences.*[14]

Not only is the interpretation of the consequences of government policy with respect to the employment relation mistaken, therefore, but profound, commonly-shared misperceptions about the magnitude of the effects of public policy on labor market flexibility are widespread.

DO MARKETS NEGATE THE NEED FOR STATE ACTION?

Much of the argument against using public policy to structure the employment relation proceeds from the presumption that markets, the capital markets in particular, are efficient in disciplining firms to adopt optimal organizational arrangements, including methods for managing the work force. The idea is that firms attempting to operate with suboptimal management practices will fare poorly in their market place and consequently, will eventually lose out to competitors. Moreover, if firms don't organize their work forces effectively, their financial performance will suffer and, as a consequence, so will their share price, leading to pressure on management to do things differently or, at the extreme limit, to a takeover by another management that will implement more effective practices.

This line of argument does seem to have some compelling logic. The data from chapter 2 demonstrated that "the role of human resources can be crucial" in producing organizational performance and competitive advantage.[15] If human resource practices matter, then organizations that don't implement high performance work practices should under-perform those that do, leading to difficulties in both the product and capital markets. But the argument also presents some difficulties. In the product or service market, as already noted, a number of factors besides human resource practices work to affect economic performance. Thus, it is possible for a firm to survive or even prosper with poor people management practices because of other bases of success, such as holding a strong technological position. Although such a firm might perform at an even higher level if it implemented a high performance management approach, it may not be forced to do so because of its competitive strength derived from other factors. Furthermore, competition is far from perfect in many markets, and, as a consequence, competitive dynamics may operate with some substantial time lag.

One empirical implication of the argument that product market com-petition produces optimal work force management practices is that firms, over time, should experience convergence in how they organize and manage the employment relationship. Just as microeconomic the-ory predicts that under conditions of perfect competition, one will observe convergence toward similar costs, prices, and production func-tions across firms, this theory would suggest convergence in employ-ment practices. But the available evidence suggests that such conver-gence in the management of the work force is not occurring and that variation in human resource practices and strategies is, at least in part, explained by the institutional and public-policy environment of the particular firms being investigated.

On the first point, reviewing a number of studies of the industrial relations practices of firms in different countries as they adapted to new competitive realities, Richard Locke noted the following:

> [T]his process of adaptation is neither universal nor uniform. In some firms, the new competitive strategies build on a variety of . . . practices which enhance the skill base and flexibility of the work place and promote greater communication, trust, and coordination among the firm's various stakehold-ers. Yet other firms have sought to adjust to increased competition by sub-contracting work . . . downsizing, and seeking to compete on the traditional basis of cost and price competition.[16]

Chapter 2 documented one example of this absence of convergence, in the form of substantial variation in the adoption of lean manufacturing principles in the automobile assembly industry, explainable in part by institutional as opposed to market factors.

On the second point, the evidence shows that "the low-cost response to market pressures and changes appears to be most frequent in countries with weak institutions, low levels of unionization, decentralized bargaining structures, and a limited governmental role in labor market affairs."[17] Whether the country has a Tayloristic, job control orientation to work organization or an institutional environment that fosters flexibility and communication is also important in understanding the different responses to the same set of competitive pressures.

What about the ability of the capital markets to compel the adoption of high performance work practices? In the capital markets, a firm's value at any given point in time is determined by the decisions made by those individuals—in today's world in the United States, primarily institutional investors—who dominate the securities market. "In 1965, individual holdings constituted 84 percent of corporate stock, institutional holdings 16 percent. By 1990, the individual fraction had declined to 54 percent, and the institutional fraction had risen to 46 percent."[18] Moreover, institutional investors trade much more frequently, thereby having a disproportionate impact on the establishment of market prices. Thus the empirical question becomes whether the capital market and its institutional investors, at least at this time, actually value or appreciate—or even understand—the impact of human resource policies on organizational performance. Some systematic evidence as well as case examples speaking to this question suggest that the answer is largely "no."

As a vivid case example of investor naïveté about managing employees, consider Greyhound, the largest bus company in the United States. In May 1993, its stock price was $22.75 a share, and in April the company had raised $90 million in a new stock offering, wowing investment analysts with the promise of a new, computerized reservation system and with the profit potential from slashing costs at the company. The three-year tenure at the company of J. Michael Doyle, the chief financial officer, and Frank Schmieder, the chief executive, however, had a deleterious effect on this company.

[T]he two executives alienated employees, damaged relations with customers and misled investors, while spending corporate funds heavily on new offices

. . . and perks for themselves and other officials. Yet for a remarkably long time, the two men won critical praise from securities analysts and investors. That praise partly reflected a knee-jerk tendency . . . to applaud anything resembling "reengineering."[19]

Only a Wall Street analyst could actually think that a company in the transportation *service* business could prosper by cutting costs even as it alienated employees and customers. By October, 1994, Greyhound stock was selling at just $2.19 a share, about one-tenth of its price of some eighteen months previously. It turns out that bad customer service and unhappy employees—the two do go together as we have seen—resulted in falling ridership and a loss of revenues that created grave financial difficulties for the company. Investors' inability to see that the company was being systematically destroyed is truly startling.

The Greyhound case illustrates how investors overvalue financial engineering and are insensitive to policies that erode a firm's human assets and, consequently, its customer service. Our next example demonstrates investors' lack of appreciation of the potential positive importance of human resource practices in creating value for the firm. In the summer of 1996, the Geron Corporation, a "biopharmaceutical company focused on discovering and developing therapeutic and diagnostic products based upon biological mechanisms underlying cancer and other age-related diseases,"[20] went public. Its technology was at an early stage of development: "The Company has not yet selected a lead compound for any of its drug development programs."[21] Once a lead compound was selected the task of formulating a deliverable drug remained, as well as the various stages of clinical trials. Suffice it to say that without question, at the time it went public, Geron was at least seven and perhaps as long as ten years away from having a product on the market and any associated revenues. What an investor was buying with a purchase of Geron stock was some patented technology but basically the human capital of its scientists and management. Clearly, this was a company whose most important assets walked out the door every night.

Ronald Eastman was the president and chief executive officer of the company. Eastman had come from American Cyanamid and had no background in the company's technology. Rather, he was an excellent manager of people. Along with his human resources manager, Ruth Grouell, Eastman was devoted to building a strong culture, a humane, innovative organization for which talented scientists would want to work, and an environment in which they would be productive. The employee handbook stated as much.

> You have joined a unique team committed to creating breakthrough solutions for diseases associated with aging. . . . As we pursue this purpose, we are guided by Geron's . . . core values: employees who respect, trust, and support one another to achieve a spirit of camaraderie and individual fulfillment, openness and honesty to achieve the highest level of integrity, ideas that change the world. . . . In pursuit of our purpose, we believe that people are our most important asset. Thus, we are committed to providing a positive work environment and creating programs to support you as you contribute your unique talents and experience to help us achieve our purpose.[22]

Geron had a good leader with a strong vision of the importance of employees to the welfare of the organization and a set of sound ideas about how to implement high performance work arrangements. One would think that this combination would sell well on the stock market. After all, in chapter 2 we saw the Welbourne and Andrews study on the substantial importance of human resources for the survival rate of initial public offerings.

As Geron was readying its offering prospectus, I met Ron Eastman and Ruth Grouell and told them about the IPO study. Since the company was already truly committed to high involvement work arrangements and had some innovative employment practices, they approached their underwriter and inquired whether they should put information about their employment policies and leadership style in the offering prospectus. This might enhance the reception the stock offering would receive. They were told, in no uncertain terms, "no." Don't blame the underwriters—J. P. Morgan, Montgomery Securities, and Salomon Brothers—too much. I am sure their advice reflected their assessment of the reactions of the investment community to such information: It might actually harm the value of the company. Amazingly, this reaction occurred in a situation where all the company really could sell was its talent and a management system for developing and retaining that talent.

Although these examples have the virtue of being vivid, more systematic quantitative evidence also exists showing the misperceptions of human resource issues by investors. Recall again the study of the five-year survival rate of initial public offerings described in Chapter 2. That study examined not only whether firms survived but also two other measures gathered at the time of the initial offering: Tobin's Q, defined as the initial stock price divided by its book value, often taken as a measure of how highly investors value a firm, and the premium obtained by the firm, measured as the difference between the initial public offering price and the tangible assets or book value of the firm, divided by the total share price to calculate the percent premium.[23] Although not necessarily perfect measures, the two, themselves highly correlated, do provide reasonable indicators of how highly investors valued the firm's future potential at the time it went public. For both measures, the human resource value scale had no significant effect, while the rewards scale was actually *negatively* related to the investor assessments of the firms' potential. "This . . . suggests that investors ignore information related to the degree to which firms value their employees, but they react negatively if firms use compensation to link pay to organizational performance."[24] Recall that the results from the study demonstrated that both of these scales were in reality *positively* correlated with firm survival and that the rewards scale had a particularly large effect. Thus, these data show that investors do not incorporate information on human resource practices in thoughtful ways, consistent with the actual demonstrated effects of these practices on firm performance.

More evidence on the criteria used by institutional investors and their appreciation, or lack thereof, of human resource factors comes from a study of 275 decision makers at 123 mutual funds and 152 institutions, including pension funds with average assets of about $500 million. The study, conducted by the Center for Business Innovation at Ernst and Young under the direction of Sarah Mavrinac, collected two forms of data. One was a survey that asked respondents to rate a number of non-financial attributes in terms of how important each was in evaluating a company, using a seven-point scale ranging from 1, not at all important, to 7, very important. Table 9-1 presents the ratings of some of these factors from the institutional investors. Overall, the investors reported that only about 13 percent of the investment decision was based on non-financial criteria, such as corporate strategy, reputation, quality of management, and so forth. The data in the table indicate that these large investors do not think the use of employee teams, the ratio of chief-executive to work-force compensation, or product or process quality recognition are very important. They also don't place much emphasis on customer complaints, the quality of employee training, or employee turnover rates. Rather, the non-financial factors they emphasize are such things as market share, management experience, quality of corporate strategy, management credibility, and research leadership. The only human resource factor that receives any significant weighting is the ability to attract and retain quality people.

The study also employed an actual decision-making task that required the respondents to make portfolio allocations among real firms in a number of industries using artificial financial data and the companies' ratings on non-financial measures. Empirically investigating the effect of the various non-financial measures on investment allocation deci-

Table 9-1   INSTITUTIONAL INVESTOR RATINGS OF THE IMPORTANCE OF NON-FINANCIAL ORGANIZATIONAL ATTRIBUTES

Attributes	Mean Rating
Comparatively More Important	
Execution of corporate strategy	6.26
Quality of corporate strategy	5.92
Innovativeness	5.77
Ability to attract and retain talented people	5.61
Market share	5.60
Management experience	5.54
Research leadership	5.40
Quality of organizational vision	5.19
Comparatively Less Important	
Quality of employee training	4.48
Employee turnover rates	4.42
Product quality awards	3.53
Process quality awards	3.39
Use of employee teams	3.26
Ratio of CEO compensation to work-force compensation	3.22

Source: Analysis of data from Ernst and Young's Center for Business Innovation, Boston, MA, 1996.

sions, the analysis showed that *none* of the human resource factors associated with high performance work systems had any statistically significant explanatory power.

In some sense, these results are really not that surprising. After all, many of these professional money managers are in their twenties and thirties. One article noted, for instance, that the average age of the portfolio managers at the thirty-two top mutual funds was thirty-six.[25] Moreover, most of these folks have never worked anywhere but in finance. The investment managers in the Ernst and Young financial measures study had spent on average only three years outside the investment industry and had less than two years of supervisory experience outside that industry. A study of the backgrounds of the top managers of the nation's fifty largest pension funds, forty largest investment managers, and ten largest foundations revealed that 0 percent of the investment company managers, 0 percent of the managers of public pension funds, and only 14 percent of the foundation money managers had any company management experience outside of finance.[26] With little or no line operating experience and with only limited managerial experience of any kind, it is small wonder that the average professional money manager has little appreciation or even understanding of how human resource management practices affect organizational performance. Occasional exceptions to this generally dismal assessment do arise, of course. In 1994, the California Public Employees' Retirement System (CalPERS), a pension system with $80 billion in assets, announced that "it will start making investment decisions in part according to how well companies treat their employees. . . . CalPERS decided [this] . . . based on research showing that a supportive attitude toward workers translates into stronger earnings."[27] But CalPERS remains an exception. Capital markets, therefore, generally demonstrate little ability to comprehend or appropriately value, at least in the short run, effective human resource management. Given this situation, reliance on the capital markets to provide effective discipline and oversight of how firms manage the employment relation would appear to be highly questionable.

Additional data on the effects of institutional investors on firm performance, or more precisely, the lack thereof, comes from a study of the performance of a random sample of *Fortune* 500 companies over the period 1990 to 1993, a time during which institutional activism in the management affairs of companies was on the rise. The study examined what link might exist between institutional influence on corporations and their economic performance. Specifically, it sought to determine the following:

> [W]hether performance was affected by the proportion of stock held by institutions on the assumption that institutions are superior monitors of corporate performance . . . the effect of ownership by public pension funds, since they include some of the most active shareholders . . . the effect of the most active institutions . . . and whether shareholder proposals meant to improve corporate governance actually lead to better performance.[28]

The study found no effect of any of this on performance. Thus, no evidence supports any effect from institutional ownership or activism on corporate performance. But this result is exactly what would be expected given the data already discussed—namely that financial institutions have no particular comparative advantage (indeed, may have some disadvantages)—in making recommendations to improve corporate performance.

Even if investors were more sophisticated and knowledgeable about the consequences of high performance work practices, free rider and collective action problems would persist that might mitigate the ability of the operation of financial markets to quickly produce optimal management practices. Consider the case of participation in organizational decision making, for instance.

> The private benefits of unchecked hierarchy are concentrated in a few managers, while the private external costs are widely scattered among many employees. . . . Thus pressure to maintain the status quo will be strong. . . . Capital markets face a set of similar problems. Any one shareholder will find very limited private value in trying to influence management or trying to organize all shareholders to do so.[29]

Although cooperation within firms may be optimal in terms of long-term performance, maintaining cooperation is difficult and requires either incentives or other forces to ensure that cooperation is maintained. An argument can be made that "from the social viewpoint the market is likely to undersupply investments in internal cooperative solutions."[30]

In addition to financial and product market limitations, labor market externalities call into question the wisdom of eschewing all forms of government intervention and relying solely on the market. After reviewing extensive evidence documenting the positive effects of participation on productivity, David Levine and Laura Tyson posed the following question: "If employee participation often has positive effects on productivity, why don't we see more of it?"[31] Their answer was, in part, a set of labor market failures and externalities that precluded individual firms from taking beneficial actions.

> [U]nder certain conditions, the market system may be systematically biased against participatory work places. Despite the potential efficiency of such workplaces, product, labor, and capital markets can all make participation unprofitable for the individual firm. As a result, the economy can be trapped in a socially suboptimal position.[32]

As one example, take the case of training. The economy as a whole would be better off with a more skilled work force—in fact, the importance of education to the economy is the reason behind public schooling. Many important skills are learned either on the job or in company-sponsored and directed training programs. A given firm may want to offer more training to its people to increase their skills and, presumably, the firm's profits. But, suppose other, directly competitive firms don't offer the same amount or quality of training. The first firm faces a dilemma. If it trains its work force, the employees may be hired away by competitors. Since these competitors have not expended the same resources on training, they will enjoy lower costs and consequently a competitive advantage. To avoid this, firms may underinvest in training, particularly in more general skills that would be of use to many other firms. Although this decision to limit training is rational for each individual firm, it can lead to a socially suboptimal level of skill development in the economy as a whole.

Nor is the foregoing scenario mere speculation. One study found that "employers in the metalworking sectors in Wisconsin regret the low level of skills among their employees, but resist engaging in extensive training because of this free-rider problem."[33] A study of the banking industry concluded that "poaching creates strong disincentives for firms to invest in training."[34] The study went on to note the following:

> Several banks . . . had recently reduced or ended their lender training programs altogether because of the poaching problem. One . . . bank had

launched a major training program in its effort to penetrate the wholesale
lending market in Los Angeles during the late 1980s. After losing eighteen
of twenty-one graduates the first year and nineteen of twenty the second
year, the bank ended the program. . . . The cycle of poaching and counter-
poaching . . . discourages training investment.[35]

Although many banks talk about customer focus, enhanced service, and
building and maintaining customer relationships, most still focus on
reducing labor costs and competing on the basis of price. Why don't
banks do what they say they should and want to do? "We argue that
the failure of more banks to integrate quality into their competitive
strategies . . . must be understood in the context of a labor market
environment that discourages managers from investing in human resources."[36]

Or consider another example: providing employment security. The
economy as a whole might be better off if most firms had people who
took a longer-term view, who were trained because of their long-term
attachments to firms that could then expect to enjoy the benefits of better trained workers, and who were motivated and committed to providing productivity-enhancing ideas because they did not fear for their
jobs. However, if all (or most) firms don't offer employment security,
those that do face a problem of adverse selection: Those employees who
most fear not being able to find work in the event of job loss—individuals who may be less skilled or motivated—will be particularly attracted
to firms offering employment security. So, unless those firms are able
to do an effective job of screening, they will wind up with a less capable
work force. Again, an individually rational choice—match what other
firms are doing—can lead to poor results for the economy as a whole.

It is difficult if not impossible to know to what extent the absence of
the diffusion of high performance work practices is attributable to the
types of problems enumerated above. But, evidence from the experience
of other countries as well as data from the United States suggests that
the possibility should not simply be dismissed out of hand.

FIRST, DO NO HARM

In considering the effect of government policy on the management of
the employment relationship and organizational performance, a good

place to begin is to note that, at a minimum, government action should do no harm. Unfortunately, this is not invariably the case. By "doing no harm" I mean that government policy and behavior should, on balance, contribute to the building of trust in the employment relationship and to fostering cooperative, as opposed to adversarial, relations among owners, managers, and rank-and-file employees. In the United States, two important approaches to government action and policy, also occasionally followed in other countries, have done harm to the objective of achieving profits through people. First, government may weigh in on one side or the other in disputes over the employment relation, thereby diminishing the willingness of the parties to negotiate directly.

Governmental action in the United States and, occasionally, elsewhere, for instance, has, all too often, taken the employers' side in labor disputes. The problem here is not in coming down on the side of the employers, but in taking sides at all. By taking a side, the state encourages that side to avoid dealing with the other: It can now hope to win by relying on the help of state action. Consequently, the need to reach accommodation and to build a relationship based on trust is lessened. Let me provide a concrete example, one that makes the Magma Copper transformation described in chapter 8 all the more remarkable.

The history of mining in the United States is not a very happy one, and the struggles of the copper-mining industry in Arizona have been particularly bitter. It is not just a matter of wages. Mining is an exceptionally dangerous occupation, in part because the government in the United States has not done much to vigorously enforce safety regulations. Between 1961 and 1973, for instance, more than twice as many disabling injuries occurred in mines as were incurred by soldiers fighting the Vietnam War. The average death rate for miners during that period of 1,080 per million was almost as high as for active duty military personnel, who experienced a death rate (during a war in which at one time more than 500,000 were fighting) of 1,270 per million.[37]

Government intervention on the side of employers in labor disputes is a theme seen throughout U.S. history. Employers were permitted to hire and equip virtual private police forces and armies (the notorious Pinkerton's security guards), and the state often called out the national guard (or the Army) to help employers fight strikes. A similar history characterized Arizona copper mining. During World War I, Phelps Dodge profits soared 200 percent due to the demand for communications cable and shell jackets. The miners, many of them of Mexican descent, tried to organize to obtain higher wages. But the state intervened forcefully to help Phelps Dodge.

> [I]n the quiet of an early July morning, a posse of sheriff's deputies and vigilantes rode into the streets of Bisbee, arrested some two thousand striking miners and sympathizers, forced them into waiting boxcars of the El Paso and Southwestern (a Phelps Dodge subsidiary), and hauled them over 173 miles of desert to a detention camp in central New Mexico, from which few ever returned to Bisbee.[38]

Nor is this pattern of behavior ancient history. In the bitter strike against Phelps Dodge that began in the summer of 1983, the state of Arizona brought the full force and power of government down on the side of the company. National Guard and Arizona Public Safety (Highway Patrol) personnel helped replacement workers enter the Phelps Dodge mine. Strikers and even their families were arrested in large numbers, often on seemingly trumped-up charges. Beverly Cole threw a paper cup on the ground at a picket line and was charged with littering, felony, fraud, and forgery.[39] By the end of the strike, some four years later, Phelps Dodge had decertified the unions and had implemented a policy of making all its mines non-union, no matter what costs or difficulties arose along the way. Of all the miners and supporters arrested, not one went to jail. In fact, most were not even prosecuted. The state of Arizona never took one case to trial.

> "Obviously, the state knew that these charges were ridiculous. The point is that they didn't care about prosecuting these people; they only wanted to intimidate them." . . . The strategy had been fairly effective. The frequent arrests and excessive bonds drained union and personal resources. . . . Perhaps the most important effect of all was that the legal offensive helped to turn away public sympathy.[40]

Eventually, Phelps Dodge lost some civil rights suits growing out of the harassment and had to pay some nominal damage claims. It is important to note that the state's actions were not financially costless: Resources were expended on the national guard and police presence, and more resources were spent on the arrests, jail detention, bail-bond hearings, and associated legal maneuvers. One wonders if this was a reasonable way to spend public funds. More importantly for the present discussion, a real question remains as to whether such state action facilitates building high performance work places. It would seem to me that it does not and, in fact, has exactly the opposite result.

As another example of the government doing harm to building management practices that enhance long-term competitiveness by "apparently" favoring business, consider the case of Korea. At 6 A.M. one morning in late 1996, without any advance notice that such changes were even contemplated, the ruling party controlling the Korea government passed changes in labor laws that provoked a prolonged series of strikes and a period of political unrest. The ostensible purpose of the changes, presumably advocated by Korean business, was to make it easier for firms to dismiss workers and replace strikers, thus helping Korean firms to compete with the lower-wage competitors emerging in the Far East and making the economy more competitive. Although the ultimate effects of these labor law changes, if they indeed even remain in force, are as yet undetermined, several things have already become clear. First, the problems with the competitiveness of the Korean economy come at least as much from the over-regulation of business and interference in the capital allocation process[41] as from labor force issues. Second, it is far from clear that preserving a low-wage system is either feasible or the best way to develop the Korean economy. To compete more effectively in the world economy, Korean firms need to develop the skills and productivity of their employees, not simply hold down wages. Observers have noted this.

> [A] policy that alienates workers might be shortsighted. Korea has left the development stage where it is competing on low wages, and entering the stage where it must compete on productivity and product quality. "We can improve the productivity rate and product quality when workers are highly motivated," said Professor Park of Sogang University. "If they are not happy it will reflect negatively in their products, and that's a disaster."[42]

The government's action is unlikely to create trust (given how the legislation was passed) and is also unlikely to create the conditions for Korean business to pursue high performance work arrangements. As such, the action, even though sought by business, will hurt their efforts to develop management practices that can create competitiveness over the long term.

Direct state intervention is, however, not the only way in which governments do harm. A second important way in which governments often impede positive development is in promulgating policies and laws governing the employment relationship that help to foster a legalistic, adversarial relationship between management and employees, a pattern of interaction that inhibits firms' ability to develop high performance work arrangements. In the United States, laws governing collective bargaining and employees' rights to organize are administered by the National Labor Relations Board using a quasi-judicial, legalistic process. "There is no mechanism under the Act for considering the effect of any decision on any other legal doctrine" because under the National Labor Relations Act, there is a "case-by-case approach to legal decision making."[43] Moreover, the legal system is a costly and uncertain venue for resolving conflicts over the employment relation. The issue of wrongful discharge and at-will employment provides a nice illustration of this problem.

The doctrine of at-will employment means that "in cases of employment of uncertain duration, 'All [employers] may dismiss their employees at will, be they many or few, for good cause, for no cause, or even for cause morally wrong, without being thereby guilty of legal wrong.'"[44] The United States is the only industrialized country that has a doctrine of at-will employment—all other countries restrict the rights of employers to discharge workers. But even in the United States the ability of employers to fire at will has been limited: not by legislation, except in the case of Montana, but by judicial interpretation. The following three exceptions have been recognized to the at-will doctrine.

> [T]he implied contract exception, the public policy exception, and the covenant of good faith and fair dealing. . . . Under the implied contract exceptions, the courts have held that the employment relationship is governed by contractual provisions. . . . The evidence of a "contract" between the employer and the employee has been construed explicitly, based on oral or written statements . . . and implicitly, based on employment practices or the context of the employment relationship. . . . The public policy exception . . . precludes employers from terminating employees for refusing to commit an act that public policy condemns or for committing an act that public policy protects.[45]

The first problem with this judicial interpretation route for the expansion of employee rights is that, because it is the product of court interpretation, diffusion is neither uniform nor consistent. Although it is clear that exceptions to strict at-will employment increased substantially during the 1980s, not all states followed the same practices. By 1989, forty of the fifty states recognized the public policy exception, thirty-six states recognized the implied contract exception, but only nine states recognized the good faith exception. Moreover, "because of the complexities of the legal doctrines themselves . . . many sources do not agree on how to characterize the status of the common law in each state."[46] Needless to say, this creates a lot of uncertainty for employers: The law governing at-will employment varies both over time and place, and is, moreover, hard to interpret even at a given place at a given time.

The second problem is with the results of the judicial process. The remedies provided for wrongful discharge take a long time to realize, are occasionally large, and, most importantly, are unpredictable. A RAND study of 120 jury trials in Los Angeles County between 1980 and 1986 found that it took more than three years for cases to come to trial. The awards ranged in size from $7,000 to $8 million. Unfortunately, it was possible to account for only about a third of this variation in the amount awarded by considering factors such as the plaintiff's age, gender, or lost earnings. On average, the typical plaintiff received just one-half year's salary, and the amount received was less than the legal fees entailed in the litigation. The legal costs were substantial, averaging $80,000 just for the defense, with the largest amount spent defending one of these cases being $650,000.[47]

The third problem is that the legal uncertainty has led employers to practice "prevention" in ways that make building a committed work force almost impossible. Labor lawyers advise their corporate clients that the phrase "permanent" employee should be avoided, as should any discussion of career prospects or future potential—because these may imply a continuing employment relationship and thereby be construed as an implicit contract. Many if not most organizations have new employees, as almost their first act (sometimes as part of the application process), sign a statement acknowledging their at-will status, an interesting signal for someone entering an organization. Other organizations may have new employees sign a mandatory binding arbitration agreement, presumably for the worthwhile purpose of reducing employer liability as well as the burden on the already overcrowded judicial system. But, again, consider the message sent, if as one of your first actions, your new employer requires you to sign away some of your legal rights, anticipating future disputes and prescribing the method for dealing with them. This would certainly seem to send a message of distrust and to signal the expectation of future employment relation disputes, thus, perhaps, creating a self-fulfilling prophecy.

But the biggest problem of all may be the consequences of the legal uncertainty and litigation costs on the level of employment in the economy. A study of employment effects at the state level reported the following:

> Our econometric analysis of state-level employment outcomes provides strong evidence that wrongful-termination doctrines have significantly affected business decisionmaking. . . . Aggregate employment drops by 2 to 5 percent. . . . Employment reductions are even higher in some nonmanufacturing industries, particularly the service sector. . . . The decline in employment appears to be greater for larger businesses.[48]

Because the reduced employment effect is so disproportionate to the actual remedies provided to terminated employees, the study's authors argued that enactment of a "proposed Uniform Employment Termination Action Act . . . would reduce the consequences of wrongful termination for business,"[49] and, presumably, the adverse impact on the level of employment in the economy. But despite the potential for state action to reduce cost and uncertainty and thereby enhance economic outcomes for all parties, only one state, Montana, has chosen to enact legislation to deal with the issues of wrongful termination and at-will employment. By leaving this and other employment relationship disputes to be settled by the courts, states foster an adversarial climate. Litigation is, if nothing else, an adversarial process, and it hinders economic efficiency and employment. This would appear to be a case of public policy—or its absence—doing harm on a grand scale.

Even as governments take sides with employers, thereby encouraging them not to deal constructively with labor unions, and even as governments eschew direct intervention in the governance of the employment relationship, leaving remedies and intervention to the courts, governments at both the state and the federal level have, over the past several decades, curtailed their enforcement of those regulations that have been passed into law. This reduction of regulatory enforcement activity makes a mockery of the frequent complaints about increasing or excessive government intervention. Furthermore, this reduction in government regulatory oversight encourages unproductive corporate behavior. With the government curtailing its role in the work place, the temptation for corporations is to try to get away with something, and to the extent that some firms succeed at this, their more scrupulous competitors, honestly adhering to regulations and safeguards, are placed at an economic disadvantage.

Table 9-2 presents the number of investigative staff in a number of federal agencies that provide oversight of various aspects of the work place and the employment relation. The trend is clear: Virtually every one of these agencies has experienced a substantial decrease in staff between 1980 and 1994. Does this impair their ability to function? Of course. Even *Business Week,* for instance, noted that understaffing at the Equal Employment Opportunity Commission has made it difficult for workers to obtain justice in sexual harassment complaints. The agency has a backlog of some 97,000 cases. The magazine noted, "For harass-

Table 9-2 CHANGES IN THE NUMBER OF INVESTIGATIVE STAFF IN FEDERAL AGENCIES DEALING WITH EMPLOYMENT RELATION ISSUES

Agency	1980	1990	1994	% Change from 1980
Occupational Safety & Health	1,388	1,271	1,128	−19%
Wage and Hour	1,098	961	727	−34%
Mine Safety and Health	1,522	1,080	1,128	−26%
Pension and Welfare Benefits	235	320	322	+37%
Equal Employment Opportunity Commission	892	762	732	−18%
National Labor Relations Board	1,122	833	783	−30%

Source: Commission on the Future of Worker-Management Relations, U.S. Department of Labor, *Report and Recommendations* (Washington, D.C.: GPO, December 1994), 54.

ment victims, an EEOC overhaul can't come soon enough. Speedy resolution of such painful cases is the best way to deliver justice—to all parties involved."[50] As government in the United States has withdrawn from its role in the work place, evidence mounts that this has not necessarily been beneficial to firms' efforts to achieve profits through people, nor has it been beneficial to the people at work.

A ROLE FOR PUBLIC POLICY

In thinking about a role for public policy in facilitating high performance work arrangements, we need to get beyond some widely-shared caricatures of economic systems. Guess which country, for instance, has the following government policies with respect to human resources and industrial relations, and imagine how competitive in world markets such a country might be.

> The SDF [Skill Development Fund] legislation requires firms employing 50 employees or more to pay 2% of their payroll costs into the SDF. Employers contributing to the SDF can recover 80% of their contributions provided they invest in training. . . . Applications for funds for training can be based on either a single training program or an entire year's training calendar.[51]
>
> Stability in industrial relations was promoted through the creation of a tripartite national governance structure. The National Trade Union Congress (NTUC) . . . and the Employers Federation (SNEF) were provided with representation in all important national bodies, including the National Wages Council, the Economic Development Board . . . and the Employees Provident Fund Board. . . . [T]he government provided funding to the labor movement for the education of union leaders and members regarding economic development issues.
>
> The Industrial Arbitration Court was empowered to ratify all collective bargaining agreements. . . . [T]he period of collective bargaining contract was fixed at five years. Wage increases were controlled via wage guidelines of the tripartite National Wages Council that took into account the competitive position of exports.[52]

It would not surprise me if you guessed a country in Northern Europe, such as Germany or one of the Scandinavian countries. The idea of tripartite cooperation among unions, employer federations, and government in an effort to manage collective economic interests certainly characterized Sweden in the recent past, and the formal governmental acknowledgment of the role of unions is also characteristic of many European countries. Australia would also be a sensible guess, given that for some time that country had a training levy to encourage skill development. Furthermore, if you are like most of the people to whom I show this description, you probably believe that such a set of policies characterizes the condition that has come to be called Eurosclerosis: too much government intervention in the economy and the labor market with a consequent rigidity that creates a system noncompetitive on world markets. What else could one think when periodicals such as *The Economist* and the *Wall Street Journal* maintain a drumbeat of criticism of governmental intervention in labor markets and treat the idea of a training tax, let alone mandated collective bargaining provisions such as that described above, as anathema or worse?

Actually, the country described is not one of those noncompetitive, European places with high unemployment and little economic growth. The description comes from an article about Singapore, a country that has virtually no unemployment and that invariably scores near the top of most listings of national competitiveness—a country that has experienced remarkable, sustained economic growth over the past several decades.

Although the amount of intervention just described may be more than is necessary or desirable in other settings, it is nevertheless the case that a number of government actions can promote the development of high performance work practices. What follows is a partial and certainly a nonexhaustive list. In each instance, I try to provide both the logic and the empirical evidence, when available, that supports the idea of a positive role for the state in promoting organizational performance through the effective management of the employment relation.

Social Security or Assistance

In a world in which both U.S. political parties are trying to outdo each other to "end welfare as we know it" and social assistance is under attack throughout Europe, it may seem strange to talk about the role of government in providing social security as a way of enhancing organizational change in work arrangements. But it is the case that one thing government policy can do to facilitate organizational change and corporate restructuring to obtain profits through people is to provide a social safety net for those harmed by losing their jobs as a consequence of rapidly increasing productivity. In fact, a clear economic rationale backs such programs: "Government programs are often justified on the grounds that society should compensate the losers for structural changes that benefit us in the aggregate."[53] The importance of such policies became clear from what I learned about the experience of the New Zealand Post. As you may recall from chapter 4, the Post shed about a third of its work force when it became a state-owned enterprise in 1987. Today, the Post is an extremely effective organization, named New Zealand's company of the year by Deloitte and Touche in 1994, operating highly profitably, that actually cut postal rates in the mid-1990s, even as it paid bonuses to its employees. Furthermore, as many readers know, New Zealand is virtually the poster child for free-market reforms. *The Economist,* for instance, has referred to the changes over the past decade as "one of the world's boldest experiments in economic reform," and noted that "New Zealand's free-market policies have been widely applauded abroad. Both foreign and New Zealand businessmen say the country has become much more attractive to invest in."[54]

Reducing staff is difficult for the management of any firm, who must put people they know and have worked with on the street. Reducing staff is also very stressful for the staff, particularly those who are redundant. Because of this, managers are sometimes reluctant to get staffing to the right level quickly, and staff, and particularly unions, are likely to fight staff reductions and resist productivity enhancements that threaten employment levels. But these problems are mitigated substantially if the "macro" environment is more benign—where, that is, economic growth is such that people believe they can find other jobs and where a social safety net exists so that individuals know their income will not fall completely. Brian Needham, the chief financial officer of the Post, described how and why the firm was able to change: "New Zealand was in crisis and everyone knew it, and because we have a social security safety net (the dole), it was easier to make the wrenching changes required."[55] In fact, almost every senior manager I talked to at the company referred to the availability of government support for individuals if all else failed as making the organizational changes substantially easier for all concerned. This "social security" as a reason that change was possible is an aspect of the New Zealand experience not frequently discussed in the business media. All too frequently commentators see only the restructuring and fail to examine why and how it was possible to restructure while leaving both the organizations and the society in a healthy condition.

A more benign macroeconomic environment also helps to curtail employment litigation and disputes. An empirical study of employment law litigation in the United States reported the following:

> In other words, good economic conditions will lead to fewer employment discrimination lawsuits, presumably because the greater availability of alternative employment serves as an attractive alternative to litigation. Also, the relative scarcity of workers will diminish the likelihood of employment discrimination, and with fewer layoffs, there will be fewer aggrieved workers who might pursue actions against former employers.[56]

Mandated Employee Participation

If individual firms are unable or unwilling to implement participatory management, as discussed by David Levine and Laura D'Andrea Tyson, but at the same time participation is effective in producing a number of positive economic benefits at the level of the firm, then, perhaps, it is more reasonable than some might think to consider some form of mandated participatory structure. It is important to first put the U.S. situation in context. "Denmark, Sweden, Austria, the Netherlands, and Luxembourg have full [codetermination] laws while Italy and most of the remaining West European countries (excepting Britain) mandate councils for employee participation at the workplace, though not on the board."[57] Nor is this practice confined to Europe. In South Korea, the law provides for "mandatory labor-management councils for all firms with 50 or more employees."[58] Thus, the United States differs from many industrialized countries in not legally requiring some form of employee participation.

If the United States is different, is its system also better? The evidence is not unequivocal but much of it suggests that it is, in fact, inferior. I am not going to cite a lot of macroeconomic statistics because of the problems of inference already mentioned above, although here, too, the record is actually better for countries such as Germany than one might imagine by reading the U.S. business press.[59] Evidence at the work-place level, however, shows that mandated codetermination and the accompanying increased level of institutionalized cooperation has a number of positive effects. In the first place, the number of days lost to strikes is lower in Germany than in countries without required participation. In 1993, 5.6 days per one thousand workers were lost to work stoppages in Germany, while the comparable figure for the United States was 69.4 and for Great Britain it was 125.6.[60]

Second, one can assess the effects of this mandated participation, in the form of codetermination, from both the statements and behaviors of managers in the various countries in which it has been imposed. When the German system of codetermination was first imposed in the early 1950s, it was vigorously resisted by employers. But in the recent past, such resistance has virtually disappeared, even though, with a trend toward more conservative governments and with the worldwide changes in industrial relations, the prospects of changing if not eliminating such regulations are brighter than they have been.

> Codetermination was resisted by corporate spokespersons in West Germany in the 1970s. But for the past decade, its repeal has not been advocated by any political party. . . . In a decade of conservative rule in West Germany, not one step was taken to water down [codetermination] law one iota. In this period, West German corporations out-invested, out-trained, and out-exported their counterparts in such countries without [codetermination] law as Britain and America.[61]

Kirsten Wever's review of industrial relations and economic performance in the United States and Germany found that German managers virtually universally mentioned five advantages of their system of employee representation:

> (1) [T]he relative merits of working with works councils versus unions; (2) the ability of the works councils to ease the conflict of interest between employers and employees; (3) the benefits of negotiating with strong bargaining partners; (4) the advantages of the German system of industrial relations over the American system; and (5) the contributions works councils can make under contemporary economic pressures.[62]

These advantages were articulated by managers, not by politicians, rank-and-file employees, union leaders, or academics. The advantages were illustrated with specific examples and based on extensive experience with working with the German system and comparing it to alternatives. A personnel manager at Bayer, for instance, a large chemical and pharmaceutical firm with over 40,000 employees in Germany, commented specifically on the effects of works councils on enhancing productivity and innovation:

> [T]he works council is a positive productivity factor regarding new technologies. If you want to introduce new technology today, it's not enough that the employees accept it because they have to, but rather that beyond that they accept it as helpful and sensible. And this certainly only is possible when [they are not afraid of] possible effects at the workplace. . . . To get them to accept it, you need the council as an interest aggregator [that] conveys the faith that . . . this will not create problems for the employees.[63]

Nor is this positive effect confined to works councils in Europe. A study of works councils in South Korea found that "effective works councils had a positive impact on labor productivity."[64] This was because they provided employees with a voice at the firm level, thereby helping to encourage high commitment personnel policies.

Wever has argued that U.S. competitiveness has been hampered by distrustful relations among business, labor, and government. While the U.S. system, compared to others, was terrific at generating innovations at the level of individual firms, it has not been very successful in getting work-place innovations widely diffused throughout the economy, an argument made earlier by Robert Cole in his study of the diffusion of small group activities in the United States, Japan, and Sweden. Wever concluded, "overall, the German experience casts doubt on the widespread assumption that the freer the market, the more competitive the firms operating within it."[65] Mandated participation or codetermination, by providing an institutionalized voice for employees, apparently solves some of the prisoner's dilemma of cooperation that arises in the absence of an institutional structure fostering trusting relations and interactions among the parties. So, although government intervention in the employment relation in this manner is not likely to occur any time soon in the United States and seems to be seriously out of fashion, evidence and logic speak to its sensibleness.

The Diffusion of Work-Place Reform and Best Practices

More than one hundred years ago when the United States was still a heavily agricultural society, the federal government funded county agents to go from farm to farm to diffuse information about farming

practices including irrigation, pest control, and information about better seeds. Even today if you visit the University of Illinois at Champaign-
Urbana, you will see the nation's oldest experimental "field," now in
the middle of campus, with a library built underground beneath it so
that this small, historically significant plot of land could continue being
used to grow corn and soybeans. In the United States, a college with A
& M (for instance, as in Texas A & M University) as part of its name
provides further evidence of the government's involvement in agriculture: The A stands for *agricultural*. The government not only funded
research on agricultural issues and funded colleges and universities to
help train knowledgeable practitioners in fields such as viticulture and
veterinary medicine useful to farming and ranching, it also actively
encouraged the diffusion of best practices in agriculture and supported
such diffusion through the efforts of federal and state employees.

One could argue that the government did not need to intervene in
agricultural technology because the market would take care at least of
diffusion. Farmers who did not employ the best and most up-to-date
methods would be disadvantaged in their competition with others who
did. Nonetheless, the government determined that this was an industry
important enough to the country and the economy that it warranted
expenditure of public money to encourage innovation based on the best
knowledge available. Today in the United States, similar efforts to promote best practices with respect to the management of the employment
relationship—and some do exist—are comparatively small in scale, extremely fragile, and are often done circumspectly to minimize visibility
and the criticism that such "governmental meddling" often invites.

In 1993, for instance, the Office of the American Workplace was
established in the Department of Labor. "The agency's mission is to
encourage good workplace practices that lead to better jobs and better
business results."[66] The agency sponsored conferences to bring business
leaders together to share their experiences and published case studies
of organizational change and research on the effects of high performance work practices on business results. The Office of the American
Workplace also published booklets that provided guidance about how
to move to high involvement work systems, including checklists and
measures to monitor progress. Although the agency was started in 1993
with much fanfare, by 1996 it was out of existence without much public
notice of its demise. The agency was a victim of the cuts in the Labor

Department's budget and congressional benign neglect as well as outright opposition. The Secretary of Labor in President Clinton's first term, Robert Reich, tried through the creation of this bureau and through sponsoring research on the effects of human resource management practices on productivity and other measures of firm performance to employ the government's resources to help in the diffusion process. His efforts were as often met by opposition as by support and, in the end, were only partly successful.

But this opposition to any government efforts to encourage the development of knowledge about effective management practices and their diffusion does not characterize most other industrialized countries. I focus here on one example from the United Kingdom because it occurred under a conservative government and illustrates one possibly useful role for state intervention. At the outset, it is important to recognize that in the 1980s under the Conservative party government, Britain's economy was less than a stellar success. By 1986, Britain had among the lowest labor rates in Europe, comparable to Spain and Portugal. Between 1960 and 1986, the average annual percentage change of value-added in manufacturing per person employed was 3.0 percent for the United Kingdom. The only country that ranked lower was the United States (at 2.7 percent), and Britain's rate of productivity growth was less than half that of Japan and was lower than the rates for France, Italy, and Belgium.[67] Moreover, the country had continued to underinvest in training and the development of human capital, increasingly important sources both for productivity growth and for finding solutions to the problem of wage erosion.

In October 1993, an organization called Investors in People UK was incorporated and began operations. The organization is a non-profit, with a twelve-person board of directors, and is led by business and funded partly through sales of Investors in People support material and partly through money from the Department of Employment. Its principal objectives include encouraging the achievement of the Investors in People Standard by organizations in the United Kingdom and helping organizations to understand how investing in people can enhance their commercial success. The Investors in People Standard, formally launched in October 1991, is a set of assessment criteria that is used to determine whether an organization merits being designated an Investor in People, a standard for employment practices that is intended to function similarly to a quality certification.[68] The Standard is intended to be a framework for improving business performance by encouraging "excellence in the field of human resources development."[69] It encourages firms to place the involvement and development of people at the heart of their business strategy. Investors in People works in partnership with Training and Enterprise Councils and industry training organizations.

By 1996, more than 10,000 organizations in the United Kingdom had achieved or were working to attain Investors in People certification. The organization published the results of a series of some fifty-nine case studies documenting the improved business results that accrued to firms from their participation in the program. But what is noteworthy is not so much the individual results—these, after all, are to be expected from organizations that seek profits through how they manage their people— but the encouragement of these organizational changes by an entity partly funded by a conservative government. This funding and encouragement of training and development clearly reflects government belief that industrial competitiveness, achieved in part through the effective management of people, is worth encouraging and stimulating through at least some degree of governmental involvement.

Such intervention in the labor market is surprisingly common, even in supposedly highly capitalistic countries. In New Zealand, for instance, the government has encouraged the development of standards and curricula for training and skill development. This is obviously done in consultation and with the participation of industry, because it is industry that best understands skill requirements and how to assess competency in them. But the government has provided a framework and stimulus for this effort. The Singapore government's intervention in the labor market was noted earlier in this chapter, and Singapore has done other things as well to influence management practice. Singapore Airlines, for instance, has developed not only a reputation for outstanding customer service but real skill in instilling a service culture and in developing operational measures to encourage service quality and improvement. When the government decided that quality was an important basis of competitive success and very useful in a country that, because of extremely low unemployment and increasing wage rates, needed to find other bases besides labor costs for competing, the government went into a joint venture with Singapore Airlines to establish the Singapore Quality Institute (SQI). This institute offers training relevant to improving quality to all organizations in the country. The idea that the only place one can observe governmental intervention to encourage training, organizational and management development, and the implementation of high performance work practices is in quasi-socialistic economies is simply wrong. It reflects an ideological bias that unfortunately inhibits a consideration of the various ways in which government action can encourage the development and diffusion of more effective ways of managing the employment relation.

Reducing Employee-Employer Conflict and Finding Mutual Interests

It is possible for the state to take actions that create a climate more favorable to developing employment relationships based on trust and mutual respect rather than conflict and distrust. It is even possible for this to occur in the United States, as an example from the city of Louisville, Kentucky, illustrates.[70] Louisville in the past had a reputation for labor-management conflict—so much so that in the 1970s it was sometimes called Strike City. The city's mayor estimates that the poor labor relations climate cost between 35,000 and 40,000 jobs in the early 1980s. As a result of these adverse economic consequences, the mayor's office "began convening a group from the labor community, the local Chamber of Commerce, and government to offer solutions to labor-management problems."[71] With the support of some large local employers, a Labor-Management Center was established at the University of Louisville.

"The results of all this was an infrastructure of labor-management government unity that created an environment for cooperation."[72] A collaborative arrangement among business, education, labor, and government annually surveys more than 1,600 employers in the local area to determine their skill requirements and has encouraged additional training. More importantly, the collaborative climate, encouraged by government, has fostered the development of more cooperative labor relations. One instance of this is Philip Morris, a company that employs about 2,700 people in the Louisville area. More than half of those employees have been represented by the Bakery, Confectionery, and Tobacco Workers Union Local 16T. In the 1970s, labor relations were very adversarial, and a six-week strike occurred in 1977. This adversarial relationship was quite costly. In anticipation of a strike each time a contract was up for bargaining, the company would operate on an overtime schedule to build up inventory. If there was no strike, the contract negotiation would be followed by shorter work weeks as the excess inventory was used. The layoffs raised the unemployment insurance costs, the overtime raised the wage costs, and the extra inventory cost money from increased carrying costs. The workers did not fare well either, alternately working extremely long hours and then being temporarily laid off.

After the 1977 strike, both sides decided to develop a different relationship. A Long-Term Agreement, signed in 1979, had a duration of nine years, with renegotiation of specific economic provisions scheduled every three years and a provision for binding arbitration if agreement could not be reached. The union was assured of transfer rights to a new plant in North Carolina, and the company did not oppose unionization in that new facility.[73] As a result of the more cooperative labor relations, grievance activity declined 90 percent, the number of job classifications went from ninety to eleven, and a no-layoff pledge, unless sales volume fell below a certain level, was implemented. Joint management-labor safety committees and a managed care health plan were instituted in the 1980s.

This change in the labor relations climate and the resulting economic benefits were in large measure a result of the intervention by the Louisville government.

> The company credited the efforts of the Mayor of Louisville in bringing labor and management together as a key factor in the improved relationship at Philip Morris. The Mayor's efforts, in the view of the company, created a new openness. Involvement in community and civic projects provided a vehicle for labor and management to work together on issues of common interest. . . . They became acquainted with each other and the good will carried over.[74]

A similar change occurred at Louisville Gas and Electric, with improving relations between management and the International Brotherhood of Electrical Workers Local 2100. This union, initially certified in 1980, settled its first two contracts only after strikes. Subsequent negotiations were also difficult, and a 1989 agreement was rejected by the members by a two-to-one margin. After 1989, the company and the union decided to change their relationship. Forty officials of the company and the union went through joint labor-management training; the bargaining process was altered from adversarial, position bargaining to mutual gains bargaining; and the parties also initiated mutual gains procedures in the grievance process. Once again, the Louisville culture and network of contacts, facilitated by government action, is credited with facilitating the change in the relationship between the company and its people.[75]

Nor is the Louisville case unique. In the Milwaukee area, the Wisconsin Regional Training Partnership, comprised of firms, unions, and public agencies, has seized the initiative in "coordinating efforts to solve the collective action problems surrounding skill formation and industrial upgrading."[76] The organization was officially launched in late 1992 under a charter that "specifies general commitments to jointly determining human resource practices, increasing investments in workplace education, improving re-employment assistance for adults, developing school-to-work initiatives for youth, and benchmarking all training efforts to advanced practices."[77]

Evaluation is difficult, because, of course, member firms join voluntarily and are undoubtedly different in many ways from firms that have chosen not to participate. Nonetheless, some data on the participating firms are instructive. Training expenditures reached a level of 2.75 percent of payroll in 1994, and "all firms are investing more heavily in workplace education and training due to new work systems associated with cell manufacturing, team work, and quality improvement."[78] Most of the firms have added employment, and "the successful transition to high performance has begun to reverse the tide and bring jobs back . . . even in the central city."[79] Other examples exist of efforts similar to those in Louisville and Milwaukee, but they are scattered, comparatively small, and inevitably face an institutional environment not conducive to their establishment. The results, however, seem to be positive when such initiatives actually occur.

CONCLUSION

It is ironic that even as many U.S. employers bemoan the legalistic, adversarial way in which the employment relation is structured, with the attendant delays, unproductive costs, and uncertainty, few seem willing to support an alternative model. It is perhaps even more ironic that the U.S. model of government non-intervention, except as a referee of disputes and to establish a general legal framework for employment, is frequently cited as a model to be adopted by others and is, in fact, diffusing, albeit with some resistance, to other countries. But eschewing direct government mediation or intervention in the employment relation, at times on a tripartite basis with business and labor, in favor of reliance on government regulation and the legal process is a risky and possibly counterproductive strategy.

> The law is associated with an adversarial process. The assertion of legal rights by one party vis-a-vis another party is, by definition, adversarial. Thus, it is not surprising that a key characteristic of innovative relationships is the absence of legalism. Innovative workplace relations do not rely on legal rights; rather they move beyond them.[80]

In the United States, what we seem to have is little or no systematic intervention in the markets for the factors of production—labor and technology—but actually quite a bit of intervention in the product markets. Other countries, notably Singapore, do exactly the reverse, leaving their product markets quite open but intervening to help firms develop their competitive strengths. During the 1980s, for example, when U.S. automobile companies had difficulty competing with the Japanese, the U.S. government pressured the Japanese government into imposing a set of "voluntary" export quotas on Japanese car makers. Textile and apparel quotas as well as quotas for agricultural products and quotas and duties on steel still exist, part of the effort to protect domestic industry, and the United States is far from the free-trader depicted by common rhetoric. Unfortunately, these quotas and tariffs cost consumers literally billions of dollars but do absolutely nothing to build more competitive companies.

Meanwhile, the government did (and does) almost nothing to enhance the capability of firms in these industries to compete more effectively. Thus, little or no state assistance and encouragement fosters the building of more cooperative labor relations, the implementation of high performance work arrangements, or changes in production systems to emphasize approaches such as lean manufacturing (as in automobile manufacturing) or modular production (as in the apparel industry) that provide competitive advantage. One can legitimately wonder whether everyone would not have been better off if the United States had left the automobile product market open but had provided encouragement and assistance in changing the employment relation, relations with unions, and the production system, all of which would have enhanced the competitiveness of the automobile companies.

In this chapter, we have reviewed evidence indicating that neither product nor financial markets always work, at least quickly and efficiently, to produce best practices in the management of the work force. And, we have reviewed arguments and evidence that suggest that most governments in industrialized and industrializing countries, even the conservative government in the United Kingdom, have come to see some role for state action, even if that role is to do nothing else but encourage training and development and the diffusion of better management practices. Evidence shows that such intervention can be useful. That is because "advanced skills and mutual trust are collective goods which individual firms, except perhaps a few of the very largest ones, are unwilling or unable to supply in adequate quantities."[81] At a minimum, government action should not have the consequence of discouraging the building of trust and the development of high performance work practices. Unfortunately, that "do no harm" standard has not consistently been observed.

10 ◆ *People, Profits, and Perspective*

*T*HE KEY TO MANAGING people in ways that lead to profits, productivity, innovation, and real organizational learning ultimately lies in how you think about your organization and its people. It lies in mind set and perspective. When you look at your people, do you see costs to be reduced? Do you see recalcitrant employees prone to opportunism, shirking, and free riding who can't be trusted and who need to be closely controlled through monitoring, rewards, and sanctions? Do you see people performing activities that can and should be contracted out to save on labor costs? Or, when you look at your people, do you see intelligent, motivated, trustworthy individuals—the most critical and valuable strategic assets your organization can have? When you look at your people, do you see them as the fundamental resources on which your success rests and the primary means of differentiating yourself from the competition? Perhaps even more importantly, would someone observing how your organization manages its people recognize your point of view in what you do as opposed to what you talk about doing?

With the right perspective and mind set, leaders can determine how to implement high performance management practices. With the wrong perspective, change efforts and new programs become gimmicks, and no army of consultants, seminars, and slogans can provide very much help.

WHAT DOES IT MEAN TO PUT PEOPLE FIRST?

What does it mean to put people first, recognizing and acting on the fact that in today's world (and probably yesterday's, as well) almost every other source of organizational success—technology, financial structure, competitive strategy—can be imitated in an amazingly short period of time?

It means, first of all, publicly and repeatedly stating the primacy and importance of people to organizational success. Richard Branson, the enormously successful entrepreneur who founded Virgin Records, Virgin Atlantic Airways, and many other enterprises, has stated in numerous speeches that at Virgin Atlantic, the people come first, the customers second, and the shareholders third.[1] The rationale for this ranking is sound, its logic firmly based on the connection between how firms manage people and the profits they achieve. In a speech in London to the Institute of Directors in 1993, Branson stated the relation this way:

> We know that the customer satisfaction which generates all important . . . recommendations and fosters a repeat purchase depends on high standards of service from our people. And we know that high standards of service depend upon having staff who are proud of the company. This is why the interests of our people come first. . . . In the end the long-term interests of shareholders are actually damaged by giving them superficial short-term priority.[2]

Another organization that has taken a similar view is Wal-Mart, the discount retailer with sales in excess of $100 billion. Over the twenty year period from 1972 to 1992, Wal-Mart was second only to Southwest Airlines among all firms publicly traded in the United States in the return earned by its shareholders, providing stockholders with a return of more than 19,000 percent over this time. Sam Walton's philosophy and perspective on Wal-Mart's people, called associates, emphasized their importance to business success:

> The more you share profits with your associates—whether it's in salaries or incentives or bonuses or stock discounts—the more profit will accrue to the company. Why? *Because the way management treats the associates is exactly how the associates will treat the customers.* And if the associates treat the customers well, the customers will return again and again, and *that* is where the real

profit . . . lies, not in trying to drag strangers into your stores for one-time purchases based on splashy sales or expensive advertising.[3]

The company's 1989 annual report stated that "We believe Wal-Mart's dynamic page in retailing continues to be written in direct proportion and as a result of our associates' involvement and contribution."[4] All the firms mentioned in this book, such as Norwest, Men's Wearhouse, ServiceMaster, Southwest Airlines, and many others, publicly and emphatically state the importance of their people to their basic strategy and to their success. Norwest, both in its annual reports and elsewhere, proclaims that people are the firm's real competitive advantage. The Men's Wearhouse states that "our success is attributable to a highly productive workforce. Our store personnel comprise one of the retail industry's finest selling organizations."[5] George Zimmer, founder and CEO, has stated that there are a number of stakeholders the firm must satisfy, but the most important are its people. Customers come second, vendors third, the community fourth, and shareholders are last—and this from the leader of an organization that has produced outstanding growth and shareholder returns.

Such public statements, by themselves, are obviously not sufficient. Many firms proclaim the importance of their people but do not manage in ways consistent with this claim. Talk, as they say, is cheap. But without the organization's affirmation through its senior leadership of the importance of people, little else will happen. It may not be a sufficient condition, but it is probably a necessary one.

Second, putting people first means fixing the firm's language to ensure consistent use of terminology that does not convey disrespect or disdain of its people. Not by accident does Branson refers to Virgin's *people*, Sam Walton to his company's *associates*, or everyone at Whole Foods to everyone else, from the CEO on down, as a *team member*. The term "worker" or even "employee" conveys someone who is in a subordinate role, and conveys less respect and concern than do these alternative terms. Dennis Bakke of AES disdains the term "human resources" because by making people sound like assets, it relegates them to the same status as machines, and, moreover, views them in mostly instrumental terms. Again, fixing the terminology is not likely, by itself, to be sufficient to guarantee the implementation of high performance management practices. But because language does influence how we see things, the right language is clearly useful in helping everyone to see people as important.

Third, leaders and organizations who believe that putting their people first is important actually act on that belief in numerous ways. One of the simplest but also most important is providing everyone access to the organization's leaders. At Southwest Airlines, every person has the home phone number of every company officer. At Virgin Atlantic, every person who works for the company has Richard Branson's home phone number. In a dramatic gesture, CEO Jack Watts of Portola Packaging, a $180 million designer and packager of bottle caps and package closures, dealt with diminishing quality and customer focus, a result of mergers and expansion, by writing in the company's newsletter, "We can best improve our operations by having each member of the team taking action. . . . If we aren't solving problems effectively, contact me and I will make sure the problem is dealt with."[6] He included his home phone number, fax number, and e-mail address.

This action symbolically tells people that all of them are important and are taken seriously in the firm. More importantly, people actually call. As Richard Branson has stated, he would much rather hear about problems from his people before he hears about them from his customers. Jack Watts learned about customer service and people issues that, before he signaled his interest in hearing from everyone and made it easy for them to reach him, had been hidden from him. Knowing what is going on in the organization is critical to leaders of large, geographically dispersed firms. Making oneself available to all kinds of information permits the leader to learn and also conveys an important message to the organization: Information is more important than the chain of command, and everyone is important to the organization's success.

Another way organizations signal their commitment to their people is through their training expenditures. In many organizations, training is viewed as a discretionary expense, something that can be readily cut or even eliminated in times of economic distress or poor profits. But other companies take a different view, because they have a different perspective on their people and on the role of training in building organizational capability as well as signaling to people that they are truly valued by and valuable to the firm. Singapore Airlines, for instance, spends about $80 million per year on training, in a company with revenues of about $4 billion. It provides an average of eleven days of training per person per year, and its core programs are "mandatory and sequentially planned—courses which staff have to attend during the various stages of their career with the company."[7] The training not only imparts skills essential to an organization that is constantly seeking productivity and service improvements, the training also reinforces the company culture and helps to build a community within the company as people get to know each other. This commitment to training is maintained virtually regardless of economic conditions.

Another such organization is USAA, a mutual insurance company begun about sixty years ago to offer insurance to military officers. USAA has since expanded its scope and now offers mutual funds to the general public, has a bank, and offers a broad range of insurance products. USAA has two unique aspects. First, it is frequently mentioned in books about excellent companies because it has continued to thrive even as its primary target population, the military, has substantially shrunk following the end of the Cold War and the subsequent cuts in the U.S. defense budget. The company has prospered by achieving an incredibly high level of customer retention by delivering high value and exceptional service and by selling additional products and services to its current customer base.

A second unique aspect of USAA is its emphasis on training. When I visited the company in 1995, I learned that it had approximately one person in its training department for every sixty-three people. The training department is separate from human resources and reports independently to the same level in the organization. And yes, you read those numbers correctly—USAA, a company with about 16,000 people, has almost three hundred people in its training department. USAA is willing to devote this level of effort to training because the firm sees training and the productivity and customer service benefits training provides as a key competitive advantage. Thus it does not outsource its training activity and it doesn't cut training when profitability diminishes. Maintaining training signals a commitment to an organization's people in a tangible way; it says, we value you enough to continue to invest in you, even when times aren't the best. Men's Wearhouse and Singapore Airlines do the same. These organizations see training not as a cost but as a key strategic weapon, and behave accordingly.

Fourth, putting people first means gathering measurements so the organization can assess how well it is doing and being willing to act on those measurements. At Hewlett-Packard, part of managers' performance evaluation depends on how well they are living up to the H-P Way, assessed through a survey of the people who work for them. One is unlikely to do well at Hewlett-Packard if the people one manages are dissatisfied with their work environment. At AES and Whole Foods Markets, surveys of attitudes and beliefs about how well the organization is living up to its values and aspirations are important enough to draw attention in the annual report. At General Electric, the company evaluates managers both by their financial performance and by assessments provided by their people. Getting outstanding results in the right way—by treating people well, developing and retaining them, and managing in a way consistent with the company's values—is the mark of success. Getting good financial numbers at the cost of people is not only not rewarded but not tolerated for very long, reflecting the company's belief that in the long run, the numbers will decline if people are not being treated properly. Citibank uses a balanced scorecard approach to measuring performance, considering dimensions besides financial. In the 1997 version of their publication describing the balanced scorecard, the category people comes first, a signal that effective teamwork and people management is important to the organization.

Fifth, and perhaps most importantly, putting people first entails ensuring that those in leadership positions have people-oriented values and manage in ways consistent with building high performance work environments. Probably no company exemplifies this practice better than ServiceMaster, a company that over a twenty-five year period, 1970 to 1995, achieved a return to shareholders of 25 percent compounded annually, more than double the return achieved by the stock market as a whole over the same period.[8] The company has been willing to invest in leadership training and courses to help people develop their communication skills and self-confidence for individuals at all levels in the organization. Developing management talent and instilling in those leaders the organization's core values is critical to the success of the firm.

ServiceMaster has grown, in part, through acquisitions, and one of the firms it acquired was Terminix, a company in the business of eliminating termites from buildings. Carlos Cantu, now the president and chief executive of ServiceMaster, was the CEO of Terminix at the time of its acquisition. His story of his meeting with William Pollard, now the chairman of ServiceMaster and at the time its CEO, is revealing.

> When I first met Bill Pollard, I was . . . presenting the company to potential buyers. . . . I was surprised when much of our conversation focused on people, leadership, and responsibility to associates in the work place. Bill was sharing his experience in a unique business environment which champions the principle that customers, associates, and shareholders should be treated with dignity and respect.[9]

How many acquisition meetings have you been in that entailed, before getting down to discussions of merger terms and finances, a general discussion of philosophy, including the company's philosophy about leadership and people? I suspect the answer is not too many.

ServiceMaster has recognized that its basic core competence, and the key to its outstanding business success in an industry with essentially no barriers to entry, is its ability to train and develop people. Having recognized this fact, the company has chosen for its leadership positions individuals who exemplify its values and who truly put people first. William Pollard has written a book, *The Soul of the Firm,* and excerpts from that book, published in the company's 1995 annual report, provide compelling evidence of both his values and the fact that those values are precisely what one would want in a leader in a company that succeeds by putting people first.

> At ServiceMaster, the task before us is to train and motivate people to serve so that they will do a more effective job, be more productive in their work, and, yes, even be better people. . . . It is more than a job, a means to earn a living. It is, in fact, our mission. . . . [I]f we focused exclusively on profit, we would be a firm that had failed to nurture its soul. Eventually . . . firms that do this experience a loss in the direction and purpose of their people, a loss in customers, and then a loss in profits. Both people and profit are part of our mission. . . . You can't run a business without people. . . . Only people—not machines—can respond to the unexpected and surprise the customer with extraordinary performance. Only people can serve. Only people can lead, only people can innovate and create.[10]

This perspective on people and organizations is, in many way, counter to that found in conventional economic perspectives with their emphasis on individual financial incentives and requirements for hierarchy, surveillance, and control. It is all too rare a perspective in the world of contemporary organizations, but essential to making the connection between people and profits. Pollard explicitly recognized the critical difference between ServiceMaster's values and philosophy and much of modern management theory:

> [B]usiness is not just a game of manipulation that accomplished a series of tasks for a profit with the gain going to a few and with the atrophy of the soul of the person producing the results. People are not just economic animals or non-personal production units. . . . [W]hen you view the person only as a production unit or something that can be defined solely in economic terms, motivational, or even incentive schemes have a tendency to be mechanical and manipulative. . . . [T]he soulless, adversarial, or work rights environment should not be the model of the future.[11]

Finally, putting people first entails recognizing the importance of people—all of a company's people in all organizations—to organizational success. A colleague reading an early draft of this book commented that much of the material covered traditional industries, such as steel, retailing, automobile manufacturing, apparel. Where, he asked, were the new, "knowledge-based" industries, such as management consulting, software, and investment banking? Other writers have emphasized the so-called new knowledge work, as though some jobs and some industries are knowledge-based and others aren't. But in 1997 and going forward, successful organizations will be those that recognize that *all work is knowledge work*. Is cleaning a hospital knowledge work? It is to ServiceMaster, which has profited in part by providing its front-line people both with high technical skills and with sales skills, permitting better customer retention and therefore enhanced profitability. Is selling men's clothing knowledge work? It is to the Men's Wearhouse, which, through its training programs, not only generates more sales revenue from people better equipped to sell but also a more committed and motivated work force with reduced turnover and inventory shrinkage, in part due to the enhanced self-esteem that comes from being taken very seriously. Is automobile assembly work knowledge work? It is to Toyota and similar companies that have both recognized and capitalized on the skills and knowledge of those people who do the work and have the best knowledge of it. The list could go on. Putting people first means, in the end, taking all of them seriously and, most importantly, recognizing the opportunities to leverage knowledge and build capability and skill in all jobs, in all organizations.

Putting people first means having articulated values and goals, organizational language and terminology, measurements, role models in senior leadership positions, and specific practices that make real the noble sentiments so often honored in the breach. It entails doing things that both reinforce the importance of people to organizational success and simultaneously make it more likely that the organization will have an advantage in attracting and retaining the best people and realizing their full potential. ServiceMaster, for the most part, treats its people, many of whom have only high school educations and who are doing relatively unskilled work, with more dignity and respect than many professional service firms I have seen—firms that rely on a more educated and more expensive work force that is also the key to their success. The Men's Wearhouse, operating in an industry, retailing, that has typically treated its people badly, calls its store salespeople "wardrobe consultants" and instills in them the belief that they can truly be "artists" in the realm of providing customer service and selling clothing that will make their customers look better. Lessons for all organizations can be found in these few that have achieved outstanding success by how they manage their people.

WHAT A PEOPLE-CENTERED STRATEGY DOES

We have talked about what putting people first entails. What does it do? Figure 10-1 diagrams what a people-focused strategy can accomplish. The diagram serves as a reminder and summary of what we have learned in this book. Basic people management practices—I have identified seven—constitute the fundamental building blocks of high performance management systems. Those practices provide competitive advantage for two interrelated reasons.

First, they are difficult to imitate. They are difficult to imitate because implementation entails changing basic views about people, organizations, and sources of success—and changing basic assumptions is always harder than altering a few superficial organizational arrangements. They are difficult to imitate because many of them defy conventional wisdom and common practice, as well as for a variety of other reasons considered in chapter 5. How do we know these practices are difficult to imitate? Because we have seen ample evidence that even when organizations know what to do to achieve higher levels of quality, productivity, and customer service, even when, as in the case of the apparel industry, a recipe exists for changing the basic competitive dynamics in ways that favor them, all too frequently implementation is slow and backsliding frequent. We also know these practices are difficult to imitate because the organizations that have followed them have, for the most part, enjoyed outstanding competitive success not just for a quarter or a year, but for many years and even for decades. This suggests that, unlike technology or other strategies, the outstanding economic returns produced are less likely to be reduced through the imitation of these strategies by competitors—at least in the short run.

The second reason these practices provide economic advantage is because they are positively related to organizational learning and skill development, innovation, customer service, labor productivity, costs—

Figure 10-1 WHAT A PEOPLE-BASED STRATEGY DOES

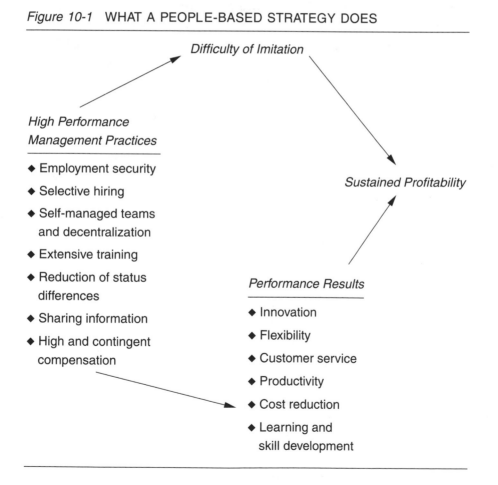

Difficulty of Imitation

*High Performance
Management Practices*

- Employment security
- Selective hiring
- Self-managed teams
  and decentralization
- Extensive training
- Reduction of status
  differences
- Sharing information
- High and contingent
  compensation

Sustained Profitability

Performance Results

- Innovation
- Flexibility
- Customer service
- Productivity
- Cost reduction
- Learning and
  skill development

including not only labor costs but also material costs such as scrap and materials handling and costs of turnover—and organizational flexibility to adapt to new competitive conditions and threats. How do we know these high performance management practices have these effects? Because in this book I have reviewed literally scores of systematic quantitative studies as well as numerous case examples that provide evidence for the business case for managing people right. We have seen evidence from studies of specific industries; from studies that span industries; from studies of manufacturing companies, service companies, and even financial service firms such as banks. We have seen evidence from research that has examined the implications of high performance management practices for learning, innovation, and customer service—not just cost and productivity.

As Figure 10-1 suggests, if a set of management practices are at once difficult to imitate and positively related to numerous sources of competitive success, the result is outstanding levels of profitability, achieved over a long time. Such a management approach produces profitability and success that is robust in that it can succeed:

1. across changes in leadership (ServiceMaster is now fifty years old and has gone through several generations of leaders);
2. across changes in the political environment (Southwest has faced airline deregulation and Norwest has confronted vast changes in financial regulation);
3. across changes in technology (Hewlett-Packard has gone from being primarily an instruments company to being a computer and printer company);
4. across changes in economic circumstances (Wal-Mart has prospered even when, in the late 1980s and early 1990s, much of the retailing industry was in bankruptcy);
5. across different cultures (AES, Virgin Atlantic, and Singapore Airlines operate globally); and
6. across changes in the competitive environment (Whole Foods' higher margins has attracted entry even from more conventional grocery store chains, but these new entrants have not had much success, so far).

It is the robustness of people as a source of competitive success—the ability of organizations that manage this way to survive and prosper in many different circumstances and to respond to numerous types of change—that has so much to recommend putting people first as a basic organizational approach.

Organizational Leverage

A people-centered strategy can provide organizational leverage that, in turn, can produce opportunities for profit. Let me explain. Consider an organization that has invested a great deal in capital resources. Many organizations operate in capital intensive businesses, such as airlines, hotels, oil refineries, pulp and paper mills, steel mills, semiconductor fabrication plants, electric power plants, and so forth. In each of these businesses, much if not most of the cost is in the fixed capital investment, and those costs continue whether or not the airlines and hotels are occupied and whether or not the manufacturing facilities are operating. Thus, the people who work in these organizations are highly leveraged, with considerable capital per person. If the people are motivated, trained, and committed, results are outstanding; if they aren't, results can be disastrous.

Here is the opportunity to profit. Find an organization that is mismanaging its people. Buy the business or facility based on what it is earning, or even at a premium. Then, implement high commitment management practices. The returns can be enormous. If this seems fanciful, let me give you a few examples. A former student told me about a diaper factory in Latin America. Although the owners had installed the most modern machinery, they had terrible policies regarding their people. They paid them poorly, gave them little training, and exercised autocratic if not despotic management. Safety in the plant was terrible, machine breakdowns were frequent, and the equipment operated less than 50 percent of the time. Then Procter & Gamble came along and offered to buy the plant. The firm was even willing to pay a premium, in the sense of being willing to pay more than would be justified on the basis of the plant's production operating at 50 percent uptime. P & G completed the acquisition and installed its typical management approach. This company has pioneered in implementing self-managing teams, emphasizing decentralization, and focusing on the safety and training of its people. Within months, the plant was operating about 95 percent of the time. That difference in productivity was all profit to P & G, as it required relatively few incremental costs to make the management in the facility more effective.

As another example, consider Whole Foods Markets. Whole Foods has grown by acquisition. A Whole Foods market, at six to seven years of age, earns about 10 percent on sales before taking out corporate overhead (which generally runs about 3 to 4 percent). Most grocery stores earn one to two percent. The profitability of a Whole Foods store is, after two years, indistinguishable between its internally-developed and acquired stores. Indeed, one of the company's core competencies is its ability to absorb acquisitions. Whole Foods has been able to buy companies such as Fresh Fields, a large, basically unprofitable competitor, purchasing the stores and sales at a discounted price because of their poor economic results. Then, by installing its people-centered management practices, the company turns the stores around and profits handsomely as a consequence. I have seen the Men's Wearhouse do similar things with its acquisitions.

Changing management practices in ways that build commitment and competence can transform poorly performing assets. By so doing, companies and entrepreneurs can profit handsomely—as can investors who understand this process and its dynamics.

THE COURAGE TO PUT PEOPLE FIRST

We have seen through both case studies and systematic evidence a compelling case for the connection between how organizations manage people and their profits. Many of the practices associated with high performance or high commitment management have been known and understood for a long time and have been subject to extensive study and discussion. Nevertheless, adoption of these ideas has proceeded slowly and sporadically. Although many of the ideas—things such as providing some sense of security for people you want to commit to the organization—are commonsensical, in their actual application they run up against a number of versions of conventional wisdom that appear to be contradictory.

In the end, doing things differently and going against conventional wisdom is difficult. Achieving profits through people thus often comes down to courage. I have been fortunate to know a number of leaders who have had the wisdom, insight, and courage to manage people effectively in spite of what their organizations or conventional wisdom has said was the right thing to do. The following is just one example.

Some years ago I met a man named Dave Spence who had joined Boise Cascade as plant manager in the company's DeRidder, Louisiana, papermaking plant. At the time he joined the company, it was involved in a contentious strike with the employees and their Louisiana union—a strike that included violence, threats, and intimidation. In the years Spence managed the plant, he worked with the people there and with the union in a different way, listening to and caring about them, while at the same time increasing production some 40 percent, an increase equivalent to the purchase of an additional $500 million in capital equipment. When I met Spence he was the head of manufacturing for the paper division. He has since been promoted to senior vice president and general manager in charge of all aspects of the paper division at Boise Cascade. He was continuing to implement his philosophy of management, nicely summarized on the first overhead he used in a presentation to my class at Stanford: "Capital and Machinery Make It Possible—People Make It Happen."

It was clear to me through my own dealings with the company that Spence's philosophy at the time he was making changes in DeRidder was not really shared by all of the senior management, despite the talk of total quality and team work. Over dinner together in Boise when I was there to do some executive education, I noted that although I thought he was on the right track, his approach seemed to be at odds with what had been the dominant management orientation and culture. Without a moment's hesitation he replied, "I took the position that I've worked at other places before, and I may have to again. I've always believed you have to do your job like you are independently wealthy; then you can do the right things all the time."

Spence's career at Boise Cascade has thrived as he and his working partners have helped turn an adversarial relationship with the union around and have harnessed the ideas and energy of more and more of the paper division's people. But executives who manage in a way not consistent with the dominant corporate ideology have no guarantees that they will prosper, regardless of the results achieved by their methods. Many, therefore, won't translate their knowledge of what needs to be done about managing people into actions that actually implement that knowledge. But for the organizations that have leaders possessing both insight and courage, the evidence demonstrates that the economic returns can be enormous.

Notes

Chapter One

1. Robert Buzzell and Bradley T. Gale, *The PIMS Principles: Linking Strategy to Performance* (New York: Free Press, 1987).
2. Richard L. Schonberger, "Is Strategy Strategic? Impact of Total Quality Management on Strategy," *Academy of Management Executive* 6 (1992): 87.
3. Ibid., 80.
4. Richard Rumelt, "How Much Does Industry Matter?" *Strategic Management Journal* 12 (1991): 167–185.
5. Charles E. Lucier and Amy Asin, "Toward a New Theory of Growth," *Strategy and Business* 1 (Winter 1996): 11.
6. Ibid., 12.
7. Ibid., 11.
8. Stephanies N. Mehta, "Low-Tech Firms Top Magazine's List of Fastest-Growing Private Companies," *The Wall Street Journal,* 11 October 1996, B2.
9. John R. Dorfman, "Oil-Drilling and Semiconductor Stocks Excel," *The Wall Street Journal,* 27 February 1997, R14.
10. "Growth Table Manners," *World Link,* March/April 1996, 47.
11. Dwight L. Gertz and Joao P. A. Baptista, *Grow to Be Great* (New York: Free Press, 1995), 1.
12. Ibid., 15.
13. Ibid., 33.
14. Glenn Ruffenach, "Which Companies Treated Their Shareholders the Best—And the Worst," *The Wall Street Journal,* 27 February 1997, R2.
15. Scott McCartney and Michael J. McCarthy, "Southwest Flies Circles Around United's Shuttle," *The Wall Street Journal,* 20 February 1996, B1.
16. G. Bruce Knecht, "Banking Maverick: Norwest Corp. Relies on Branches, Pushes Service—And Prospers," *The Wall Street Journal,* 17 August 1995, A9.

17. Norwest Corporation, *1996 Annual Report,* Minneapolis, MN, 11.
18. Robert H. Waterman, *What America Does Right* (New York: W. W. Norton, 1994), 21–22.
19. Brent Keltner, "Divergent Patterns of Adjustment in the U.S. and German Banking Industries: An Institutional Explanation," (Ph.D. diss., Stanford University, 1994).
20. Brent Keltner, "Relationship Banking in the U.S. and Germany," *California Management Review* 37 (Summer 1995): 55.
21. Barry Meier, "Need a Teller? Chicago Bank Plans a Fee," *The New York Times,* 27 April 1995, C1, C9.
22. Norwest Corporation, *1995 Annual Report,* Minneapolis, MN, 7.
23. Keltner, "Divergent Patterns of Adjustment," 120.
24. Ibid., 121.
25. Keltner, "Relationship Banking," 48.
26. Keltner, "Divergent Patterns of Adjustment," 94.
27. Ibid., 46.
28. Keltner, "Relationship Banking," 50.
29. Peter H. Lewis, "Apple's Best Hope: On-Line Sales," *The New York Times,* 13 August 1996, B9.
30. Apple Computer, *Apple Employee Handbook* (Cupertino, CA: Apple Computer, 1993), 1.
31. Anonymous employee, quoted in Apple Computer, "Human Resource Policies and Practices at Apple Computer," 20 May 1994, 18.
32. Ibid., 19.
33. Ibid.
34. Eileen Appelbaum and Rosemary Batt, *The New American Workplace* (Ithaca, New York: ILR Press, 1994), 159.

Chapter Two

1. John Paul MacDuffie, "Human Resource Bundles and Manufacturing Performance: Organizational Logic and Flexible Production Systems in the World Auto Industry," *Industrial and Labor Relations Review* 48 (1995): 199.
2. Thomas Bailey, "High Performance Work Organization in the Apparel Industry: The Extent and Determinants of Reform," working paper 1, National Center for the Workplace, Berkeley, CA, October 1996, 1.
3. Mark A. Huselid, "The Impact of Human Resource Management Practices on Turnover, Productivity, and Corporate Financial Performance," *Academy of Management Journal* 38 (1995): 645.
4. Ibid., 647.

5. Ibid., 667.
6. Mark A. Huselid and Brian E. Becker, "The Impact of High Performance Work Systems, Implementation Effectiveness, and Alignment with Strategy on Shareholder Wealth," unpublished paper, Rutgers University, New Brunswick, NJ, 1997, 18–19.
7. Linda Bilmes, Konrad Wetzker, and Pascal Xhonneux, "Value in Human Resources," *Financial Times*, 10 February 1997, 10.
8. Theresa Welbourne and Alice Andrews, "Predicting Performance of Initial Public Offering Firms: Should HRM Be in the Equation?" *Academy of Management Journal* 39 (1996): 891–919.
9. Ibid., 901.
10. Ibid., 910–911.
11. John Paul MacDuffie, "International Trends in Work Organization in the Auto Industry: National-Level versus Company-Level Perspectives," in *The Comparative Political Economy of Industrial Relations,* eds. Kirsten S. Wever and Lowell Turner (Madison, WI: Industrial Relations Research Association, 1995), 64.
12. Ibid., 77. List used by permission.
13. Frits K. Pil and John Paul MacDuffie, "The Adoption of High-Involvement Work Practices," *Industrial and Labor Relations Review* 35 (1996): 434.
14. MacDuffie, "International Trends," 105.
15. Casey Ichniowski, Kathryn Shaw, and Giovanna Prennushi, "The Effect of Human Resource Management Practices on Productivity," working paper, Graduate School of Business, Columbia University, New York, New York, 16.
16. Ibid., 29.
17. Ibid., 32.
18. Ibid., 41.
19. Casey Ichniowski, Thomas A. Kochan, David Levine, Craig Olson, and George Strauss, "What Works at Work: Overview and Assessment," *Industrial Relations* 35 (1996): 325.
20. Jeffrey B. Arthur, "Effects of Human Resource Systems on Manufacturing Performance and Turnover," *Academy of Management Journal* 37 (1994): 672; emphasis added.
21. John T. Dunlop and David Weil, "Human Resource Innovations in the Apparel Industry: An Industrial Relations Systems Perspective," unpublished paper, Harvard University, 1992, 1–2.
22. Thomas Bailey, "Organizational Innovation in the Apparel Industry," *Industrial Relations* 32 (1993): 34.
23. Dunlop and Weil, "Human Resource Innovations," 1.

24. Sid Riley, "The Industrial Revolution: Our Time Has Arrived," *Bobbin* 28 (April 1987): 76; quoted in Bailey, 38.
25. John T. Dunlop and David Weil, "Diffusion and Performance of Modular Production in the U.S. Apparel Industry," *Industrial Relations* 35 (1996): 337.
26. Bailey, 36–37.
27. Dunlop and Weil, "Diffusion and Performance," 337–338.
28. Ibid., 338.
29. Ibid, 334.
30. Ibid., 335.
31. Vinay Sohoni, "Workforce Involvement and Wafer Fabrication Efficiency," in *The Competitive Semiconductor Manufacturing Human Resources Project: First Interim Report,* ed. Clair Brown (Berkeley, CA: Institute of Industrial Relations, 1994), 112.
32. Clair Brown, "Executive Summary," in *The Competitive Semiconductor Manufacturing Human Resources Project: First Interim Report,* ed. Clair Brown (Berkeley, CA: Institute of Industrial Relations, 1994), 5.
33. Richard Ricketts, "Survey Points to Practices that Reduce Refinery Maintenance Spending," *Oil and Gas Journal,* 4 July 1994, 38.
34. Ibid.
35. Ibid., 40.
36. Ibid., 41.
37. Agis Salpukas, "New Ideas for U.S. Oil," *The New York Times,* 16 November 1995, C1, C18.
38. Benjamin Schneider and David E. Bowen, "Employee and Customer Perceptions of Service in Banks: Replication and Extension," *Journal of Applied Psychology* 70 (1985): 431.
39. Benjamin Schneider, "Service Quality and Profits: Can You Have Your Cake and Eat It, Too?" *Human Resource Planning* 14 (1991): 151.
40. B. Schneider, J. J. Parkington, and V. M. Buxton, "Employee and Customer Perceptions of Service in Banks," *Administrative Science Quarterly* 25 (1980): 252–267.
41. Schneider and Bowen, 430.
42. R. H. Johnson, A. M. Ryan, and M. J. Schmit, "Employee Attitudes and Branch Performance at Ford Motor Credit" (paper presented at the Ninth Annual Conference of the Society of Industrial and Organizational Psychology, Nashville, TN, April 1994).
43. Mark J. Schmit and Steven P. Allscheid, "Employee Attitudes and Customer Satisfaction: Making Theoretical and Empirical Connections," *Personnel Psychology* 48 (1995): 521–536.

44. Anne Moeller and Benjamin Schneider, "Climate for Service and the Bottom Line," in *Creativity in Services Marketing*, eds. M. Venkatesan, D. M. Schmalansee, and C. Marshall (Chicago: American Marketing Association, 1986), 68–70.

45. Jeffrey B. Arthur, "The Link Between Business Strategy and Industrial Relations Systems in American Steel Minimills," *Industrial and Labor Relations Review* 45 (1992): 488–506.

46. MacDuffie, 218.

47. Huselid, 667–668.

48. John E. Delery and D. Harold Doty, "Modes of Theorizing in Strategic Human Resource Management: Tests of Universalistic, Contingency, and Configurational Performance Predictions," *Academy of Management Journal* 39 (1996): 821.

49. Ibid., 825.

50. Mark A. Youndt, Scott A. Snell, James W. Dean, Jr., and David P. Lepak, "Human Resource Management, Manufacturing Strategy, and Firm Performance," *Academy of Management Journal* 39 (1996): 836–866.

51. See, for instance, chapter 3 in Jeffrey Pfeffer, *Competitive Advantage Through People* (Boston: Harvard Business School Press, 1994).

52. Barry A. Macy and Hiroaki Izumi, "Organizational Change, Design, and Work Innovation: A Meta-Analysis of 131 North American Field Studies, 1961–1991," in *Research in Organizational Change and Development*, Vol. 7, eds. W. A. Passmore and R. W. Woodman (Greenwich, CT: JAI Press, 1993), 235–313.

53. Casey Ichniowski, "Human Resource Practices and Productive Labor-Management Relations," in *Research Frontiers in Industrial Relations and Human Resources*, eds. David Lewin, Olivia Mitchell, and Peter Sherer (Madison, WI: Industrial Relations Research Association, 1992), 239–271.

54. Delery and Doty, 825.

55. Huselid, 640.

56. Peter Berg, Eileen Appelbaum, Thomas Bailey, and Arne L. Kalleberg, "The Performance Effects of Modular Production in the Apparel Industry," *Industrial Relations* 35 (1996): 369.

57. Ichniowski, Kochan, Levine, Olson, and Strauss, 324.

58. National Center on the Educational Quality of the Workforce, *EQW Issues*, Vol. 10 (Philadelphia, PA: National Center on the Educational Quality of the Workforce, 1995), 4.

59. Richard M. Locke, "The Transformation of Industrial Relations? A Cross-National Review," in *The Comparative Political Economy of Industrial Rela-*

tions, eds. Kirsten S. Wever and Lowell Turner (Madison, WI: Industrial Relations Research Association, 1995), 16.

Chapter Three

1. See chapter 2 in Jeffrey Pfeffer, *Competitive Advantage Through People: Unleashing the Power of the Work Force* (Boston: Harvard Business School Press, 1994).
2. Richard M. Locke, "The Transformation of Industrial Relations? A Cross-National Review," in *The Comparative Political Economy of Industrial Relations,* eds. Kirsten S. Wever and Lowell Turner (Madison, WI: Industrial Relations Research Association, 1995), 18–19.
3. Herb Kelleher, "A Culture of Commitment," *Leader to Leader* 1 (Spring 1997): 23.
4. John E. Delery and D. Harold Doty, "Modes of Theorizing in Strategic Human Resource Management: Tests of Universalistic, Contingency, and Configurational Performance Predictions," *Academy of Management Journal* 39 (1996): 820.
5. Ling Sing Chee, "Singapore Airlines: Strategic Human Resource Initiatives," in *International Human Resource Management: Think Globally, Act Locally,* ed. Derek Torrington (New York: Prentice Hall, 1994), 152.
6. "Southwest Airlines," Case S-OB-28 (Palo Alto, CA: Graduate School of Business, Stanford University, 1994), 29.
7. Brian O'Reilly, "The Rent-a-Car Jocks Who Made Enterprise #1," *Fortune,* 28 October 1996, 128.
8. Laurie Graham, *On the Line at Subaru-Isuzu* (Ithaca, New York: ILR Press, 1995), 18.
9. See, for instance, C. A. O'Reilly, J. A. Chatman, and D. F. Caldwell, "People and Organizational Culture: A Profile Comparison Approach to Assessing Person-Organization Fit," *Academy of Management Journal* 34 (1991): 487–516; and J. A. Chatman, "Managing People and Organizations: Selection and Socialization in Public Accounting Firms," *Administrative Science Quarterly* 36 (1991): 459–484.
10. Graham, 31.
11. Ibid.
12. Ibid., 33.
13. Rosemary Batt, "Outcomes of Self-Directed Work Groups in Telecommunications Services," in *Proceedings of the Forty-Eighth Annual Meeting of the Industrial Relations Research Association,* ed. Paula B. Voos (Madison, Wisconsin: Industrial Relations Research Association, 1996), 340.
14. Rajiv D. Banker, Joy M. Field, Roger G. Schroeder, and Kingshuk K. Sinha,

"Impact of Work Teams on Manufacturing Performance: A Longitudinal Field Study," *Academy of Management Journal* 39 (1996): 867–890.

15. "Work Week," *The Wall Street Journal*, 28 May 1996, A1.

16. Batt, 344.

17. Ibid.

18. Ibid., 346.

19. Graham, 97.

20. M. Parker and J. Slaughter, "Management by Stress," *Technology Review* 91 (1988): 43.

21. Whole Foods Market, Inc., *1995 Annual Report*, Austin, TX, 3, 17.

22. Charles Fishman, "Whole Foods Teams," *Fast Company*, April–May 1996, 104.

23. Ibid., 107.

24. Harley Shaiken, Steven Lopez, and Isaac Mankita, "Two Routes to Team Production: Saturn and Chrysler Compared," *Industrial Relations* 36 (January 1997): 31.

25. Alex Markels, "Team Approach: A Power Producer Is Intent on Giving Power to Its People," *The Wall Street Journal*, 3 July 1995, A1.

26. Kirsten Downey Grimsley, "The Power of a Team," *Washington Business*, *The Washington Post*, 12 February 1996, F12.

27. Mark van Beusekom, *Participation Pays! Cases of Successful Companies with Employee Participation* (The Hague: Netherlands Participation Institute, 1996), 7.

28. Rhonda Thompson, "An Employee's View of Empowerment," *HR Focus*, July 1993, 14.

29. Ibid.

30. Thomas R. Bailey and Annette D. Bernhardt, "In Search of the High Road in a Low-Wage Industry," *Politics and Society* (1997, in press).

31. Glenn Collins, "In Grocery War, the South Rises," *The New York Times*, 25 April 1995, C5.

32. Verne C. Harnish, "Company of Owners," *Executive Excellence*, May 1995, 7.

33. Mary Rowland, "Rare Bird: Stock Options for Many," *The New York Times*, 1 August 1993, F14.

34. David Jacobson, "Employee Ownership and the High-Performance Workplace," working paper no. 13, National Center for the Workplace, Berkeley, CA, 1996.

35. Bill Gurley, "Revenge of the Nerds: The Stock Option Square Dance," World Wide Web, www.upside.com/texis/archive/search/article.html?UID= 970314003. 14 March 1997.

36. Fishman, 105.
37. Ibid., 104.
38. John Paul MacDuffie and Thomas A. Kochan, "Do U.S. Firms Invest Less in Human Resources? Training in the World Auto Industry," *Industrial Relations* 34 (1995): 153.
39. Ibid., 163.
40. Shaiken, Lopez, and Mankita, 25.
41. Catherine Truss, Lynda Gratton, Veronica Hope-Hailey, Patrick McGovern, and Philip Stiles, "Soft and Hard Models of Human Resource Management: A Reappraisal," *Journal of Management Studies* 34 (1997): 60.
42. Ibid., 60–61.
43. Bailey and Bernhardt, 5.
44. Men's Wearhouse, *1994 Annual Report,* Fremont, CA, 3.
45. Michael Hartnett, "Men's Wearhouse Tailors Employee Support Programs," *Stores,* August 1996, 47.
46. Ibid., 48.
47. Thomas A. Stewart, "How a Little Company Won Big by Betting on Brainpower," *Fortune,* 4 September 1995, 121.
48. Ibid., 122.
49. Graham, 107–108.
50. Suzanne Schlosberg, "Big Titles for Little Positions," *San Francisco Chronicle,* 29 April 1991, C3.
51. "Doing the Right Thing," *The Economist,* 20 May 1995, 64.
52. Whole Foods Market, Inc., *Proxy Statement,* 29 January 1996, 15.
53. Scott McCartney, "Salary for Chief of Southwest Air Rises After 4 Years," *The Wall Street Journal,* 29 April 1996, C16.
54. Fishman, 106.
55. Ibid., 104.
56. Ibid., 105.
57. "Jack Stack (A)," Case 9-993-009 (Stanford, CA: Business Enterprise Trust, 1993), 2–4.
58. Ibid.
59. Ibid., 5.
60. Tim R. V. Davis, "Open-Book Management: Its Promise and Pitfalls," *Organizational Dynamics* 25 (Winter 1997): 7–20.
61. "Jack Stack (A)," 3.
62. Brian Becker and Barry Gerhart, "The Impact of Human Resource Management on Organizational Performance: Progress and Prospects," *Academy of Management Journal* 39 (1996): 786.

Chapter Four

1. Brian Becker and Barry Gerhart, "The Impact of Human Resource Management on Organizational Performance: Progress and Prospects," *Academy of Management Journal* 39 (1996): 786.
2. "Human Resources at the AES Corporation: The Case of the Missing Department," Case SHR-3 (Stanford, CA: Stanford University, Graduate Business School, 1997, 16–17).
3. AES Corporation, *1996 Annual Report,* Arlington, VA, 12.
4. Beth Benjamin, letter to author, 1997.
5. Jeffrey Pfeffer, *Managing with Power: Politics and Influence in Organizations* (Boston: Harvard Business School Press, 1992).
6. Employees of AES, interview by author, tape recording, Thames, Connecticut, 25 September 1996.
7. Ling Sing Chee, "Singapore Airlines: Strategic Human Resource Initiatives," in *International Human Resource Management,* ed. Derek Torrington (New York: Prentice-Hall, 1994), 157.
8. Marvin B. Lieberman, Lawrence J. Lau, and Mark D. Williams, "Firm-Level Productivity and Management Influence: A Comparison of U.S. and Japanese Automobile Producers," *Management Science* 36 (October 1990): 1195.
9. Ibid., 1212.
10. Ibid., 1209.
11. Ibid., 1212.
12. Bill Osborne, New Zealand Post, interview by author, Wellington, New Zealand, 2 April 1996.
13. David A. Morand, "Forms of Address and Status Leveling in Organizations," *Business Horizons,* November–December 1995, 37.

Chapter Five

1. Investors in People, *The Benefits of Being an Investor in People* (London: Investors in People, undated), 4.
2. Ibid., ii.
3. Barry Gerhart and Charlie O. Trevor, "Employment Variability Under Different Managerial Compensation Systems," *Academy of Management Journal* 39 (1996): 1692.
4. Eileen Appelbaum and Rosemary Batt, *The New American Workplace* (Ithaca, New York: ILR Press, 1994), 147.
5. Edward E. Lawler III, Susan G. Cohen, and Lei Chang, "Strategic Human

Resource Management," in *Building the Competitive Workforce,* ed. Philip H. Mirvis (New York: John Wiley, 1993), 43.

6. Neil Fligstein, *The Transformation of Corporate Control* (Cambridge, MA: Harvard University Press, 1990), 109.

7. Ibid., 226.

8. Neil Fligstein, "The Intraorganizational Power Struggle: Rise of Finance Personnel to Top Leadership in Large Corporations, 1919–1979," *American Sociological Review* 52 (1987): 47.

9. Fligstein, *Transformation of Corporate Control,* 226.

10. Michael A. Hitt, Robert E. Hoskisson, Richard A. Johnson, and Douglas D. Moesel, "The Market for Corporate Control and Firm Innovation," *Academy of Management Journal* 39 (1996): 1110.

11. Ibid.

12. Ibid., 1110–1111.

13. Ibid., 1090.

14. Ibid., 1112.

15. Lawler, Cohen, and Chang, 36.

16. Ibid., 36–37.

17. Ibid., 35.

18. J. R. Meindl and S. B. Ehrlich, "The Romance of Leadership and the Evaluation of Organizational Performance," *Academy of Management Journal* 30 (1987): 91–109.

19. Jeffrey Pfeffer, Robert B. Cialdini, Benjamin Hanna, and Kathleen Knopoff, "Faith in Supervision and the Self-Enhancement Bias: Two Psychological Reasons Why Managers Don't Empower Workers," *Basic and Applied Social Psychology* (in press).

20. Ibid.

21. Ibid.

22. Alan Sloan, "The Hit Men," *Newsweek,* 28 February 1996, 44–45.

23. Brian Dumaine, "America's Toughest Bosses," *Fortune,* 18 October 1993, 39.

24. Steven Flax, "The Toughest Bosses in America," *Fortune,* 6 August 1984, 19.

25. Peter Nulty, "America's Toughest Bosses," *Fortune,* 27 February 1989, 54.

26. "Albert J. Dunlap: Following the Paper Trail," *Journal of Business Strategy* 16 (September–October 1995): 48.

27. "The Shredder," *Business Week,* 15 January 1996, 58.

28. Albert J. Dunlap, "If You're Going to Be a Director . . .," *Directors and Boards* (Winter, 1995): 5.

29. Andrew Cassel, "After the Fall," *Across the Board,* April 1996, 30.

30. Matt Krantz, "How Sweet It Is: Al Dunlap Gets Sunbeam Deal," *Investor's Business Daily,* 23 July 1996, A4.

31. "For Markets, A Good Quarter on Paper," *Investor's Business Daily,* 1 October 1996, A1.

32. Glenn Collins, "Sunbeam to Halve Work Force of 12,000 and Sell Some Units," *The New York Times,* 13 November 1996, C1.

33. Thomas Petzinger Jr., "Does Al Dunlap Mean Business, or Is He Just Plain Mean?" *The Wall Street Journal,* 30 August 1996, B1.

34. "The Shredder," 56.

35. Jonathan Kaufman, "In Name Only: For Richard Thibeault, Being a 'Manager' Is a Blue-Collar Life," *The Wall Street Journal,* 1 October 1996, A1.

36. David Halberstam, *The Best and the Brightest* (New York: Random House, 1972), 53.

37. Jeffrey Pfeffer, *Competitive Advantage Through People* (Boston: Harvard Business School Press, 1994), 53.

Chapter Six

1. John Kotter, *The General Managers* (New York: Free Press, 1982).

2. John Kotter, *The New Rules* (New York: Free Press, 1995).

3. Anthony Carnevale, "Preface," in Stephen J. Rose, *Declining Job Security and the Professionalization of Opportunity* (Washington, DC: National Commission for Employment Policy, 1995), iii.

4. Daniel C. Feldman, "The Nature, Antecedents, and Consequences of Underemployment," *Journal of Management* 22 (1996): 386.

5. Courtney von Hippel, Stephen L. Mangum, David B. Greeberger, Robert L. Heneman, and Jeffrey D. Skoglind, "Temporary Employment: Can Organizations and Employees Both Win?" *Academy of Management Executive* 11 (1997): 1.

6. Gerald E. Ledford, Jr., Edward E. Lawler III, and Susan A. Mohrman, "Reward Innovations in *Fortune* 1000 Companies," *Compensation and Benefits Review* 27 (July–August 1995): 78.

7. Sun Microsystems, *Organizational Profile: Sun Microsystems Building Employee Self-Reliance: Career Services at Sun* (Woodside, CA: California Strategic Human Resource Partnership, 1996), 2.

8. Laurie Hunter, Alan McGregor, John MacInnes, and Alan Sproull, "The 'Flexible Firm': Strategy and Segmentation," *British Journal of Industrial Relations* 31 (1993): 396–398.

9. Kathleen Christensen, *Contingent Work Arrangements in Family-Sensitive Corporations* (Boston: Center on Work and Family, Boston University, 1995), 23.

10. Louis Uchitelle, "More Downsized Workers are Returning as Rentals," *The New York Times*, 8 December 1996, 22.
11. Ibid.
12. Princeton Survey Research Associates, *Worker Representation and Participation Survey: Report on the Findings* (Princeton, NJ: Princeton Survey Research Associates, 1994), 16.
13. Ibid., 18.
14. R. S. Belous, *The Contingent Economy* (Washington, DC: National Planning Association, 1989).
15. Peter Cappelli, "Rethinking Employment," *British Journal of Industrial Relations* 33 (1995): 581.
16. Christensen, 7.
17. Cappelli, 580.
18. Mike Bresnen and Carolyn Fowler, "The Organizational Correlates and Consequences of Subcontracting: Evidence from a Survey of South Wales Businesses," *Journal of Management Studies* 31 (1994): 849.
19. Cappelli, 571.
20. Joel Cutcher-Gershenfeld, "The Impact on Economic Performance of a Transformation in Workplace Relations," *Industrial and Labor Relations Review* 44 (1991): 244.
21. See Cappelli, 577.
22. Christensen, 2.
23. Cappelli, 563.
24. Sanford M. Jacoby, *Employing Bureaucracy* (New York: Columbia University Press, 1985), 13.
25. Ibid., 14.
26. Ibid., 15.
27. Ibid.
28. Ibid., 21.
29. Ibid., 22.
30. Ibid., 34.
31. Ibid., 35.
32. Robert Lacey, *Ford: The Men and the Machine* (New York: Ballantine Books, 1986), 130.
33. Ibid., 128–129.
34. Ibid., 129.
35. Ibid., 131.
36. Ibid., 128.
37. James B. Rebitzer, "Job Safety and Contract Workers in the Petrochemical Industry," *Industrial Relations* 34 (1995): 41.

38. Denise M. Rousseau and Carolyn Libuser, "Contingent Workers in High Risk Environments," *California Management Review* 39 (Winter 1997): 113.

39. Ibid., 111.

40. Jone L. Pearce, "Toward an Organizational Behavior of Contract Laborers: Their Psychological Involvement and Effects on Employee Co-Workers," *Academy of Management Journal* 36 (1993): 1093.

41. J. R. Dorfman, "Stocks of Companies Announcing Layoffs Fire Up Investors, But Prices Often Wilt," *The Wall Street Journal,* 10 December 1991, C1, C2.

42. Martin Neil Baily, Eric J. Bartelsman, and John Haltiwanger, "Downsizing and Productivity Growth: Myth or Reality?" working paper 4741, National Bureau of Economic Research, Cambridge, MA, May 1994, 13.

43. American Management Association, *1994 AMA Survey on Downsizing: Summary of Key Findings* (New York: American Management Association, 1994), 4.

44. Ibid., 1.

45. Wayne F. Cascio, "Downsizing: What Do We Know? What Have We Learned?" *Academy of Management Executive* 7 (1993): 97.

46. Mitchell Lee Marks, "Restructuring and Downsizing," in *Building the Competitive Workforce: Investing in Human Capital for Corporate Success,* ed. Philip H. Mirvis (New York: John Wiley, 1993), 60–94.

47. "Fire and Forget?" *The Economist,* 20 April 1996, 51.

48. Leonard A. Schlesinger and Jeffrey Zornitsky, "Job Satisfaction, Service Capability, and Customer Satisfaction: An Examination of Linkages and Managerial Implications," *Human Resource Planning* 14 (1991): 143.

49. Ibid., 146.

50. Dave Ulrich, Richard Halbrook, Dave Meder, Mark Stuchlik, and Steve Thorpe, "Employee and Customer Attachment: Synergies for Competitive Advantage," *Human Resource Planning* 14 (1991): 96.

51. Ibid., 97.

52. Ibid.

53. Ibid., 100.

54. Ibid., 101.

55. Ibid.

56. Jeffrey A. Alexander, Joan R. Bloom, and Beverly A. Nuchols, "Nursing Turnover and Hospital Efficiency: An Organization-Level Analysis," *Industrial Relations* 33 (1994): 506.

57. Ibid., 517.

58. Frederick F. Reichheld, *The Loyalty Effect* (Boston: Harvard Business School Press, 1996), 91.

59. Ibid., 97.

60. Ibid., 97–98.

61. Gretchen M. Spreitzer and Robert E. Quinn, "Empowering Middle Managers to Be Transformational Leaders," *Journal of Applied Behavioral Science* 32 (September, 1996): 256.

62. "Writing a New Social Contract," *Business Week,* 11 March 1996, 60.

63. Francy Blackwood, "Using Benefits to Tame the Turnover Beast," *San Francisco Business Times,* 19 August 1994, 10A.

64. "Jack Stack (A)," Case 9-993-009. (Stanford, CA: Business Enterprise Trust, 1993), 6.

65. Frits K. Pil and John Paul MacDuffie, "Japanese and Local Influences on the Transfer of Work Practices at Japanese Transplants," in *Proceedings of the Forty-Eighth Meeting of the Industrial Relations Research Association,* ed. Paula B. Voos (Madison, WI: Industrial Relations Research Association, 1996), 282.

66. American Management Association, 3.

67. Barry Gerhart and Charlie O. Trevor, "Employment Variability Under Different Managerial Compensation Systems," *Academy of Management Journal* 39 (1996): 1692–1712.

68. Dawn Amfuso, "3M's Staffing Strategy Promotes Productivity and Pride," *Personnel Journal* 74 (February 1995): 31.

69. G. James Francis, John Mohr, and Kelley Andersen, "HR Balancing: Alternative Downsizing," *Personnel Journal* 71 (January 1992): 71–78.

70. Valerie Frazee, "Share Thy Neighbor's Workers," *Personnel Journal* 75 (June 1996): 81–84.

71. Valerie Frazee, "Insourcing Saves Jobs at Harman," *Personnel Journal* 75 (June 1996): 85–86.

72. Ibid., 86.

73. Ibid.

74. Gillian Flynn, "A Strike Puts Employees Up to Bat," *Personnel Journal* 75 (July 1996): 71.

75. Marks, 79.

76. Clair Brown, Michael Reich, and David Stern, "Becoming a High-Performance Work Organization: The Role of Security, Employee Involvement and Training," *The International Journal of Human Resource Management* 4 (1993): 271.

77. Ibid.

78. Ron Christian, New Zealand Post, interview by author, Wellington, New Zealand, 2 April 1996.

79. Marks, 79–80.

80. Peter Hartz, *The Company that Breathes* (Berlin: Springer-Verlag, 1996), 20–21.

81. Ibid., 98.

82. Ibid., 107.

83. Ibid., 110–111.

84. Ibid., 112–113.

85. Ibid., 118–119.

86. Ibid., 96; emphasis added.

87. Brown, Reich, and Stern, 249–250.

88. Jennifer J. Laabs, "Share the Pain to Share the Gain," *Personnel Journal* 75 (June 1996): 91.

89. Elmar Toime, interview by author, Wellington, New Zealand, 2 April 1996.

Chapter Seven

1. Melinda Grenier Guiles, "Ford to Defer Merit Raises for 1st Quarter," *The Wall Street Journal,* 24 January 1990, A3.

2. Ibid.

3. Thomas Teal, "Not a Fool, Not a Saint," *Fortune,* 11 November 1996, 204.

4. Dana Milbank, "U.S. Productivity Gains Cut Costs, Close Gap with Low-Wage Overseas Firms," *The Wall Street Journal,* 23 December 1992, A2.

5. Ibid.

6. Alan Neale, "Are British Workers Pricing Themselves Out of Jobs? Unit Labour Costs and Competitiveness," *Work, Employment, and Society* 6 (1992): 271.

7. Ibid., 275.

8. Ibid.

9. Karel Williams, John Williams, and Colin Haslam, "Do Labour Costs Really Matter?" *Work, Employment, and Society* 3 (1989): 300.

10. Stephen Wood, "High Commitment Management and Payment Systems," *Journal of Management Studies* 33 (1996): 55.

11. Michael Beer, Bert Spector, Paul Lawrence, D. Quinn Mills, and Richard Walton, *Managing Human Assets* (New York: Free Press, 1984), 114.

12. Wood, 55.

13. Barbara B. Buchholz, "The Bonus Isn't Reserved for Big Shots Anymore," *New York Times,* 27 October 1996, F10.

14. J. Storey and K. Sisson, *Managing Human Resources and Industrial Relations* (Buckingham: Open University Press, 1993), 140–141.

15. Peter Passell, "Paid by the Widget, and Proud," *New York Times,* 16 June 1996, F12.

16. Ibid., F12.
17. Herbert A. Simon, "Organizations and Markets," *Journal of Economic Perspectives* 5 (1991): 33.
18. M. H. Bazerman, R. I. Beekun, and F. D. Schoorman, "Performance Evaluation in a Dynamic Context: A Laboratory Study of the Impact of Prior Commitment to the Ratee," *Journal of Applied Psychology* 67 (1982): 873–876.
19. F. David Schoorman, "Escalation Bias in Performance Appraisals: An Unintended Consequence of Supervisor Participation in Hiring Decisions," *Journal of Applied Psychology* 73 (1988): 58.
20. Ibid., 61.
21. Hewitt Associates, *Compensation Guide: Benefits and Compensation Update* 4 (January 1997): 4.
22. William Mercer, *Leader to Leader* 1 (Winter 1997): 62.
23. Ibid., 61.
24. Peter Nulty, "Incentive Pay Can be Crippling," *Fortune*, 13 November 1995, 235.
25. Ibid.
26. Gregory A. Patterson, "Distressed Shoppers, Disaffected Workers Prompt Stores to Alter Sales Commissions," *The Wall Street Journal*, 1 July 1992, B1.
27. Ibid.
28. Ibid., B2.
29. Wood, 56.
30. Passell, F12.
31. Larry Hatcher and Timothy L. Ross, "From Individual Incentives to an Organization-Wide Gainsharing Plan: Effects on Teamwork and Product Quality," *Journal of Organizational Behavior* 12 (1991): 174.
32. Ibid., 169.
33. Jone Pearce, William B. Stevenson, and James L. Perry, "Managerial Compensation Based on Organizational Performance: A Time Series Analysis of the Effects of Merit Pay," *Academy of Management Journal* 28 (1985): 271.
34. Nulty, 235.
35. Gerald E. Ledford, Jr., Edward E. Lawler III, and Susan A. Mohrman, "Reward Innovations in *Fortune* 1000 Companies," *Compensation and Benefits Review* 27 (July–August 1995): 78.
36. Alfie Kohn, "Why Incentive Plans Cannot Work," *Harvard Business Review* 71 (September–October 1993): 54–63.
37. "Air Products Announces Management Compensation and Stock Ownership Initiatives," *Yahoo! On the Money PR Newswire*, 31 October 1996, 1.

38. Value Line, *The Value Line Investment Survey, Part 3, Ratings and Reports* (New York, NY: Value Line Pub., 1996), 1886.

39. Alfie Kohn, *Punished by Rewards* (Boston: Houghton Mifflin, 1993).

40. Ibid., 46.

41. Jude T. Rich and John A. Larson, "Why Some Long-Term Incentives Fail," *Compensation Review* 16 (1984): 26–37.

42. Graef Crystal, *In Search of Excess* (New York: Norton, 1991).

43. ´Simon, 33–34.

44. Bob Nelson, "Dump the Cash, Load on the Praise," *Personnel Journal* 75 (July, 1996): 65–66.

45. Kohn, "Why Incentive Plans Cannot Work."

46. Ibid.

47. Quoted in Richard Donkin, "Sharing the Action Without Conflict," *Financial Times*, 2 May 1997, 9.

48. Ibid.

49. Gerald Marwell, "Altruism and the Problem of Collective Action," in *Cooperation and Helping Behavior: Theories and Research*, eds. V. J. Derlega and J. Grzelak (New York: Academic Press, 1982), 208.

50. Terry L. Besser, "Reward and Organizational Goal Achievement: A Case Study of Toyota Motor Manufacturing in Kentucky," *Journal of Management Studies* 32 (1995): 387.

51. Ibid., 388.

52. Ibid., 389.

53. Ibid., 395.

54. Jeffrey B. Arthur and Lynda Aiman-Smith, "Gainsharing as Organizational Learning: An Analysis of Employee Suggestions Over Time," *Proceedings of the Forty-Eighth Annual Meeting*, Industrial Relations Research Association, Madison, WI, 1996, 271.

55. "Disunited Families," *The Economist*, 11 January 1997, 60.

56. Adam Bryant, "No Longer Flying in Formation," *The New York Times*, 17 January 1997, C2.

57. Ibid.

Chapter Eight

1. Andrea Adelson, "Physician, Unionize Thyself: Doctors Adapt to Life as H.M.O. Employees," *The New York Times*, 5 April 1997, 21.

2. Richard N. Block, John Beck, and Daniel H. Kruger, *Labor Law, Industrial Relations and Employee Choice* (Kalamazoo, MI: Upjohn Institute, 1996), 33.

3. William N. Cooke, "Product Quality Improvement Through Employee

Participation: The Effects of Unionization and Joint Union-Management Administration," *Industrial and Labor Relations Review* 46 (1993): 122.

4. T. A. Kochan, H. C. Katz, and R. B. McKersie, *The Transformation of U.S. Industrial Relations* (New York: Basic, 1986).

5. Block, Beck, and Kruger, 3.

6. David G. Blanchflower and Richard B. Freeman, "Unionism in the United States and Other Advanced OECD Countries," *Industrial Relations* 31 (1992): 58.

7. Ibid.

8. Jeffrey H. Keefe, "Do Unions Influence the Diffusion of Technology?" *Industrial Relations* 27 (1988): 336–351.

9. Thomas Karier, "Unions and the U.S. Comparative Advantage," *Industrial Relations* 30 (1991): 1–19.

10. See, for example, chapter 7 in Jeffrey Pfeffer, *Competitive Advantage Through People* (Boston: Harvard Business School Press, 1994), or Richard Freeman and James Medoff, *What Do Unions Do?* (New York: Free Press, 1984).

11. Steven G. Allen, "Unionization and Productivity in Office Building and School Construction," *Industrial and Labor Relations Review* 39 (1986): 187–201.

12. Steven G. Allen, "The Effect of Unionism on Productivity in Privately and Publicly Owned Hospitals and Nursing Homes," *Journal of Labor Research* 7 (1986): 59–68.

13. Blanchflower and Freeman, 68.

14. "Study of Corporate Performance in the UK Manufacturing Sector," unpublished paper, Centre for Economic Performance, London School of Economics and Political Science, London, 4.

15. Ibid.

16. Eileen Appelbaum and Rosemary Batt, *The New American Workplace* (Ithaca, New York: ILR Press, 1994), 152.

17. Robert Drago, "Quality Circle Survival: An Exploratory Analysis," *Industrial Relations* 27 (1988): 336–351.

18. Cooke, 129–130.

19. Ibid., 130.

20. Margaret Gardner, "Labor Movements and Industrial Restructuring in Australia, New Zealand, and the United States," in *The Comparative Political Economy of Industrial Relations,* eds. Kirsten S. Wever and Lowell Turner (Madison, WI: Industrial Relations Research Association, 1995), 45.

21. Paul Osterman, "Skill, Training, and Work Organization in American Establishments," *Industrial Relations* 34 (1995): 141.

22. Appelbaum and Batt, 152.

23. Ibid., 134. See also W. M. Boal, "Unionism and Productivity in West Virginia's Coal Mining," *Industrial and Labor Relations Review* 43 (1990): 390–405.

24. Harry C. Katz, Thomas A. Kochan, and Mark R. Weber, "Assessing the Effects of Industrial Relations Systems and Effort to Improve the Quality of Working Life on Organizational Effectiveness," *Academy of Management Journal* 28 (1985): 519.

25. Casey Ichniowski, "The Effects of Grievance Activity on Productivity," *Industrial and Labor Relations Review* 40 (1986): 75–89.

26. Harry C. Katz, Thomas A. Kochan, and Kenneth R. Gobeille, "Industrial Relations Performance, Economic Performance, and QWL Programs: An Interplant Analysis," *Industrial and Labor Relations Review* 37 (1983): 3–17.

27. Joel Cutcher-Gershenfeld, "The Impact on Economic Performance of a Transformation in Workplace Relations," *Industrial and Labor Relations Review* 44 (1991): 241–260.

28. Ibid., 245.

29. Ibid., 249.

30. Ibid., 254.

31. Paul S. Adler, "The 'Learning Bureaucracy': New United Motor Manufacturing, Inc.," *Research in Organizational Behavior* 15 (1992): 120.

32. Ibid., 122.

33. Kirsten S. Wever, *Negotiating Competitiveness* (Boston: Harvard Business School Press, 1995), 5.

34. John Holusha, "LTV's Weld of Worker and Manager," *The New York Times*, 2 August 1994, C4.

35. Ibid.

36. Ibid.

37. George W. Bohlander and Marshall H. Campbell, "Problem-Solving Bargaining and Work Redesign: Magma Copper's Labor-Management Partnership," *National Productivity Review* 12 (1993): 520.

38. William H. Miller, "Metamorphosis in the Desert," *Industry Week*, 16 March 1992, 30.

39. Barbara Kingsolver, *Holding the Line: Women in the Great Arizona Mines Strike of 1983* (Ithaca, New York: ILR Press, 1989).

40. Marsh H. Campbell, "Magma: A Cultural Revolution—A Short Course," (paper presented at the Cooper 95-Cobre 95 International Conference, Santiago, Chile, November 1995), 1.

41. Miller, 30.

42. Ibid.

43. Campbell, 2.

44. Bohlander and Campbell, 521.
45. Ibid.
46. Miller, 30.
47. Bohlander and Campbell, 523.
48. Campbell, 3.
49. Ibid.
50. Miller, 27.
51. Ibid.
52. Ibid., 30.
53. Bohlander and Campbell, 532.
54. Campbell, 5.
55. Bohlander and Campbell, 531.
56. Miller, 33.
57. Bohlander and Campbell, 524.
58. Ibid.
59. Campbell, 9.
60. The material that follows is from "AT&T: The Dallas Works (A)," Case 9-492-023 (Boston: Harvard Business School, 1991).
61. Ibid., 2.
62. Ibid., 5.
63. Elmar Toime, interview with author, Wellington, New Zealand, 2 April 1996.
64. "United Parcel Service (A)," Case 9-488-016 (Boston: Harvard Business School, 1987), 3.
65. Louis Uchitelle, "A New Labor Design at Levi Strauss," *The New York Times*, 13 October 1995, C1, C2.
66. Ibid., C1.
67. Oscar Suris and Robert L. Rose, "UAW Is Boosting Efforts to Organize Workers at Major Auto Parts Suppliers," *The Wall Street Journal*, 28 June 1996, A2, A4.
68. Robert L. Simison and Robert L. Rose, "Divided Detroit: In Backing the UAW, Ford Rankles Many of Its Parts Suppliers," *The Wall Street Journal*, 13 February 1997, A1.
69. Ibid., A2.
70. Appelbaum and Batt, 152.
71. Garth L. Mangum and R. Scott McNabb, *The Rise, Fall, and Replacement of Industrywide Bargaining in the Basic Steel Industry* (Armonk, New York: M. E. Sharpe, 1997), 63.
72. Ibid., 133.

Chapter Nine

1. Eileen Appelbaum and Rosemary Batt, *The New American Workplace* (Ithaca, New York: ILR Press, 1994), 146.
2. John J. Donohue III and Peter Siegelman, "The Changing Nature of Employment Discrimination Litigation," *Stanford Law Review* 43 (1991): 983.
3. "Stakeholder Capitalism," *The Economist,* 10 February 1996, 23–25.
4. Ibid., 24–25.
5. Harold L. Wilensky, "The Great American Job Creation Machine in Comparative Perspective," *Industrial Relations* 31 (1992): 475.
6. Ibid.
7. Ibid., 476.
8. Ibid., 477.
9. Ibid., 478.
10. Ibid., 480.
11. Ibid., 484.
12. Christopher F. Buechtemann, "Introduction: Employment Security and Labor Markets," in *Employment Security and Labor Market Behavior,* ed. Christopher F. Buechtemann (Ithaca, New York: ILR Press, 1993), 3.
13. Ibid., 23.
14. Ibid., 44.
15. Brian Becker and Barry Gerhart, "The Impact of Human Resource Management on Organizational Performance: Progress and Prospects," *Academy of Management Journal* 39 (1996): 779.
16. Richard M. Locke, "The Transformation of Industrial Relations? A Cross-National Review," in *The Comparative Political Economy of Industrial Relations,* eds. Kirsten S. Wever and Lowell Turner (Madison, WI: Industrial Relations Research Association, 1995), 11.
17. Ibid., 24.
18. Michael Useem, *Investor Capitalism* (New York: Basic Books, 1996), 25.
19. Robert Tomsho, "Real Dog: How Greyhound Lines Re-Engineered Itself Right Into a Deep Hole," *The Wall Street Journal,* 20 October 1994, A1.
20. Geron Corporation, *Geron Corporation Prospectus* (Menlo Park, CA: Geron Corporation, 30 July 1996), 4.
21. Ibid., 7.
22. Geron Corporation, *Geron Employee Handbook* (Menlo Park, CA: Geron Corporation, March 1996), 1.
23. Theresa M. Welbourne and Alice O. Andrews, "Predicting the Performance of Initial Public Offerings: Should Human Resource Management Be in the Equation?" *Academy of Management Journal* 39 (1996): 904–905.

24. Ibid., 907–909.
25. Dan Dorfman, "Bear: '1929 Can Happen Again,'" *USA Today,* 11 June 1993, 4B.
26. Useem, 94.
27. Asra Q. Nomani, "Calpers Says Its Investment Decisions Will Reflect How Firms Treat Workers," *The Wall Street Journal,* 16 June 1994, A4.
28. "Not Awakening the Dead," *The Economist,* 10 August 1996, 47.
29. Stephen C. Smith, "On the Economic Rationale for Codetermination Law," *Journal of Economic Behavior and Organization* 16 (1981): 273.
30. Ibid., 272.
31. David I. Levine and Laura D'Andrea Tyson, "Participation, Productivity, and the Firm's Environment," in *Paying for Productivity: A Look at the Evidence,* ed. Alan S. Blinder (Washington, DC: Brookings, 1990), 184.
32. Ibid., 235–236.
33. Kirsten S. Wever, *Negotiating Competitiveness* (Boston: Harvard Business School Press, 1995), 21.
34. Brent Keltner and David Finegold, "Adding Value in Banking: Human Resource Innovations for Service Firms," *Sloan Management Review* 38 (Fall 1996): 64.
35. Ibid.
36. Ibid., 58.
37. Barbara Kingsolver, *Holding the Line* (Ithaca, New York: ILR Press, 1989), 4.
38. Ibid., 9.
39. Ibid., 192.
40. Ibid., 193.
41. Andrew Pollack, "Seoul Takes Its Cue From Mrs. Thatcher," *The New York Times,* 12 January 1997, E5.
42. Ibid.
43. Richard N. Block, John Beck, and Daniel H. Kruger, *Labor Law, Industrial Relations, and Employee Choice* (Kalamazoo, MI: Upjohn Institute, 1996), 42.
44. Benjamin Aaron, "Employee Voice: A Legal Perspective," *California Management Review* 34 (1992): 129.
45. James N. Dertouzos and Lynne A. Karoly, *Labor-Market Responses to Employer Liability* (Santa Monica, CA: The Institute of Civil Justice, RAND, 1992), 5–6.
46. Ibid., 11.
47. James N. Dertouzos, Elaine Holland, and Patricia Ebener, *The Legal and Economic Consequences of Wrongful Termination* (Santa Monica, CA: RAND, 1988).
48. Dertouzos and Karoly, 62–63.

49. Ibid., 64.
50. "Getting Justice is No Easy Task," *Business Week,* 13 May 1996, 98.
51. Sarosh Kuruvilla, "Linkages Between Industrialization Strategies and Industrial Relations/Human Resource Policies: Singapore, Malaysia, The Philippines, and India," *Industrial and Labor Relations Review* 49 (July 1996): 641.
52. Ibid., 640.
53. Bruce C. Fallick, "A Review of the Recent Empirical Literature on Displaced Workers," *Industrial and Labor Relations Review* 50 (1996): 5.
54. "New Zealand: Into Unknown Territory," *The Economist,* 5 October 1996, 39.
55. Brian Needham, New Zealand Post, interview with author, Wellington, New Zealand, 2 April 1996.
56. Donohue and Siegelman, 988.
57. Smith, 262.
58. Morris M. Kleiner and Young-Myon Lee, "Works Councils and Unionization: Lessons from South Korea," *Industrial Relations* 36 (January 1997): 4.
59. A number of analyses of macroeconomic performance comparing the relative strength of Germany and either the United States or other European economies can be found in Wever, chapter 2.
60. Ibid., 37.
61. Smith, 276.
62. Wever, 120.
63. Ibid., 124.
64. Kleiner and Lee, 14.
65. Wever, 3.
66. See the inside front cover of Office of the American Workplace, U.S. Department of Labor, *Road to High-Performance Workplaces: A Guide to Better Jobs and Better Business Results* (Washington, DC: GPO, 1994).
67. Steve Evans, Keith Ewing, and Peter Nolan, "Industrial Relations and the British Economy in the 1990s: Mrs. Thatcher's Legacy," *Journal of Management Studies* 29 (1992): 571–589.
68. "Background to Investors in People" (press release from Countrywide Communications, London, 22 May 1995).
69. "Investors in People—The Journey" (press release from Countrywide Communications, London, 22 May 1995), 1.
70. The following discussion relies on information found in Block, Beck, and Kruger, 48–51.
71. Ibid., 48.
72. Ibid.
73. Ibid., 49.

74. Ibid., 50.

75. Ibid.

76. Joel Rogers and Eric Parker, "The Wisconsin Regional Training Partnership: Lessons for National Policy," working paper 3, National Center for the Workplace, Berkeley, CA, October 1996, 2.

77. Ibid., 11.

78. Ibid., 30.

79. Ibid., 32.

80. Block, Beck, and Kruger, 56.

81. Rogers and Parker, 1.

Chapter Ten

1. Tim Jackson, *Richard Branson: Virgin King* (Rocklin, CA: Prima Publishing, 1996), 5.

2. INSEAD, *Branson's Virgin: The Coming of Age of a Counter-Cultural Enterprise. Case Supplement: Extracts from Richard Branson's Speech to the Institute of Directors, 1993* (Fontainebleau, France: INSEAD, 1995), 1.

3. Sam Walton with John Huey, *Made in America* (New York: Bantam, 1992) 163–164.

4. Wal-Mart, *1989 Annual Report,* Bentonville, Arkansas, 3.

5. Men's Wearhouse, *1995 Annual Report,* Fremont, CA, 3.

6. "Message from Jack Watts, Chairman and CEO," *Portola Planet,* Winter/Spring 1997, 1.

7. Ling Sing Chee, "Singapore Airlines: Strategic Human Resource Initiatives," in *International Human Resource Management: Think Globally, Act Locally,* ed. Derek Torrington (New York: Prentice-Hall, 1994), 157.

8. ServiceMaster, *1995 Annual Report,* Downers Grove, Illinois, 2.

9. Ibid., 18.

10. Ibid.

11. Ibid.

Index

About the Author

Jeffrey Pfeffer is Thomas D. Dee Professor of Organizational Behavior in the Graduate School of Business, Stanford University. He received his B.S. and M.S. from Carnegie-Mellon University and his Ph.D. in business administration from Stanford. Dr. Pfeffer has served on the business school faculties at the University of Illinois, the University of California at Berkeley, and as a visiting professor at the Harvard Business School. He has directed executive programs and management development programs and has taught executive seminars in twenty-one countries around the world, in addition to lecturing in management development programs in companies, associations, and universities in the United States. He is also a member of many professional organizations, has served on the editorial boards of scholarly journals, and is the author of *New Directions for Organization Theory, Competitive Advantage through People, Managing with Power, Organizations and Organization Theory, Power in Organizations, Organizational Design,* and co-author of *The External Control of Organizations: A Resource Dependence Perspective,* as well as more than eighty articles and book chapters.